Renault and Art

A Modern Adventure

Renault and Art

A Modern Adventure

Editor
Ann Hindry

Photographer for the collection
Georges Poncet

Translator from the French
Charles Penwarden

HAZAN

Ann Hindry would like to thank Pierre Buraglio, Christian Dor, Erró, Hélène Fraiseau, Bernard Hanon, Simon Hantaï, Christian Husson, Guy Lebez, Freddy Moustacchi, Claude-Louis Renard, Philippe Royer, Patricia Rozet, Hélène et Jesús Rafael Soto, Pierre Souleil, Takis, Serge Van Hove, Pierre Zigmant.

Foreword

The contemporary art collection built up by Renault from 1966 to 1985 is an integral part of the company's heritage. As an outstanding reminder of a period when the corporation sought to express its engagement with its times through the art of the day, Renault's involvement with the visual arts remains exemplary in more ways than one. It is therefore fitting to preserve its memory.

There was a real need to restore its place in history – in the history of the company, but also in the history of art. The importance of this collection speaks for itself. Renault was in contact with artists of international renown, who are representative of a number of important tendencies in the art of that time.

The conditions in which this collection was assembled can also be considered remarkable, whether for the quality of the collaboration between the artists and the corporation in the case of commissions, or for that of the support given to personal projects.

This book will enable a wider audience – the men and women who work for Renault, but also art professionals and the general public – to gain access to the works of this collection, most of which have rarely been seen until now.

LOUIS SCHWEITZER
Chairman and CEO of Renault

Contents

Preface

Looking back, these works in the Renault art collection which so impressively strike – and, in a sense, test – our gaze, can be seen to constitute a coherent and important chapter in the history of the art of the sixties and seventies. This is art made for the urban environment, art that aims to make an impact. Dubuffet, Tinguely, Vasarely and Soto all sought to go well beyond the simple canvas. The element of play in their work made these artists extremely popular. What they were doing found an echo in a contemporary culture in which the Nouveau Roman and the films of Godard which, instead of the traditional narrative exploration of psychology, assigned a central role to the exact description of the surface of things. After the exclusive reign of Art Informel, with its emphasis on an elusive subjectivity, their concern was to legitimise the effect produced by works grounded in present reality and the period's belief in irreversible progress. The most striking structural features of these works – montage, simple visual alphabets, juxtapositions and the use of series – no longer reflected the artist's personal style or technique but, rather, his ability to organise and standardise.

The end result of this change was that the psychic dimension was displaced towards the object. At first glance, what could be easier to describe or more unambiguous than these works? In them, aesthetic feeling and interpretation are brought into the realm of the measurable. The objective conditions of perception and the physiological reflexes of vision were like a palette used by the different artists who contributed to the development of this new stylistic tendency. It became possible to establish an inventory of optical laws. There are some privileged elements which exercise such strong pressure on the eye that vision is subordinated to an aggressive domination. Contrasts, radiance, retinal persistence, the effects of simultaneous colours and labyrinthine perspectives – such are the means used here. They prevent the formation of a harmonious balance between vision and understanding. The goal is a state of alertness and not of meditation. In the terminology of the times, which measured artistic contributions on a scale of social relevance, the idea was to stimulate a keen critical awareness, an awareness which came to a head in Paris during the month of May, amidst colours redolent of the Chinese New Year. The observation that our relation to these works cannot be domesticated constituted the crux of the argument which upheld the importance of the anti-cultural effect of kinetic art and Op art.

There is no superstructure to embellish what is seen. With these works, it is the reaction of our eyes that is all-determining. The eyes are confronted with their own reality, testing themselves in a pure act of vision. The repetition of small-scale elements creates a kind of agitation which prevents the viewer from concentrating on a global form. And if forms do happen to appear, these emerge through the constant repetition of one unchanging element. The giant scale which covers the field of vision and absorbs the viewer, supports the constraint of perspective. Something ineluctable and compelling is expressed. One could describe it in terms of pointillism without a fixed subject.

Op art, kinetic art – a rejection of tradition? The history of an illusion? It is time to recall the optimism of those turbulent years. The artists who stood out from the phalanx were not just aware of themselves: they communicated self-awareness to a whole generation. From a historical point of view, one reason why this movement had its moment of glory was because, in France, Constructivism and the Bauhaus had had very little real influence. Let us not forget that, during all the years he spent in Paris, Mondrian lived in a state of unimaginable isolation. This lost tradition enabled Parisian artists and artists who had settled in Paris during the fifties to rewrite the history of geometric and concrete art. Let us be sure not to miss this rendezvous with the return of history.

WERNER SPIES

Director of the Musée national d'art moderne,
Centre Georges Pompidou

RENAULT

Renault : the History of a Collection

When Louis Schweitzer became chairman and chief executive officer of Renault in 1992, he and a mere half-dozen colleagues in senior management were about the only people who knew about the company's modern art collection. He was aware that the collection was a sizeable one, that it included works of great quality produced by major contemporary artists. And, without knowing exactly how it was built up, he also knew that it was the fruit of what was, in many ways, an exceptional history. He therefore took the decision to "exhume" it, to give it a new life. For while the major realizations integrated into the spaces of the corporate headquarters at Quai du Point-du-Jour had remained on daily view to employees for the quarter of a century since their installation, the overall significance of the collection had become somewhat diluted. The lobby and the staff restaurant, designed by Jesús Rafael Soto, were passed through and used by hundreds of people every day; the cafeteria with its fifty-meter frieze painted by Julio Le Parc was similarly frequented; and upstairs, the executive hospitality rooms boasted eighteen cutout paintings from Jean Dubuffet's *Roman Burlesque*, while the corridors on the general management floors featured two impressive *Accumulations* of car parts by Arman. Yet, in general, the population of the building was uninformed and had remained or become oblivious to these works. As for art professionals and the general public, logically enough, they were unaware even of their existence. Orphaned of their own history, deprived of an organized context, lacking "explanatory notes," so to speak, and isolated from the other complementary works that had been acquired as part of the same dynamic but were now meticulously stored out of harm's way but also out of sight and mind, these artistic environments had lost their specific identity. Louis Schweitzer realized this and saw the need to give this singular group of works a historical status – in art history, in company history, and in a human history. He and his close colleagues were also aware of the duties that went with their responsibility for a large collection of contemporary – and therefore living – art. And so, at Louis Schweitzer's instigation, this unique collection began to emerge from an almost decade-long hibernation that had been initiated under the chairmanship of Georges Besse in 1985, in circumstances that will later be discussed in greater detail.

The choice of the term "hibernation" is not arbitrary here, for it implies a deliberate *and* necessary decision to put a living entity into a state

Arman
Accumulation Renault n° 129, 1967, Logos Renault (detail)
D.R., Courtesy archives Denyse Durand-Ruel

In the foreground, from left:
Pierre Dreyfus (2nd), Arman (4th), Claude-Louis Renard (5th)
Exhibition *Arman, accumulations Renault*, 1969
Musée des Arts Décoratifs, Paris

of suspended animation. Renault is a car maker with a rich history, a company that employs thousands of men and women and that, since its foundation, has symbolized the industrial potential of an entire nation. Consequently, a great deal hangs upon what it does and the hazards, both large and small, are inevitably amplified. This is what makes Renault's involvement with the art of its time so exemplary in all its assumptions, difficulties, crises, and accomplishments. If we consider that, up to the beginning of the nineteenth century, fostering and keeping advanced forms of art was pretty much the preserve of princes or popes, then, with a little hindsight, we can say that, for their period, Renault's adventures (and misadventures) with art and their undeniably signifiant result, define the nature of the relationship between the prince of modern times, that is industry, and the artist. There is one key difference, however: the personal choices made by the industrial prince of the twentieth century implicate not only his successors and his court but hundreds of families and, possibly, the image of his entire company. The exercise is all the more difficult because by essence contemporary art has a delayed action. Moreover, while the captain of industry always makes his decisions about art, in which "everything is subjective," alone, these decisions cannot hope for the incontestability or permanence of those taken by church or monarch.

How It Started

In 1967 Claude-Louis Renard, an executive in personnel relations, presented the chairman Pierre Dreyfus with a corporate plan for contemporary art. The project was original, as indeed, all things being equal, was the status of the Renault factory as a state-owned, nationalized company. The idea was not to amass, to invest cannily in art objects that were likely to gain in value (a flourishing bourgeois activity), nor to construct an enlightened image by appropriating modern works that lend themselves to promotional uses. The objective was more ambitious than that, the perspectives were more long-term and more challenging and the human dimension much richer: the goal was to try to bring the worlds of art and industry closer together. *"What is the role of art in an industrial civilization that now concerns us all and seems to be generating a new way of life? In a world that is constantly evolving, should it simply reflect the ideas and ways of living of the past? Is it a distraction usually reserved to our more wealthy contemporaries? Do artists still have a role to play when the objects produced by machines have attained such a degree of perfection? The answer is clear. On its own, the machine cannot replace man's creative imagination. While it is capable of satisfying his material needs, its role cannot be to express the sum of his aspirations."* This was the view of the then executive vice-president, Christian Beullac, who was approached at the beginning of the project and supported it throughout.[1] In its broad outlines, the project was based on an exchange between parties rather than the classic patron-artist relationship. The company would offer the artist support in the form of technical, logistical, human, and financial

1. *Renault Magazine*, October 1974.

Arman
Accumulation Renault n° 101, La victoire de sale motrice, 1967
R4 side panels (view of studio)

Courtesy Archives Denyse Durand-Ruel

Arman
Accumulation Renault n° 153, 1968
Gray R 16 fenders
D.R., Courtesy Archives Denyse Durand-Ruel

Nicolas Schoffer
SCAM I leaving the factory, 1971
D.R.

assistance and in exchange, so to speak, would make him aware of the realities, possibilities, and restrictions of its particular socioeconomic world. The works produced as a result of this grant would initially remain the property of the artist.[2] Furthermore, Renault would ensure that its own personnel were informed while collaborating with museums on exhibitions in external venues not under its aegis. Thus defined, activities began in that same year, 1967, overseen by a specially created department: Recherches, Art et Industrie, directed by Claude-Louis Renard.

All exceptional events or flowerings can be put down to an ideal convergence of distinct factors. The birth and development of Recherches, Art et Industrie is no exception. Beginning with the human factor: Pierre Dreyfus, a high-ranking civil servant, was a free spirit sensitively attuned to the subjective world of artistic creation;[3] Claude-Louis Renard, a friend of André Malraux, had just as much exposure to the life of the arts as he did to the life of industry; Christian Beullac, a man of wide-ranging and curious intellect with an appetite for sharing his discoveries, played a vital role in facilitating relations between his two colleagues. We can also suppose that both the unique history of state control and the specific context in which the initiative took shape helped to make the project plausible. On the one hand, as a cutting-edge company and national industrial powerhouse, Renault already played an emblematic, "pathbreaking" role, and its social history also reflected its traditional emphasis on the human dimension; on the other, although a nationalized industry, it enjoyed an autonomy that was most unusual in postwar France. Astutely negotiated by Renault's first chairman, Pierre Lefaucheux, this status was certainly highly prized by his successor, Pierre Dreyfus.[4] No doubt Dreyfus recognized the value, however relative compared to other concerns, of being involved in a venture that was at once singular on a human scale, progressive, and supranational. Besides, the contemporary art scene of the sixties seemed to lend itself particularly well to the harmonious interaction of the worlds of art and industry. Since the mid-fifties, artists everywhere had been revisiting the conventional attributes of their practice. Painting and sculpture were abandoning their immemorial immobility and beginning to move both literally and optically. The traditional noble materials, such as wood, bronze, stone, pigment, and canvas, were being augmented by objects or bits of objects, industrial substances and materials taken from everyday life. Moreover, the artist, traditionally a solitary

Jean-Pierre Raynaud
Exhibition *Rouge Vert Jaune Bleu*, 1972
Musée des Arts Décoratifs, Paris (partial view)
© André Morain

2. As of 1975, Renault acquired a number of works in exchange for payment.

3. Pierre Souleil, then Director of Finance, who, along with his colleague and future successor, Christian Dor, gave unstinting support to the project, wrote of Pierre Dreyfus: *"His goal? Was it not to make people understand that there can be no taboos in art? It was not patronage. He used to say rather mischievously that the workers were more interested than the white-collar staff in the artists who came to work in the workshop. The works committee was also favorably inclined, and that delighted him." Pierre Dreyfus* (Paris: Gallimard, 1995). We should also note that Pierre Dreyfus's decision to approve C.-L. Renard's project was all the more remarkable because, though a great lover of literature, he was much more reticent about contemporary art.

4. See Jean-Louis Loubet, *Renault, cent ans d'histoire* (Paris: Editions E.T.A.I., 1998).

demiurge, was beginning to "delegate his powers" and collaborative work was gaining a new legitimacy. This development went hand in hand with the fact that the finished object, long seen as the immutable, tangible result of a unique genius, was losing its absolute supremacy in favor of the founding idea, which was now often as highly valued as its material realization.
The protagonists of art were increasingly receptive to the concrete, metamorphosing world around them. In France, a number of artists from different backgrounds were beginning to set sculpture and painting "in motion."
The most important of these, including Victor Vasarely, Jean Tinguely, and Jesús Rafael Soto, were brought together by the Galerie Denise René for a seminal exhibition entitled *Le Mouvement*. At the turn of the sixties, the Nice-based group of Nouveaux Réalistes, of which Yves Klein and Arman were leading representatives, had begun to explore the lessons of the American proto-Pop artist Robert Rauschenberg while taking care to distinguish themselves from Pop itself, which they considered too polished. They developed

Jesús Rafael Soto
Exhibition *Soto*, 1969
ARC/Musée d'Art Moderne
de la Ville de Paris

a style of art involving the ironic manipulation of the debris left behind by a contemporary industrial society, which both fascinated and repelled them. All these artists privileged the idea, allowing the artistic object to become impoverished as a distinct physical entity, while at the same time being enriched by the new, broader external input. Established artists such as Jean Dubuffet were developing the scope of work already based on both personal spontaneity and the organized use of new industrial materials such as polystyrene and vinyl paint. Dubuffet established the practice of having the final object made by assistants. Completed in the early seventies, his *Coucou bazar* theatre, in which sculptures and paintings serve as both actors and set, was one of the great moments in this expansion of the artistic field toward other territories.

The new-found eclecticism and transversality of the artistic domain also drew on more general philosophical ideas, on an idealistic and often utopian strain of thought. As a result of the fast economic growth of the postwar decades, the mood of the times was highly positive, and it was no doubt shared by many in industry. The situation, it would seem, was propitious. And yet, this idealistic aspiration to a meeting of worlds was accompanied by a political awareness, which, in the case of many artists, took the form of an intense mistrust of economic decision-makers and, at best, led to a lack of interest on the part of industrialists for an activity they saw as the plaything of the privileged. The political situation was, without a doubt, tense. The events of May 1968 and the social unrest of the years that followed had real impact on the activities of Recherches, Art et Industrie. As a "social showcase," Renault made an ideal scapegoat for politically engaged artists, whose sympathies naturally went with the workers and against the bosses, in cases of conflict. Arman, one of the first artists contacted by Renault and the partner in one of Recherches, Art et Industrie's most successful collaborations, remembers the period with a touch of humor: *"For an artist, working with Renault wasn't politically correct. I still don't know why."*[5] Jean-Pierre Raynaud, also one of the first artists at Quai du Point du Jour, experienced the political pressures of the day rather more directly.[6]

The Pioneering Years, 1967–1973

In spite of the difficulties, once this generous goal of inventing a new kind of relationship between a major corporation and the world of art had been set, it was pursued with great fervor. The choice of Arman was both logical and emotionally satisfying. By 1967 his reputation was established and the movement he had helped launch, the Nouveaux Réalistes, was highly influential in the French scene. After starting out in Nice, he now moved between France and the United States, where he was well integrated into the American artistic community. Most importantly, one of the main strands in his work centered on the accumulation of objects, notably mass-produced standard objects. In the United States, his interest in the car, the "super-object" of modern society, had already prompted him to make an eventually fruitless proposal to Ford.[7] He therefore accepted Claude-Louis Renard's proposition with enthusiasm. In the first years he produced some hundred sculptures or reliefs from mechanical parts and sheet metal panels. Each was given the title

5. See Daniel Abadie, "Entretien avec Arman," in *Arman, Accumulations Renault, 1967–1970,* (cat.), Galerie Georges-Philippe Vallois, Paris, 1995.

6. In 1972, on the eve of Raynaud's exhibition at the Musée des Arts Décoratifs in Paris, organized with Renault Recherches, Art et Industrie, a Renault worker, Pierre Overney, was shot dead by a watchman named Tramoni. At the opening, Raynaud was taken to one side and threatened by some of his artist friends. It was a particularly stormy evening and, at the end of the exhibition, Raynaud, who was deeply affected, decided to demolish all the works he had made in that particular context, of which he was still the owner. Only three pieces survived, these having been sold to private collectors by prior agreement.

7. Arman, *Mémoires accumulés,* interview with Otto Hahn, (Paris: Belfond, 1992).

Julio Le Parc
Wall paintings, 1974
Acrylic on canvas
Renault corporate headquarters,
Quai du Point-du-Jour,
staff cafeteria (detail)

Accumulation Renault and a number. The terms of the collaboration stipulated that while Renault would provide material support for Arman to make these works (parts, workshops, etc.), these would remain the property of the artist. Exhibitions were then organized by Recherches, Art et Industrie with the support of Ileana Sonnabend, Arman's gallery in Paris, in a number of major European museums, starting in 1969 with the Musée des Arts Décoratifs in Paris. *"The encounter between Arman and the state-owned Renault company has given rise to the important body of work we are presenting here,"* wrote its director, François Mathey, in his preface to the catalogue, *"but also to the beginnings of an adventure that concerns not only Arman, but all artists and, in the future, perhaps even their very condition."* [8] In 1970, Arman made a new series of works for the French pavilion at the World Exposition in Osaka, and, in 1973, he made the integrated panels for the new Renault headquarters, which were then under construction. The relationship between Arman and Renault was symbiotic to an exceptional degree, in that it most certainly had a direct influence on the course taken by the artist's work (see the essay by Catherine Francblin).

As of 1969, Renault began calling upon young, almost unknown artists, such as Alain Jacquet, Jean-Michel Sanejouand, and Jean-Pierre Raynaud. The idea was to give them the resources to produce original work and then, as far as possible, to help them exhibit it in a recognized structure. The radical nature of their art-making meant that it was impossible to anticipate the final form taken by their work, but the risk was worth taking and they were given a free hand to pursue their explorations. While Jacquet worked on the atomization of the image, a technique he continued to develop throughout his career, by producing a series entitled *Fragmentations* out of the front parts

8. François Mathey, in *Arman, accumulations Renault* (cat.), Union Centrale des Arts Décoratifs, Paris, 1969.

of vans, Sanejouand began a cycle of theoretical investigations in the *Organisations d'espace* (Organizations of Space) in the Seine valley, which were then shown at the Centre National d'Art Contemporain in March 1973. As for Raynaud, he threw himself headlong into the adventure, working intensively in a studio lent to him by Renault and, after abandoning several projects, produced a monumental set of sculptures. Working in his characteristic manner, he isolated and immobilized each component of an object (in this case, the Renault 4 car), presenting them quite apart from their usual context, serialized and differently colored. The superb exhibition of these works at the Musée des Arts Décoratifs in Paris, simply entitled *Rouge Vert Jaune Bleu,* was sadly overclouded by social and political conflict and most of the works were destroyed after the exhibition (see note 6). It seems highly likely that these particularly stressful circumstances were enough to put an end to Raynaud's collaboration with Renault.

Beyond the question of aesthetic affinities and shared ideals, the creation of a true bond between artists and the world of industry also implied that together

Julio Le Parc
Peintures formant frise, 1974
Acrylic on canvas
Renault corporate headquarters,
Quai du Point-du-Jour,
staff cafeteria (partial view)
© Georges Poncet, 1997

they explored the possibilities of technical collaboration. So it was that in 1971 Jean Dubuffet began working with the assistance of Renault technicians using a new machine for transposing the coordinates of car designs for the creation of new models. Similarly, Nicolas Schoffer, with his *Scam* car-sculpture, and Pol Bury, with his *Colonnes animées* (Animated Columns), both posed logistical problems, which the Renault engineers readily set about solving. Schoffer's car was built according to national vehicle standards and was driven in Paris and Milan, while the technicians elaborated a prototype of Bury's *Column*, which served to produce the masterpiece now exhibited at the Fondation Maeght. Back in 1969, when working on a particularly monumental project, Victor Vasarely was able to rely on the technical brio of Jean Prouvé's design office and the technological know-how of a Renault subsidiary with whom Claude-Louis Renard had put him in contact. Then in 1972, as part of this relationship built upon genuine reciprocity, Vasarely and his son, Yvaral, designed the new company logo at the request of Pierre Dreyfus.[9]

9. The logo was commissioned in July 1971 and completed in April 1972. It was put into use in September 1972.

During this period, a number of others artists came into Renault's orbit for short periods but, as foreseen under the terms defined for the activities

Luis Tomasello
Renault corporate headquarters, Quai du Point-du-Jour, lecture room, 1974 (detail)

of Recherches, Art et Industrie, their presence left no tangible traces within the company. However, these encounters may still be attested by works existing elsewhere in the art world. Among temporary companions, one notable example is that of César, who was fascinated by the adventure but whose spontaneous way of working was ill-suited to an organized project, however free in principle.[10] His proposition, which consisted in making *Compressions* of the entire Renault range, was met with a simple refusal, due not to any narrow-mindedness but to a well considered feeling that this would be an act of self-destruction – of auto-destruction, one might say. Still, Renault readily provided César with the mechanical parts and panels he used in a number of his *Expansions* at the end of the sixties. And it was in the company's laboratories that he made some of his first painted *Compressions.*

With Jean Dewasne, it was different inasmuch as he made a significant contribution to the artistic enhancement of the new corporate headquarters after 1973. Nevertheless, his first collaborative undertaking with Renault, a historic if now underestimated event, took place completely out of company bounds, so to speak. Dewasne had always been interested in the role of new technologies in the visual arts. A determined artist who was militantly in favor of uncompromising but applied abstraction, he founded the Atelier d'Art Abstrait in 1950 (an initiative which had won him renown) and taught the "technology of painting, new chemical components, and modern visual techniques." The sculptor Jean Arp, who was considered one of the founders of Concrete Art, professed a great liking for his "gay, anti-tragic, and anti-dirty" works. These certainly fit very smoothly into a highly structured universe. In the first months of 1972, Dewasne started working on twenty-four painted monumental sculptures using chassis parts from Saviem trucks, which he had discovered during a visit to the factory in Blainville and which had been altered in accordance with his instructions. The ensemble, which Dewasne worked on between 1972 and 1975 and included in the series of *Antisculptures* begun in 1951, was shown at the Musée National d'Art Moderne in 1975 as part of the activities of Recherches, Art et Industrie.[11]

The Construction of the Headquarters at Quai du Point-du-Jour

In 1973 plans to build a new Renault corporate headquarters provided an opportunity to invite artists to make a direct contribution to the company's actual physiognomy. Claude-Louis Renard's guiding idea was to call upon

10. Conversation with the author in June 1997.

11. Dewasne represented France at the 1968 Venice Biennale alongside Arman, Piotr Kowalski, and Nicolas Schoffer.

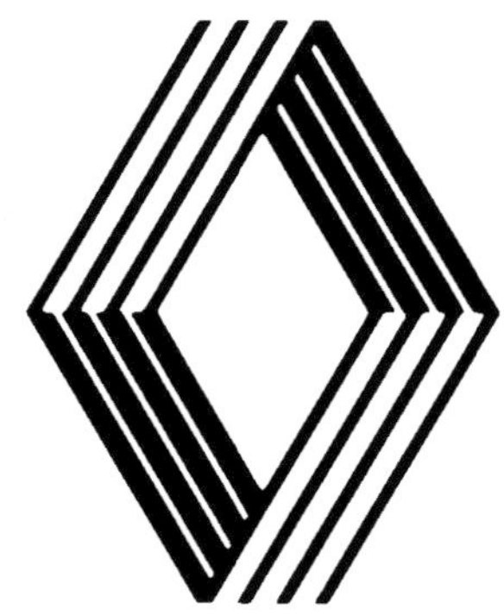

J.-P. Yvaral
Renault logo, 1972

outstanding artists whose visual language was compatible with a site designed to house hundreds of men and woman doing work that was totally outside the artistic sphere. Thus they began with the protagonists of kinetic art. This movement, which, as we have seen, was promoted with great zeal in Paris by the prominent gallerist Denise René, based its explorations on the use of real or optically induced movement, and tended to dissolve the object in order to create "environments," to encourage viewer interaction, and to advocate the use of "modern" materials such as aluminium, chrome, and plastic. Consequently, Jesús Rafael Soto, a then relatively unknown Venezuelan artist, was commissioned to design two complete environments for spaces that were of primary importance for both Renault's personnel and the company's public image – the large lobby and the staff restaurant, two areas occupying contiguous spaces on the ground floor. Soto had already worked on an environment for an earlier architectural project and now set about adapting this to the head offices as they were being built.[12] The result remains one of the artist's most impressive and successful architectural creations (see the essay by Christophe Domino). At the same time, the Argentinean artist Julio Le Parc produced a set of forty-seven paintings constituting a broad frieze running along the walls of the staff cafeteria. A member of the radical Groupe de Recherche d'Art Visuel (GRAV) which also included Vasarely's son Yvaral, Le Parc designed works that used highly colored geometrical drawings and linear scales of colors of varying intensity in order to have an immediate retinal impact. These works were often physically broken up by the division of their surfaces into geometrical modules. Another Argentinean, Luis Tomasello, who also worked on modular surfaces and the effect of light on optical movement induced by the changing position of the viewer, was commissioned to design a lecture room and applied his principles there with great subtlety. Takis, the Greek artist who made special use of magnetic fields to create sculptures whose implicit movement was expressed in the tension between the different elements, made a large two-part work to be installed on opposite sides of the corridor running between the central lifts and the cafeteria (see the essay by Maïten Bouisset). *"I have a very vivid memory of the conditions in which I made that large piece,"* recalls Takis today. *"All the Renault technicians and workers who were helping my assistant and myself, seemed highly motivated by the presence*

12. An earlier project for the building at 34, Quai du Point-du-Jour had been entrusted to the Brazilian architect Oscar Niemeyer. Soto had worked on the basis of Niemeyer's plans, which were ultimately scrapped. Meanwhile, history has marched on and Renault is again moving in December 1999. Soto's work will be readapted once more.

Victor Vasarely

Wooden panel, 1974

Silk-screen on aluminium

Renault corporate headquarters, Quai du Point-du-Jour, former engineers' and executives' restaurant

D.R.

of artists and artworks. The atmosphere was remarkably dynamic."[13] On the eighth floor, for the engineers' and executives' restaurant, Victor Vasarely designed an environment rhythmically punctuated by anodized aluminium panels on which he silk-screened transfers of the "constellar" geometrical combinations in which he was particularly interested at the time. Such is the naturalness and balance exuded by these 2 by 2 meter or 1.5 by 2 meter panels that we tend to overlook the technological and formal prowess that made them possible. After all, these works were more or less made in the pre-computer age (see the essay by Arnauld Pierre).

While, outside the area of kinetic art, it seemed natural to think of Arman, who came up with two large, almost flat *Accumulations* made of sawn-off engine parts for the corridors of the eighth floor, it also made sense to choose the exponents of rigorous abstraction. On the four landings occupied by the computing sections, Jean Dewasne integrated four long mural panels (oil-based paint on wood) whose geometrical designs, comprising abstract and highly graphic variations on the world of cars, were all interlinked. A few years later, Dewasne added a big mural environment for what, at the time, was the "computer room," home to a now extinct professional category, the "card-punch checkers."

Given the stated intention not to limit these artistic creations exclusively to the headquarters, plans were soon being made to integrate artworks into other Renault sites under construction or renovation. Thus, the coming years saw the company solicit two uncompromising abstract artists, Jean Degottex and Simon Hantaï, for the Centre de Recherches in Rueil-Malmaison. In 1981 Degottex – whose meditative and silent work, whatever the medium, reflects his quest for a radical economy of signs and of intervention in pictorial space – designed a long wall made of cast industrial bricks for the functions room, a boxed-in and windowless place on the ground floor. The horizontal distribution of these "natural-colored," i.e., terracotta, bricks, was punctuated and at the same time subverted by fine white diagonal notches, which, by creating subtle stripes across the plane, opened it up to space. As for Hantaï, in 1976 he began work on four integrated mural works for the restaurant and cafeteria, which remain his biggest environmental ensemble to this day (see the essay by Eric de Chassey). Gottfried Honegger, a Swiss artist initially originally trained in the Zurich school of Concrete Art by Max Bill and Alfred Lohse, applied a strict pictorial vocabulary based

13. From a conversation with Maïten Bouisset, September 1998.

Jean Dewasne
Oil-based industrial paint on wood, 1974
Panels fitted on the ground floor and 1st, 2nd, and 3rd floor work areas of the computer building, Renault corporate headquarters, Quai du Point-du-Jour

Jean Degottex
Les obliques, 1980
Brick wall
Rueil-Malmaison technical center, functions room

on serial systems and modular structures. Using a painting-object with a "programmatic" structure and a limited range of colors, he tried to make the work invisible to the spectator so that the latter would be surreptitiously placed in a relationship with the space of his work. For similar reasons, he carried out what he called a "coloring" of the Renault complex in Caccia, Portugal. For the lobby of the Renault Alpine factory in Dieppe, he created the project for an imposing mural composition to be related to an ensemble of smaller works.*

*As for Soto, he designed a "Progression" for the plant at Flins which was later built by the workers.

Thus in 1973 and 1974, Renault took a major step by commissioning works that were to be an integral part of the building. Until then, the art inspired by Renault had remained outside the company, limited to artists' studios or official exhibition spaces. As the preserve of the directorship, the activities of Recherches, Art et Industrie took place more in the art milieu than they did in the industrial one. Contacts between artists and industrial personnel remained sporadic and limited to certain professional categories. Now, with the inauguration of the new building, art became a permanent physical presence at the heart of the company.[14] However, while the kinetic artists, with their predilection for pure forms and modern materials – for what we would now call a high-tech world – seemed very much at one with the vision of a smooth-surfaced, efficient professional environment, and while Takis, Dewasne, and Arman integrated the world of the motor vehicle by using its various ingredients in their art, the intensely colored images of chaotic proliferation in the work of Jean Dubuffet grated on the sensibility of many. Claude-Louis Renard knew and admired Dubuffet and was eager that his work should occupy a prominent position on the general management floor. He therefore made a proposition, which Dubuffet enthusiastically accepted, that he design a work for the hospitality rooms on the eighth floor. Showing remarkable generosity for an artist of his renown, Dubuffet produced two successive projects and some fifty preparatory drawings.[15] The eighteen finished works, set out with great precision in the series of six rooms for which they were designed, has the same formal verve and wit as *Coucou bazar*. Powerfully present in their rather small surroundings, they can be said to reverse the effect of Dubuffet's first theatre design by surrounding each dining table and making the guests, in spite of themselves, actors in a rather "turbulent" set (see the essay by Didier Semin).

14. This situation will not be changed by the planned move; the works will simply be relocated into various Renault buildings.

15. For more on the history of these projects and drawings, the first series of which Dubuffet entitled *Le roman de Renard,* see the *Catalogue des travaux de Jean Dubuffet,* Roman burlesque, Sites tricolores, part XXVIII, (Paris: Editions de Minuit, 1979) and, of course, Didier Semin's essay in the present volume.

16. The contract for the dining rooms, dated 26 November 1973, also mentions plans for "a wall about 100 meters long with, possibly, one or several complementary elements." An added provision dated 13 June 1974 was drawn up for "a site including a pool and surrounding area."

17. For more information on the habitable works, see the *Catalogue des travaux de Jean Dubuffet*, "Habitats, burlesque, Closerie Falbala, Salon d'été," part XXXI, (Paris: Editions de Minuit, 1981). It may be of interest here to observe that the *Site scripturaire* project was left to hang for several years before being finally abandoned for financial reasons. The impact of the decision to abandon the *Salon d'été*, compared to the virtual silence surrounding the termination of the *Site* project, speaks volumes about the symbolic importance of Renault in French national life.

1975–1985. Activities Develop. Triumph and Tribulation for a Great but Difficult Idea.

Inaugurated in February 1975, the suite containing Dubuffet's *Roman burlesque* was coolly received by many Renault staff. Nevertheless, more or less concurrently with his first commission, Dubuffet had also started work on a monumental project requested by Pierre Dreyfus on the suggestion of Claude-Louis Renard. This was a rest and relaxation area measuring some fifty by sixty meters to be located on the esplanade at the foot of the building on Quai du Point-du-Jour.[16] The desire to create habitable spaces, to transpose artistic reality from its mental elaboration to the experiential reality of the spectator, is something that Dubuffet felt more and more strongly during the sixties. Construction work on the *Closerie Falbala* had just come to an end, and the project for the *Site scripturaire*, commissioned by the EPAD (the public body in charge of developing the new Défense area, west of Paris) was still in the preliminary stages.[17] He therefore threw himself passionately into the new project. Echoing the *Jardin d'hiver* of 1969–1970, he called it the *Salon d'été*. This huge, open-air habitable sculpture was formally configured in such a way as to pick up the layout of the hospitality

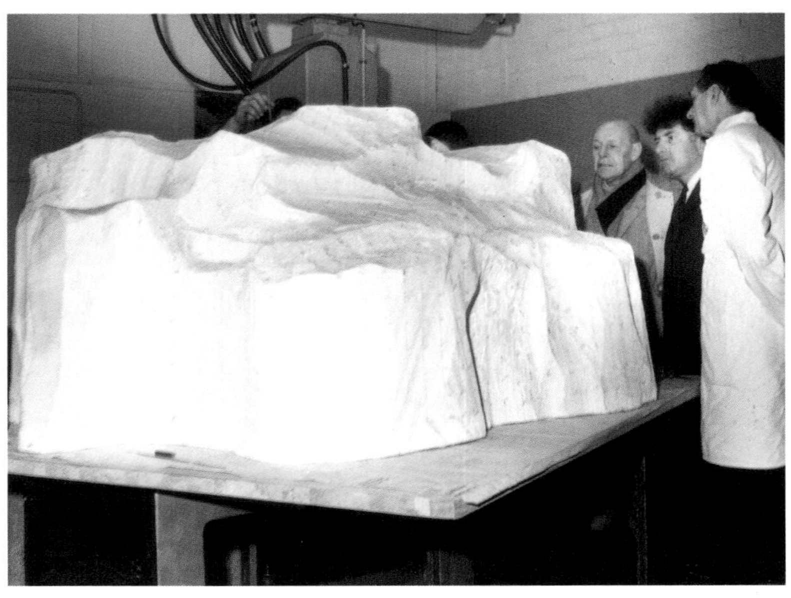

Jean Dubuffet and Claude-Louis Renard
in the Renault design office with the Delta 3D machine, 1971
D.R.

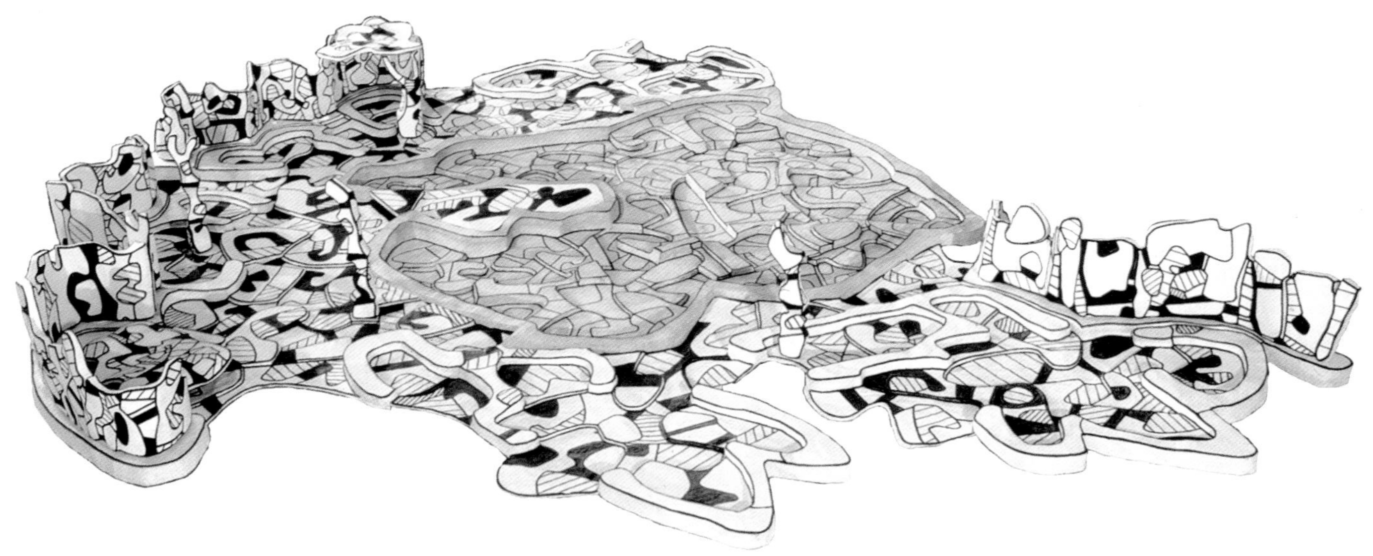

Jean Dubuffet
Salon d'été, maquette 1/10, 1974, expoxy painted with polyurethane (black and blue)
© Georges Poncet, 1998

rooms on the eighth floor. The model presented in August 1974 was approved and work began in September that year. However, it would seem that both the scale of the technological challenge and the lack of enthusiasm among many of Renault's senior management had been underestimated. In September 1975 Pierre Dreyfus asked that the work be stopped, even though it had reached an advanced stage, in order to leave his successor a "clear-cut situation" and the freedom to take a definitive decision. Bernard Vernier-Palliez took over from Pierre Dreyfus in January 1976. In September 1976, observing the scale of the difficulties in this project that he had inherited and not initiated, he decided not to continue. The rest is history. It is a sad yet constructive chapter of history, which saw the artist and the company become involved in an eight-year legal battle pitting the patron's rights as owner against the artist's moral rights over his work. It was sad because the superb monument was never made, and relations between Dubuffet and Renault were severed for good. But it was constructive because the final decision, made in 1981 and confirmed in 1983, established the legal precedent for an artist's moral rights over his project. In the meantime, however, passions reached a pitch on both sides and, by a cruel irony, Renault, which was no doubt the most receptive of any company at the time to contemporary art, became a symbol of obscurantism for art world professionals.[18] For while the first judgement, rendered in March 1977, went in favor of Renault, who now proceeded to cover over the already much damaged work site, the following month there was a new exhibition at the Musée des Arts Décoratifs, where Recherches, Art and Industrie had organized a good number of shows, entitled *Model for the* Salon d'été *and other projects.* The affair now went beyond art circles and became

18. In August 1977, while proceedings were under way, Dubuffet launched a monthly publication, *Le petit messager du Salon d'été*, run by a support association directed by the journalist Chantal Gaulin. The supporters of the monument were also vocal within the company: Jacques de Chambrun and Marc de Beaumont created the Renault Committee "Pour que vive le *Salon d'été*."

From left: **Simon Hantaï, François Mathey, and Robert Bordaz**
Exhibition *Hantaï*, 1976
Musée d'Art Moderne
de la Ville de Paris

a national cultural scandal exasperating the Renault management. In June 1978 the Paris Court of Appeal dismissed Dubuffet's claims and it was not until the decision of 8 July 1981 by the Court of Appeal in Versailles, confirmed by the Court of Referral, that the legal saga came to an end to the artist's advantage. The decision stated that *"the monumental work designed and created by Jean Dubuffet, at the present time unfinished . . . constitutes a work of art in the sense of articles 3 and 7 of the law of 11 March 1957. . ."* Dubuffet decided not to insist on the work being built. "*I disliked the idea of forcing them to build my work when it seemed so little desired,*" explained Dubuffet soon after, "*and I therefore decided not to press my claim.*" Whatever the rights and wrongs, the vicissitudes of this affair show how very complex a project on such a scale can be. Today, with a little detachment and looking beyond this specific case, the fact that similar difficulties continue to arise gives pause for thought. One example of this would be the recent disputes surrounding the *Tilted Arc*, the large-scale sculpture installed in 1981 by the American Richard Serra on Federal Plaza in New York.[19]

19. Here, in a country reputedly the most open to contemporary art, we have a monumental work by an internationally renowned artist, commissioned by the authorities of one of the most culturally dynamic cities in the world, but ultimately rejected by a number of local inhabitants who lodged a complaint. In 1992, after numerous juridical ins and outs, and strenuous efforts by artistic and cultural circles, the sculpture was finally removed from the place for which it had been designed.

During these years, the activities of Recherches, Art et Industries continued, but in a context that was obviously less propitious. Within the company, those who had always been opposed to any kind of involvement with art, or those who were simply skeptical, found ample confirmation of their forebodings in the catastrophic death throes of a grand project that could so easily have been the crowning highlight of a scheme begun fifteen years earlier. At the same time, the mutual trust and understanding that had gradually been built up between Renault and the art world had been shaken – even if Claude-Louis Renard did continue to enjoy privileged relationships with artists. Since 1975, Recherches, Art et Industrie had in fact extended its activity across a broad range of contemporary practices. It had approached members of the Supports-Surfaces group such as Claude Viallat and Marc Devade, and then Dominique Thiolat and Dominique Gauthier.[20] And, among major exponents of experimental abstract painting, Renard approached not only Jean Degottex and Simon Hantaï but also the American Sam Francis and the Frenchman Martin Barré. In 1978, realizing that he would need a fixed space in order to house his growing number of exhibitions, Renard created the Centre International de Création Artistique in a set of rooms

20. The movement Supports-Surfaces was the subject of an exhibition at the Galerie Nationale du Jeu de Paume in 1998. See the exhibition catalogue, *Supports-Surfaces*, (Paris: Editions du Jeu de Paume, 1998).

Martin Barré
77/78 series, or *Renault Series*
Exhibition *Martin Barré*, 1979
Musée d'Art Moderne de la Ville de Paris
© André Morain

Eduardo Chillida and Pierre Alechinsky at the Abbaye de Sénanque, 1984
© André Morain

allotted to him in the Cistercian abbey at Sénanque, which was temporarily without religious function and being managed by Berliet (which fused with SAVIEM and gave birth in 1975 to Renault Véhicules Industriels). The center opened with an exhibition by a young abstract artist with radical theories, Marc Devade, and followed up with an artist of growing renown, Jesús Rafael Soto, who also had strong links with Renault. These events set the tone for a regular exhibition program that helped put Sénanque on the contemporary art map. At the same time though, the link between art and industry so ardently desired at the outset by Renard but also by Pierre Dreyfus and Christian Beullac (who, like Dreyfus, left the company in 1975) was growing increasingly tenuous. In 1980 a non-profit society named Incitation à la Création was set up in view of giving Recherches, Art et Industrie greater leeway with regard to cultural circles on the one side and to Renault hierarchy on the other. In fact, the activities of Recherches, Art et Industrie were now, in a manner of speaking, paralleled by those of Incitation à la Création. The latter, which had its own distinct budget, was above all responsible for managing external events, while the former controlled grants. This reorganization had been made necessary by the greater complexity of the internal context for such operations. In any case, the program was impressive. The quality of the exhibitions and the publications that usually accompanied them was of museum standard. Contracts of various kinds proliferated.[21] Up and coming artists of all nationalities participated: figures such as Christian Boltanski and Pierre Buraglio in France, as well as Jan Dibbets, Mel Bochner, and Antonio Saura, to name but a few. Established artists such as Antoni Tàpies, Pierre Alechinsky, and Henri Michaux conceived works specially for the occasion. The story of Michaux's participation is especially touching because, during the year he spent preparing paintings

21. From 1975 onwards, roughly a hundred creative grants involving donations of works were organized in the framework of Recherches, Art et Industrie's Incitation à la Création scheme. A certain amount of confusion arises here from the decision to give the association the ideologically attractive name Incitation à la Création.

for his exhibition at Sénanque, 1983, this important and now ageing artist discovered that his old allergy to turpentine had ceased. He made ten oil paintings but died in 1984 before the exhibition could take place, leaving Renault some thirty works, including these ten doubly unique oils (see the essay by Claire Stoullig).

In 1985 the Cistercian monks returned, as expected, to the abbey at Sénanque and the association moved to the Abbaye de Montmajour in the region of Bouches-du-Rhône, with the agreement of the ministry of culture and the municipal council of Arles. There, it continued organizing exhibitions through to 1987. Claude-Louis Renard's Incitation à la Création program (run by the association of the same name and Recherches, Art et Industrie) had its apogee in the first half of the eighties. Although its ties with Renault were relatively discreet, the association was presided over by the company's chairman and chief executive officer, Bernard Hanon, as of 1981. Already long familiar with its work, he was an enlightened supporter of its activities and, as a great lover of contemporary art and connoisseur of the United States, was pleased to see the program extended to American artists – Robert Rauschenberg, James Rosenquist, and Roy Lichtenstein, all leading figures or precursors of Pop – at a time when Renault

From left: **Antoni Tàpies, Micheline Renard, and Claude-Louis Renard at the Abbaye de Montmajour, 1986**

was preparing to have a second go at the American market.[22] These were the years when the formula conceived by Claude-Louis Renard really fulfilled its potential. The lightweight structure (Renard worked alone, with help from his wife, Micheline Renard) and its organizational flexibility worked wonders, allowing for several simultaneous collaborations with artists from a wide variety of countries. The artists were contacted, an agreement was reached, and they were left to work at their own rhythm on new works, which the association later exhibited at Sénanque or Montmajour, or perhaps in a museum, according to a highly flexible timetable.

In 1984 this fragile edifice was swept away by Renault's disastrous economic results. Bernard Hanon was forced to hand over the reins to Georges Besse. Totally dedicated to the survival of the company that had been entrusted to him and to the exclusion of any secondary considerations, Besse decided to stop all artistic activities at once and mark a symbolic break with the previous management. Given the urgency of the situation, of which he was well aware, every detail counted. Anything that might seem extravagant in any way or suggest a possible laxity had to disappear.

Nevertheless, the association Incitation à la Création continued to be given free office space (but no budget) at Quai du Point-du-Jour until 1988. It was up to Claude-Louis Renard, who was no longer with Renault, to find a new base and source of finance. Faithful to his enduring engagement, Bernard Hanon would stay on as chairman of the association until then. In 1986 an urgent selection was made. Renault brought its relations with artists to an amicable end. The company wrote to each one, offering them ownership of the works then under its responsibility.[23] For projects still under way, the artists kept the sums already paid to them by way of compensation for the termination of the collaboration. Having discharged Renault in these terms, the artists could then choose whether to keep the works returned to them or to entrust them to the Incitation à la Création, which would continue to exist. In 1989 this association and the works it held (and most of the artists decided to maintain their links), was taken up by a private entrepreneur, Jean Hamon, a passionate collector who undertook to manage and conserve the works and to preserve their status, in agreement with the artists. As for Renault, it of course kept the integrated works and the works acquired with a view to building up a collection for the foundation

22. Jean-Louis Loubet, *op. cit.*, note 4.

23. There are forty artists in the collection, to whom all or some of their works were returned. These include: V. Adami, P. Alechinsky, Arman, E. Arroyo, M. Barré, T. Berlant, M. Bochner, C. Boltanski, P. Briggs, P. Buraglio, E. Chillida, A. Clément, J. Degottex, M. Devade, J. Dibbets, H. Di Rosa, Erró, S. Francis, D. Gauthier, E. Hanani, S. Hantaï, G. Honegger, A. Jacquet, J. Monory, G. Noël, J. Olitski, B. Pagès, L. Pang, J.-P. Pincemin, L. Poons, M. Raysse, J. Rosenquist, J. R. Soto, Takis, A.Tapiés, S. Tanger, J. Tinguely, Télémaque, van Hoek, C. Viallat.

it had planned at the time, but also various works that were spared because they were physically less voluminous, less difficult to keep or more reassuring in terms of the maker's reputation. These items were put into storage.

And so, in 1986, the first chapter of this remarkable story came to an end. With its highs and lows, it illustrates the difficulties besetting a project that could hardly be accused of lacking vision. Once again, today, it is Takis who sums it up most clearly: *"It was a unique experiment for the period, inasmuch as this very major industrial enterprise was taking an enormous risk, wagering on the future. It is important to understand how little chance artists of our generation had in those years of being involved in that kind of public or private commission."*[24] The fact remains that a major corporation and art do not operate in the same time frames. The second exists in a continuum made up of a constellation of individual stars that shine when one comes near, the first beats to the rhythm of the complex skein of factors that constitute an organized company. There is no reason to believe that the two may not meet once again with similarly fertile results. By its great quality and coherence, the lasting trace of their past meeting – the Renault Collection as it now exists and as it is presented here – can but make one optimistic.

ANN HINDRY

24. *Op. cit.*, note 13.

1 **Victor Vasarely, 1971**
© André Morain

2 **Jean Degottex, 1977**
© André Morain

3 **Julio Le Parc, 1971**
© André Morain

4 **Erró, 1982**
© André Morain

5 **Jean Dubuffet, 1971**
D.R.

6 **Takis, 1968**
© A. de Andrade, Magnum, Archives Takis

7 **Jean Dewasne** (on the right), **1975**
© André Morain

1

2

3

4

5

6

7

An introduction to the Renault Art Collection

As we have seen, the Renault art collection as it exists today was not built up in a linear, progressive fashion with the overarching objective of assembling an exhaustive concert of reputed contemporary works. Nor was it formed by successive, isolated acquisitions. Rather than a collection in the strict sense of the term, it is the result of an original patronage scheme whose eventful history is told in the preceding essay. *"The goal was never to make a collection,"* insists Claude-Louis Renard, *"none of the works associated with the activities of Recherche, Art et Industrie existed beforehand; they were all created specially for the occasion. True, at a given moment, with a view to setting up a foundation, we did start buying works in order to complete the ensembles we already had. But, apart from that, during the first six years, from 1967 to 1973, Renault did not keep a single work resulting from the activities of Recherches, Art et Industrie. Each one belonged to the artist. Later, it was agreed that we could choose a few of the works that had been made so as to constitute an ensemble that could not be resold."*[1]

The collection includes both major groups of several dozen works by artists such as Dubuffet, Arman, Vasarely, and Michaux (spanning one or several distinct periods) and architectural works designed specifically for Renault's buildings by Soto, Takis, Hantaï, Dewasne, Degottex, Le Parc, Tomasello, and Honegger, but also "individual" works like the paintings by Rauschenberg and Sam Francis, the sculpture by Niki de Saint-Phalle or the small groups of two or three pieces by Alechinsky, Erró, or Matta. (A complete catalogue can be found at the end of this volume.) The disparities in the ways different artists, movements, and periods are represented are due to the diverse circumstances in which these works entered the collection – although nearly all of them were acquired in the framework of a collaborative undertaking or project with the artist.

The group of works by Erró dating from 1984 and consisting of two large 200 × 300 cm canvases, *Renault Scape* and *Motor Scape (Renault 5)*, and a series of sixty small collages conflating Renault cars with the great tradition of Western painting, come out of a concern to link the two different worlds. The collages are made with banal images or fragments of images showing Renault cars or parts of Renault cars alongside famous classic paintings. The incongruous union of two remote worlds within the same iconic register – journalistic or professional reproduction – in which they are

1. Conversation with the author, December 1998.

Niki de Saint-Phalle
The White Goddess, 1963
Objects, wool and paint on pannel
178 × 110 cm

Erró
Renault Scape, 1984
Oil on canvas
200 × 300 cm

Erró
Motor Scape (Renault 5), 1984
Oil on canvas
200 × 300 cm

subverted and broken up, is at once scathing, humorous, and touching. It is also wholly characteristic of Erró's basic method. All these pictures are based on a collage of different elements. As for *Renault Scape* and *Motor Scape (Renault 5)*, they belong to the recurrent series of "scapes" made from accumulations of images selected, this time, from within a single family of objects. Both works show a phantasmagorical heap of (Renault) cars, motors, and parts, fitted together in such a way that they look like a perspective view of a landscape or a ruined megalopolis. Started in the early sixties, the relatively homogenous "scapes" punctuate an output that consists mainly of large, deliberately overloaded and eclectic pictorial spaces packed with highly disparate bits of popular imagery usually distorted or violated by their form and content. Erró's figurative world is a simultaneously apocalyptic and ironic representation of modern society and its systems of production and communication; of its prodigal, unthinking use of the image. In fact, the technique used by Erró to elaborate his paintings – the computer system known as "iron rule," for modelling forms in a 3D lead line, which he then transposes onto the canvas – can be said to link him with the industrial world of the time, which, as he recalls today, was a pleasure for him to frequent: "*I remember it as a kind of idyll without the slightest false note. I was taken to Flins to see the Renault 5 and the Espace being assembled, so I could get the spirit of the place, so to speak. As always, I needed images, lots of images. The documentation service provided me with every catalogue they could find concerning the cars and their parts. This was the material with which I got down to work.*"[2]

If Erró can be seen as a leading representative of a certain kind of European Pop Art, then the Texan Robert Rauschenberg is the great inspiration of American Pop. In accordance with what, from the outset, was always his stated aim, *"to act in that gap between . . . art and life,"* Rauschenberg began in the early fifties to form composite works – the now famous "combine paintings" – by bringing together on the same support the most heterogeneous materials from all areas of experience. While this collapsing of registers and worlds is not devoid of affinities with Erró's method, Rauschenberg, as an heir to the Dadaist revolution at the beginning of our century, moved beyond the purely pictorial dimension to include real chunks of life (be it car tires, stuffed animals, or plants in soil). In the sixties he started making silk-screen paintings in which, silk-screen and photographic

2. In an interview with Maïten Bouisset, September 1998.

Robert Rauschenberg
Untitled, 1984
Silk-screen and acrylic on canvas
258 × 206 cm

Roberto Matta
60-Quand ?, 1970
Oil on canvas
154 × 139 cm

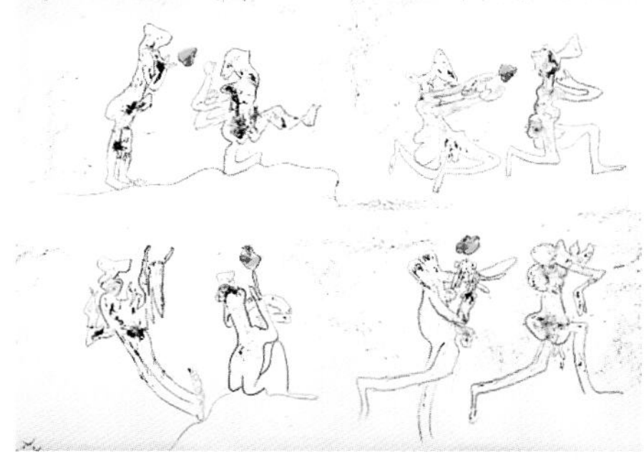

Roberto Matta
From left to right and from top to bottom:
Faire resonne un obstacle, 1978
Graphite and wax crayons on paper
50 × 66 cm

Pen totototo, 1967
Graphite and wax crayons on paper
50 × 65 cm

Les feux du psycho-obstacle, 1972
Graphite and wax crayons on paper
50 × 65 cm

Wieser tennis, tennis anyone, 1974
Graphite and wax crayons on paper
50 × 71 cm

transfers were often brought together on the canvas with paint applied using a house-painter's or artist's brush. Rauschenberg's contacts with Recherches, Art et Industrie began in the early seventies. His first project, a wholly transparent car built in conformity with technical standards whose mechanical parts would all be visible, alongside silk-screened images by the artist, was enthusiastically taken up by the design office but proved impractical on economic grounds. Relations continued, however, and in 1981 Rauschenberg accepted Claude-Louis Renard's invitation to visit the site of the American Motors–Renault plant in Kenoscha, Wisconsin. Some of the many photographs he took there were used to make four large works on paper that, along with two canvases of which one is now in the collection, constitute an ensemble entitled *Renault Series* (1984). The image is "classic Rauschenberg" with his signature juxtaposition of techniques: photographic reproductions, silk-screen, and painting. The most noteworthy characteristic of this piece is its cross shape (is the cross

Pierre Alechinsky
Roue d'herbe, 1983
Acrylic on paper mounted on canvas
155 × 170 cm

borne by the painter as an heir to Abstract Expressionism and its bold brushstrokes here parodied by the surprising painting-over of the images?) with an ENTRANCE sign where one would expect to read INRI. The sociocultural and religious allusions, together with the subtle shift of codes, endows the ensemble with an explosive irony.

Of the autonomous works that entered the collection in the ten years from 1975 to 1985, few bear such a direct or explicit relation to the world of industry, or to Renault in particular, as the ones by Erró and Rauschenberg. Jean Tinguely, though, was fascinated by movement and mechanics, by cars in general and Formula 1 in particular, and he and his wife, Niki de Saint-Phalle, had always been fervent supporters of Recherches, Art et Industrie. *"Jean Tinguely was a close friend who was also a linchpin of the new structure,"* recalls Claude-Louis Renard. *"He spent a lot of time at Renault and brought*

3. Cf. note (1)

Pierre Alechinsky
Escalator, 1983
Acrylic on paper mounted on canvas
150 × 120 cm

people together."[3] A number of projects were worked out but for various reasons, none of them were carried through. However, when the idea of setting up a Renault Foundation began to be aired, Renard offered to buy one of Tinguely's masterpieces, *Requiem pour une feuille morte* (see the essay by Margrit Hahnloser). Tinguely agreed at once and at the same time donated three other companion sculptures, *Bascule V, Eos VIII,* and *Eos XII.* The collaboration was pursued in 1981 when Tinguely produced some twenty new sculptures for an exhibition at the art center in Sénanque. Then, in 1985, Renault provided the support to enable the artist to realize his project for a video/sculpture on the theme of Formula 1, the famous *Pit Stop*, now at the Tinguely Museum in Basel.

At the same time as *Requiem*, Renault also bought an important work by Niki de Saint-Phalle, *The White Goddess* from 1963. (Saint-Phalle also produced a large number of collaborative works with her husband. In Paris,

Antoni Tàpies
Untitled, 1950
Ink with gouache highlights and black tape on paper
68 × 197 cm

the *Stravinsky Fountain*, outside the Pompidou Center, is the most striking and accessible example of their collaboration, which was as intense as it was erratic.) *The White Goddess* (1963) is one of the large monochrome assemblages she made between 1962 and 1964. It marked the end of the "tirs" (shootings), the large reliefs of big female figures in plaster, which were hung with bags of paint and then colored when these bags were burst open by rifle bullets. The large female figures that began to appear in 1962, literally made out of bits of junk – wire, textiles, found objects, kitsch toys, artificial flowers, etc. – and covered in plaster, perpetuated the idea of woman as victim, as already violently expressed in the "shot" women, but also introduced the idea of the woman as womb, bearer of life. They come a few years before the multicolored *Nana* figures, Saint-Phalle's better-known totems of triumphant feminity.

"For me, Matta is one of the greatest artists of our age," declared Erró.[4] The affinities between these two artists can be understood on the level of their common determination to bring about a veritable shift in the viewer's perceptions. Starting out as a member of the Surrealists, Matta subsequently perpetuated their spirit in his attempt to illustrate a world that is inaccessible to our perceptions, yet as real as anything our eyes can see. Painting (and

4. Maïten Bouisset, "Entretien avec Erró," *Le Matin*, 6 May 1985.

drawing) are sensuous creations that propose other forms of knowledge of the world. The painting entitled *60-Quand ?* (1970) presents a space of movement, a moment in the metamorphosis of a "machine" that we know without recognizing. The transformation of the strange forms shown here is also metaphorical; it is the mutation of our mental space. Moving away from the more abstract, gestural quality of the paintings, the four drawings, from roughly the same period – *Pen totototo* (1967), *Les feux du psycho-obstacle* (1972), *Wieser tennis, tennis anyone* (1974), and *Faire resonne obstacle* (1978) – are typical of Matta's graphic work, showing small, tightly packed figures that are human beings or fragments of human beings or instruments traced in graphite and wax crayon. These meager anthropomorphic or mechanical sign-persons and sign-objects are laid out without any depth on the rectangular surface of the paper in a circular pattern established by their postures, the positioning of the fragments of objects, or by the colored marks on the ground. The overall effect suggests the speed of thought, the fragmentation of a fleeting perception, and *"forms that are unknown to us: the liver or heart of a butterfly, the deformations of an ant's intestines, the vibrations of a fly's wings."* [5] None of these figures can be identified as existing in reality, but each of its constituent elements can. The resulting impression of the familiar yet previously unseen is both paradoxical and unsettling – life according to Matta.

The collaboration between Pierre Alechinsky and Recherches, Art et Industrie lasted for only one year but it was a particulary fruitful one. The two paintings in the collection, *Roue d'herbe* (1983) and *Escalator* (1983) belong to a group of works made between 1981 and 1984 and shown for the first time at *Alechinsky, Encres et Peintures*, an exhibition organized by Recherches, Art et Industrie at the Abbaye de Sénanque in 1984. A painter but also a writer and printmaker, Alechinsky has always been interested in the plastic qualities of script. This concern is characteristic not only of CoBrA, of which he was the youngest member from the late forties onwards, but also of other artists whose work grew out of this dual practice, such as Henri Michaux and Antoni Tàpies. His paintings always constitute a kind of visual polyphony, with the rhythms of vision and reading dissociated by the division of the pictorial space into a center and perimeter. The series made between 1982 and 1984 are exceptionally graphic, with a "black and white" central area containing a fine gray wash constituting a figure outlined in a very "written"

5. Alain Sayag, *Matta, Dessins*, Galerie de France, Paris, 1990.

black line contrasting with the nonfigurative, gestural, and colorful periphery. Whereas the center can be read and mentally interpreted, the abstract touches in the margin make a sensuous visual impression. Given the context, the motif of *Roue d'herbe* (Grass Wheel) can be taken as an allusion to the automobile, but the wheel theme has been treated by other artists in very different contexts. For example, there are Duchamp's *Bicycle Wheel* and *Rotoreliefs* from the beginning of the century, *The Wheel of Fortune* (1951–52) by Asger Jorn, the dominant figure of CoBrA, and Alberto Giacometti's *Chariot* (1950). As for Alechinsky, in 1970 he devoted a whole book to the theme, *Roue libre* (Freewheeling). No doubt the idea of movement is more important here than the actual reference to a machine. This is confirmed by *Escalator*, in which the figure seems to be moving in the direction of the (Western) reading eye, thus indicating how the gaze should read the painting, an effect subtly blurred by the fluctuating fictive frame.

Antoni Tàpies's large drawing from 1950 occupies a similar position at the junction of image and word. It features the staple elements of the Catalonian artist's formal vocabulary: the cross, which anchors and designates but that is without religious connotations; elementary signs; and poor materials (here, two sheets of paper roughly glued together). Like an ideogram, the loose yet assertive black line charged with fluid and dripping pigment, unifies the whole into a big banner-like calligraphy. Tàpies's pictorial writing is inspired by both Oriental calligraphy and graffiti.

Oriental culture was also a pervasive influence in the work of the American abstract painter Sam Francis, from whom the collection acquired a large-format work done in 1978. From their inception, Francis was *au fait* with the activities of Recherches, Art et Industrie. *"By virtue of his already considerable reputation, he helped make our activities gain credibility in the american art world,"* explains Claude-Louis Renard, who remembers the painter's *"unfailing support."*[6] This very cordial working relationship came to fruition at the beginning of the eighties with an exhibition at Sénanque. There was also another project for Montmajour, which remained on the drawing board.

The painting of Sam Francis owes much to American Abstract Expressionism – a movement that approaches the canvas as an empirical space, a field to be

6. *Op. cit.*, note (1)

Sam Francis
Untitled, 1978
Acrylic on canvas
120 × 365 cm

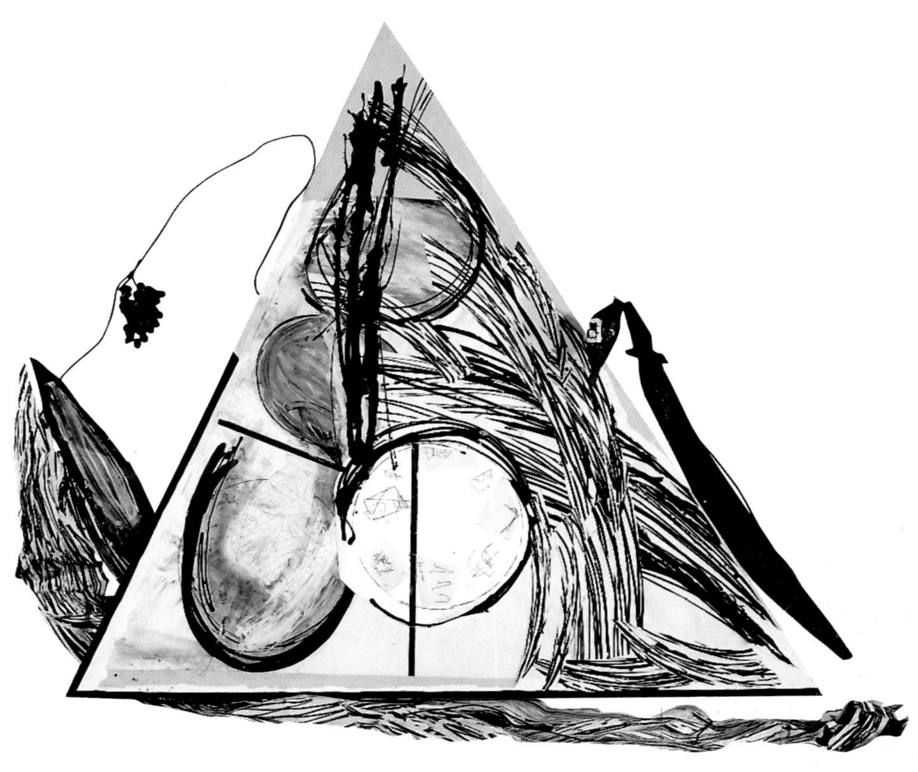

Dominique Gauthier
Médée n° 13, 1982
Oil and acrylic on canvas, felt pen and pencil on paper glued on canvas, metal rods and plastic parts fixed to the stretcher
230 × 275 cm

filled, and not a theoretical space, an inert ground on which painted forms are to be deposited – as well as to Matisse's use of big, flat patches of color. As he said, *"For me, color is true substance, the point of departure, and not drawing or line."*[7] His overriding interest was in the elementary relations between the ingredients of painting: color and surface. Like many of the works from this period, the powerfully present white in this large painting has a luminous density, which enables it to hold its own with the explosions of brightly colored paint. The space of the canvas opens beyond the edges and while its forms signify no more than the dynamic tension between them, the ensemble asserts a spirituality that transcends its materiality.

The abstract painting that followed in the wake of the great breakthrough that was Abstract Expressionism is also represented in the collection by the paintings of the French artist Dominique Thiolat. His large canvases with big motifs against intensely painted, warm-hued grounds are like a Europeanized echo of Robert Motherwell. From the same generation as Thiolat, Dominique Gauthier deliberately revisits the physical components

7. *Sam Francis, peintures récentes* (cat.), Musée national d'Art moderne, Centre Georges-Pompidou, 1978.

Dominique Thiolat
Untitled, 1978-1979
Acrylic on canvas
206 × 193 cm

of painting in a intensely engaged body of work that moves blithely from Abstract Expressionism to the most overtly narrational figuration. Finally, the Chinese-American Liga Pang, close to Sam Francis, attempts to reconcile this modern Western experimentation involving the different material elements of painting with an Oriental pictorial tradition more concerned with the sign.

ANN HINDRY

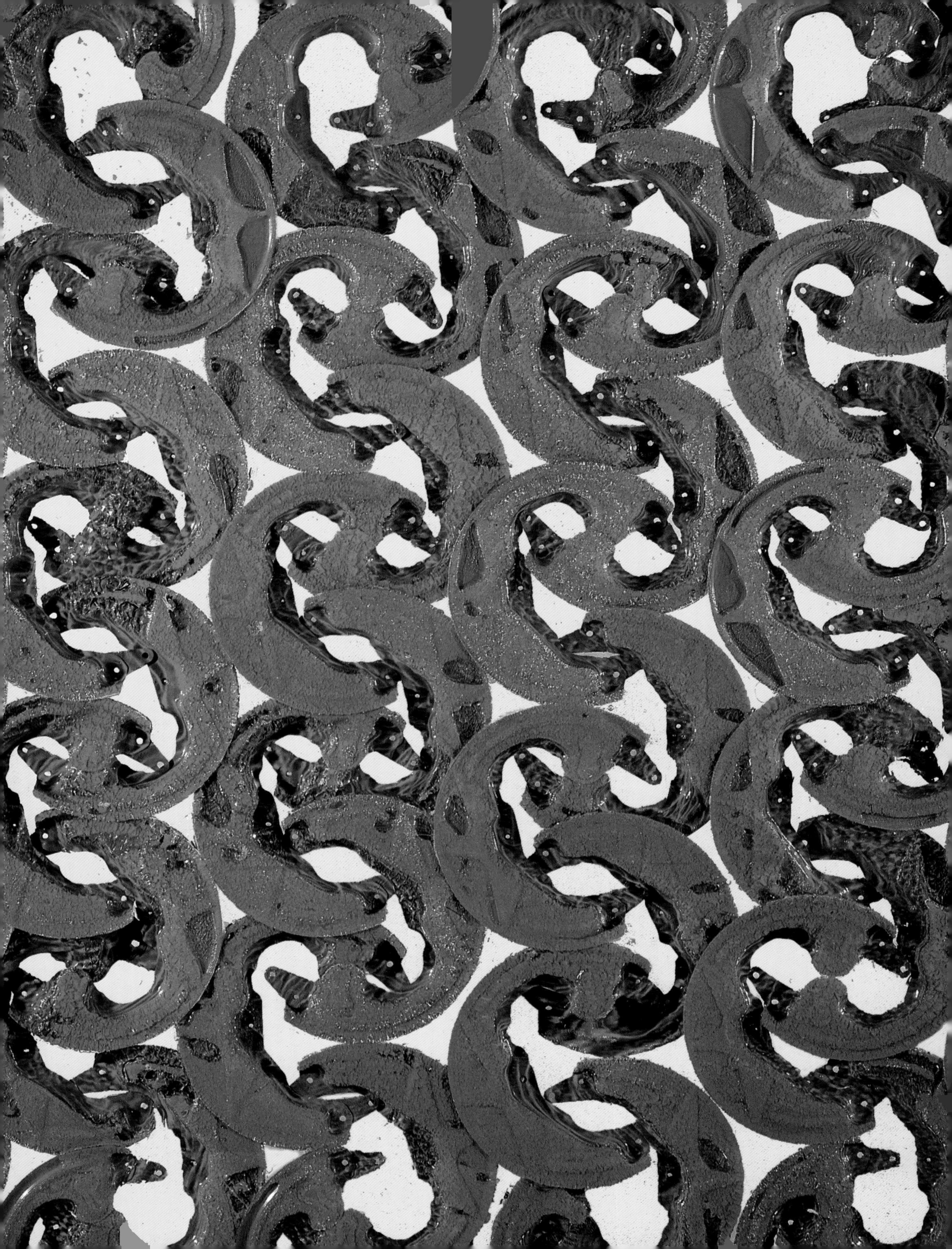

Arman
Arman's Treat

"It was as if they had opened the doors to a palace and I was free to help myself."

ARMAN

These words clearly indicate the kind of circumstances under which Arman began his collaboration with Renault in 1967. At the time, the artist had already come a certain way but was, relatively speaking, at the beginning of his career. He had made his first "accumulation" less than ten years earlier, in 1959. Now nearly forty, Arman was still a young artist at the height of his abilities with a powerful creative appetite. One can imagine what a pleasure it was for him to be able to work with a major car manufacturer.

In fact, the partner in Arman's collaborative venture with the motor industry was very nearly Ford: he had been in contact with the American firm not long before his meeting with Claude-Louis Renard and had already been out to Detroit and brought in three of his friends: Roy Lichtenstein, Robert Rauschenberg, and Frank Stella. However, after much hesitation, Ford decided that this kind of collaboration with artists might not be appreciated by the public and dropped the project.

In 1967, although a permanent resident of the United States (where the Sidney Janis Gallery in New York regularly exhibited his sculptures), Arman was still considered a French artist (he became an American citizen in 1972). While this consideration may have been of some importance to a nationalized company like Renault, the nature of Arman's work also made him an obvious choice. The idea of inviting him to come and choose his materials from the factory flowed naturally from his characteristic approach to industrial objects. As Arman himself put it, *"the factory [was] one of the churches of [my] religion."*

Of all the Nouveaux Réalistes, Arman was certainly the one who was most fascinated by industrial objects. The use of mass-produced items for aesthetic ends is a classic theme of twentieth-century art. From Marcel Duchamp to Jeff Koons, from the Surrealists to today, Arman is neither the first nor the last representative of the trend that Pierre Restany described as the *"adventure of the object."* However, it would seem that his work has a much stronger relation to the industrial mode of production than that of Duchamp, César, Daniel Spoerri, or Jeff Koons. For to talk about industrial production is not the same thing as to talk about the objects themselves. You could even

Accumulation of mechanical elements, 1974
Brake parts in plexiglass (detail)
200 × 200 × 12 cm

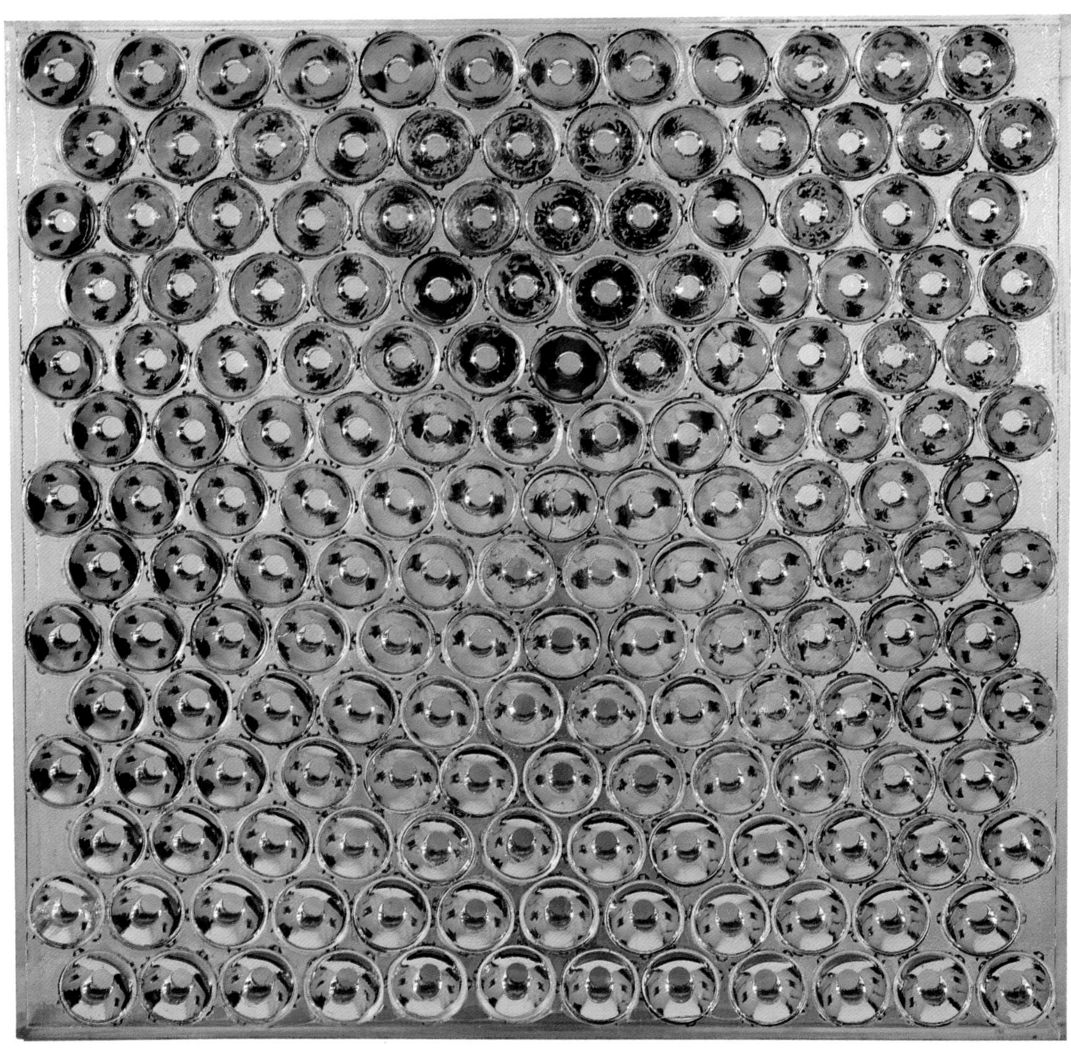

Accumulation of mechanical elements, 1974
Headlights in plexiglass
200 × 200 × 16 cm

Accumulation of mechanical elements, 1974
Joints in plexiglass
200 × 200 × 16 cm

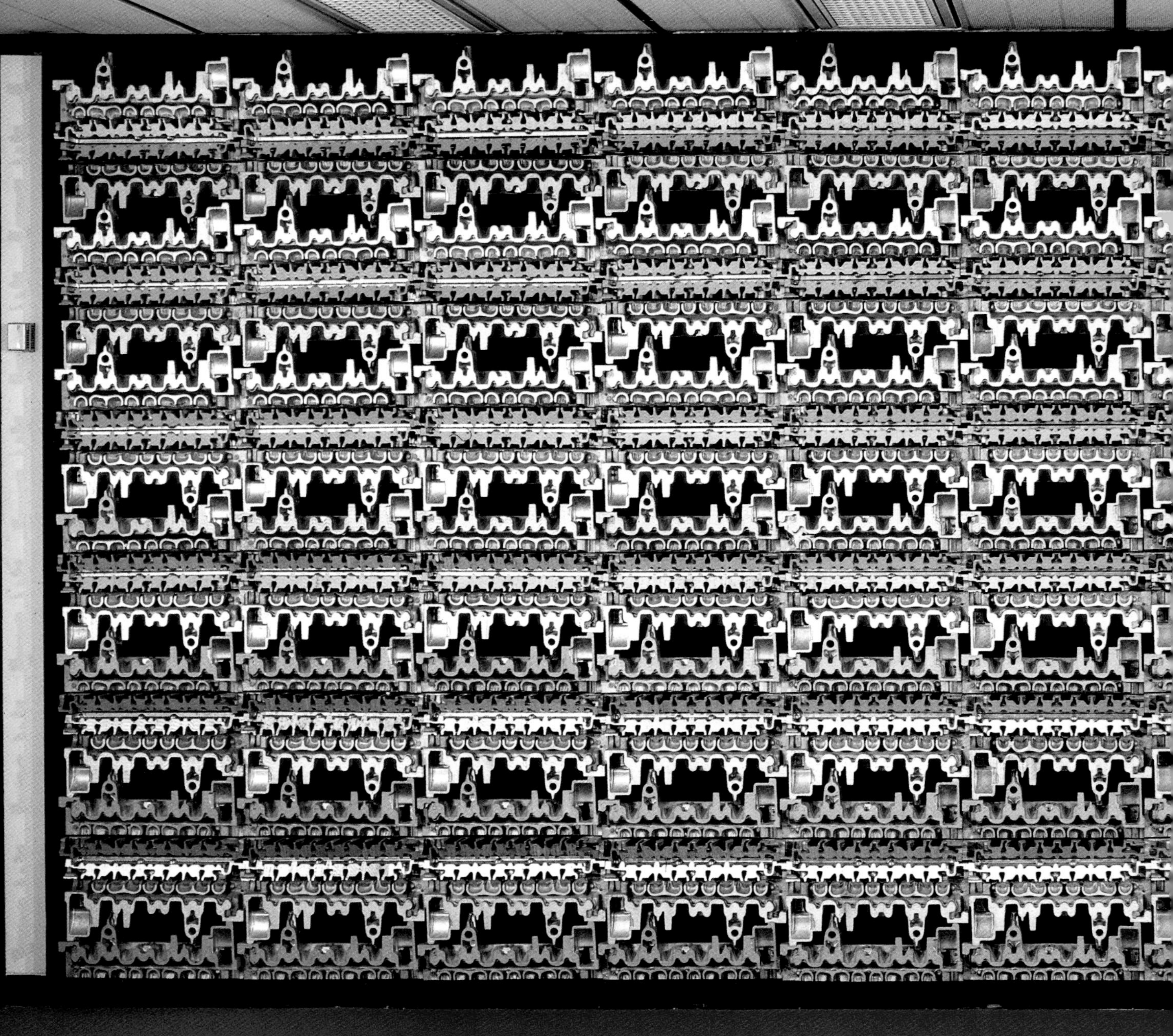

Accumulation Renault, 1974
Renault engine parts (cylinder heads) screwed on painted wooden panel
247 × 628 cm
Renault corporate headquarters, Quai du Point-du-Jour, 8th floor

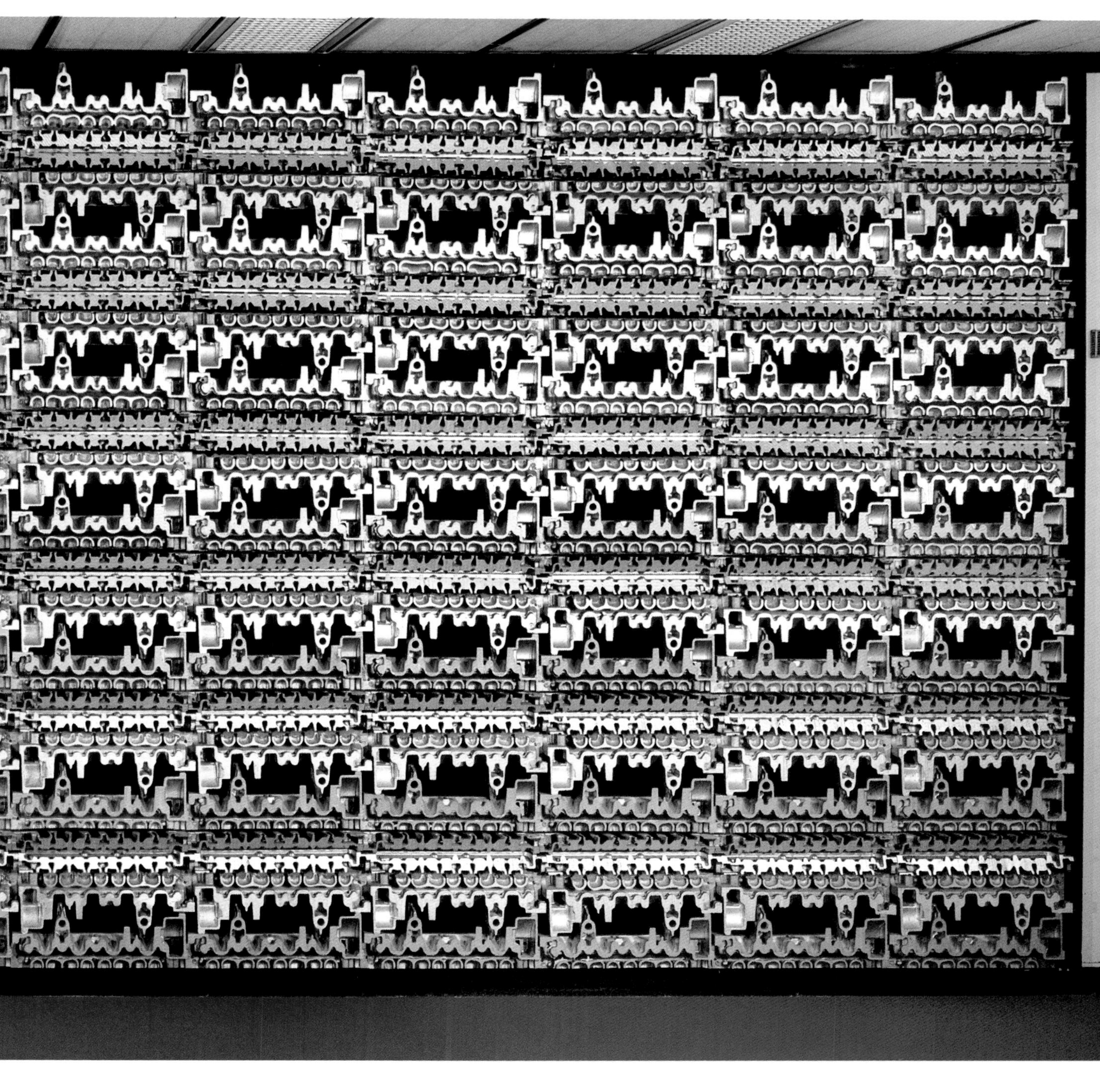

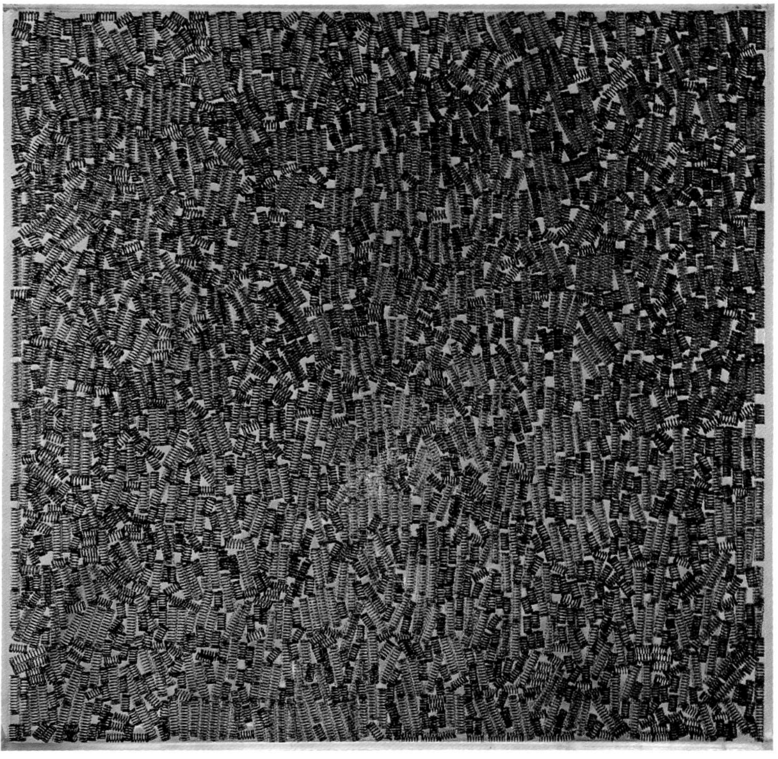

Accumulation of mechanical elements, 1974
Springs in plexiglass
200 × 200 × 16 cm

say that objects as such do not exist in industry, firstly because each object is only the sum of a number of parts, and secondly because when an object is multiplied ad infinitum it loses its own identity and forms a new entity.

This is how the artist spoke of the project in 1969: *"In a way, dealing with a system of production like Renault's has put me in the kind of landscape that I have always been out to render in my work [since] one of its goals has always been production-consumption-destruction."* I would like to insist on these three terms, particularly the last, which commentators on Arman's work often tend to neglect. Contrary to what is sometimes said about Arman's glorification of the object, it should be noted that in most of his works he degrades the objects he uses. This is obvious in the case of the "rages" or "combustions", but can the same be said about the "accumulations"? Yes, emphatically so. That is precisely what distinguishes his gesture from Duchamp's invention of the readymade. By choosing an object and presenting it on a pedestal like a sculpture, Duchamp magnified it. In contrast, by gathering together a large quantity of identical objects, Arman denies their singularity, which tends to dissolve in the ensemble. Indeed, Arman himself noted that while Duchamp baptized a urinal *Fountain* and thus gave it a new name, what he did in his accumulations was to unbaptize.

Underpinning these works is the idea that quantity modifies the quality of objects and, beyond a certain threshold, causes them to disintegrate. When Arman speaks of the *"the kind of landscape that I have always been out to render,"* he is talking above all about a landscape shaped by quantity. Rather than Duchamp, it is Warhol who comes to mind here, in whose work the repetition of the same image not only ruins its emotional significance but also takes the place of any other content. *"I have always been attracted by what is multiple,"* remarks Arman. *"I love camera shop windows or tool or toy shop windows. When I used to take photographs, I liked to repeat the same images."* [1]

Arman's taste for the serial and the repetitive naturally found plenty of outlets in the work done under the aegis of Renault's Recherches, Art et Industrie. In fact, it would appear that the benefits of this collaboration exceeded his expectations. For it was only now that he undertook to *"do real sculptural work."* Having come to art through painting, Arman's accumulations up to this stage had involved only objects small enough to fit in a box, and the painter continued to express himself in works that, although not always hung on the wall, were nevertheless presented frontally like paintings. In contrast to these, the accumulation of Renault 16 car fenders

1. I take the liberty here of referring readers to my own book *Les Nouveaux Réalistes*, (Paris: Editions du Regard, 1997).

Accumulation of mechanical elements, 1974
Fan blades in plexiglass
200 × 200 × 7 cm

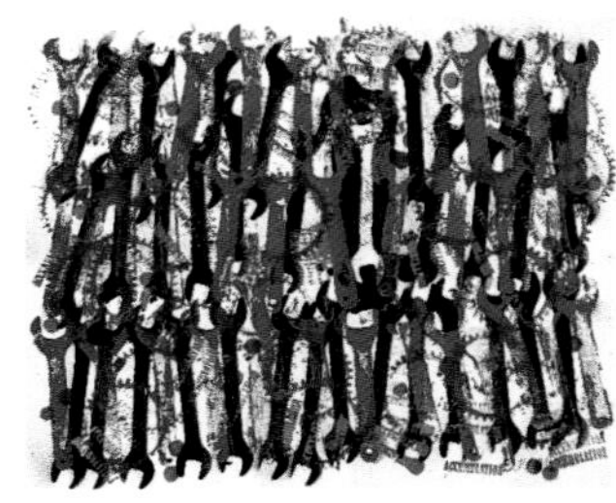

Composition, 1974
Oil with imprints from objects on canvas
70 × 80 cm

(*Accumulation Renault n° 153*) and the fine spiralling accumulation *Le Murex (Accumulation Renault n° 103)* very much belong to sculpture, in terms of both their scale and the configuration of the parts. Significantly enough, *Accumulation n° 153* is also known as *La cathédrale* because of its imposing scale on the one hand and, on the other, because, seen from the front, the arrangement of its parts suggest the arches of a barrel vault. As for *Accumulation n° 103*, it reflects Arman's interest in the Futurists and, above all, the man who designed the *Monument to the Third International*, Vladimir Tatlin.

Another source of surprise and satisfaction for Arman was the fact that Renault gave him a chance to use new objects. This marked an important step away from the supposed specificity of Nouveau Réalisme. One need only think of the torn posters collected in the street by Raymond Hains and Jacques de Villeglé, or indeed the rusty alarm clocks Arman bought at the flea market and the dentures he recuperated from a hospital bin. One measure of the significance of these new objects for Arman will be given if we recall, for one thing, that his father was an antique dealer and, for another, that it was precisely the small format of their work and the inclusion of used objects that distinguished the Nouveaux Réalistes from the American Pop artists at the famous comparative show put on by the Sidney Janis Gallery in October 1962.[2] Next to the Americans, recalls Arman, the Europeans *"looked puny and dusty,"* like *"antique dealers."*

But this experience with Renault was more than just an opportunity to work systematically with new objects. It also allowed Arman to appropriate all kinds of bits of engine and coachwork whose nature he would have otherwise found hard to grasp. As we have seen, his desire to create an art in harmony with the system of industrial production – a system that inevitably includes a consumption phase and a destruction phase – implied the disappearance of the object as such in favor of the new entity constituted by the accumulation. Now, in a factory, the object is only the last link in a very long chain. In other words, before the car-object come other objects such as electrical wires, springs, air filters, joints, spark plugs, fans, bumpers, gear boxes, hoods, rear-view mirrors, etc. Moreover, before converging as part of the car, all these elements go through different stages of development liable to cause yet more proliferation. This is what seems to have struck Arman most forcibly: *"Up to then, I had a preconceived image of the way in which*

2. Among the artists featured in this show, *The New Realists*, were Arman, Christo, Raymond Hains, Yves Klein, Daniel Spoerri, Jean Tinguely, James Rosenquist, Roy Lichtenstein, Claes Oldenburg, Andy Warhol, George Segal, and Tom Wesselmann.

Composition, 1974
Oil with imprints from objects on canvas
149 × 200 cm

a car may be assembled . . . The real discovery was to find all these objects in states in I was not expecting, intermediary states which surprised me."

Thus, thanks to Renault, Arman not only discovered the possibility of working with an incalculable number of brand-new items that were so many abstract fragments, but also found that he could use various fragments at various stages of their production. Thus, as he requested them so he was provided with hoods ready to be cut from the sheet metal, or items at the holing stage (when elements such as screw holes are put in), or at the enamelling stage. The accumulations of fenders and hoods mentioned contain groups of sprayed elements, but this paint is totally artificial since in normal circumstances it is only applied when assembly is complete – not item by item. Clearly then, Arman did not just use already existing elements; he also used elements that had been specially prepared for him by workers at the factory. *"I didn't take this or that gear or mechanical piece just as they were,"* he recalls. *"I chose a particular part of them that interested me, then I asked them to cut it in two."* This no doubt explains his words to Claude-Louis Renard in 1969: *"By showing me how these elements were made and prepared before being assembled in the factory, they truly whetted my appetite."*

Arman's activity matched his hunger. In all, he made over a hundred accumulations with the pieces and materials provided by Renault. A selection of these works was presented at the Musée des Arts Décoratifs in Paris in 1969. They were accompanied by the artist's "Accumulative Poem,"

ACCUMULATIVE POEM

Extract from the exhibition catalogue
Arman, accumulation Renault,
1969, Musée des Arts Décoratifs, Paris.

SIXTEEN R FOUR SIDE PANELS
TWENTY-FOUR R FOUR FENDERS
TWENTY-NINE YELLOW R FOUR FENDERS
ONE THOUSAND ASSORTED WIRES ALL COLORS LENGTH ZERO POINT SIX ZERO METERS VARYING THICKNESSES
FIVE R SIXTEEN PANELS RIGHT SIDE
FIVE R SIXTEEN PANELS LEFT SIDE
THIRTY-FOUR DAUPHINE ROOF TOPS
TWO HUNDRED AND FIFTY REAR-VIEW MIRRORS
TWENTY-FOUR GLOSSY BLACK R FOUR HOODS
EIGHTEEN FRÉGATE CRANKSHAFTS
FORTY AIR FILTERS
TWO HUNDRED HAND GRIPS
EIGHTY R FOUR IGNITION HARNESSES
SIXTY-SIX R TEN CRANKSHAFTS
THIRTY SAWN-OFF R SIXTEEN CYLINDER HEADS
ONE THOUSAND RED ELECTRICAL WIRES LENGTH ZERO POINT SIX ZERO METERS BARE TIPS
ONE HUNDRED AND FORTY CONTROL BUTTONS REF. EIGHT MILLION FIVE HUNDRED AND FIFTY-EIGHT THOUSAND SEVEN HUNDRED AND FIVE
ONE HUNDRED AND FORTY CONTROL BUTTONS REF. EIGHT MILLION FIVE HUNDRED AND FIFTY-EIGHT THOUSAND SEVEN HUNDRED AND FOUR
ONE HUNDRED AND FORTY CONTROL BUTTONS REF. EIGHT MILLION FIVE HUNDRED AND FIFTY-FIVE THOUSAND FOUR HUNDRED AND FORTY-NINE
TEN SETS OF R EIGHT GASKETS
TEN SETS OF R FOUR GASKETS
ONE HUNDRED AND THIRTY-FIVE R FOUR TAIL LIGHTS
TWENTY-FOUR R SIXTEEN HOODS
EIGHTY-FOUR R FOUR FRONT FENDERS
FORTY R SIXTEEN AIR FILTERS
ONE HUNDRED AND TWENTY-FIVE SOFICA FAN TURBINES
FIVE SHEETS OF COPPER AND CHROME PARTS
TWO HUNDRED HANDLES
ONE HUNDRED R FOUR FAN BLADES
SIX SAWN – OFF ENGINE BLOCKS
SIXTY SAWN-OFF R TEN CYLINDER HEADS
FORTY R SIXTEEN AIR FILTERS
FORTY R FOUR RADIATORS
TEN R SIXTEEN FRONT FENDERS
FIVE HUNDRED R FOUR RADIATOR BADGES
TWO HUNDRED AND FIFTY R SIXTEEN RENAULT LOZENGES
ONE HUNDRED R TEN TEN MARKINGS
ONE HUNDRED R EIGHT EIGHT MARKINGS
ONE HUNDRED R FOUR FOUR MARKINGS
ONE HUNDRED R FOUR "PARISIENNE" MARKINGS
FIVE THOUSAND DARK GRAY WIRES LENGTH ZERO POINT TWO ZERO METERS WITH COPPER COLOR CONTACTS AT EACH END
TWO THOUSAND BLACK WIRES LENGTH ZERO POINT SIX ZERO METERS BARE TIPS
FIVE THOUSAND RED WIRES LENGTH ZERO POINT TWO ZERO METERS WITH COPPER COLOR CONTACTS AT EACH END
TWO THOUSAND WHITE WIRES LENGTH ONE METER BARE TIPS
TEN SETS OF R SIXTEEN ENGINE GASKETS
TEN SETS OF GASKETS REF. NINE MILLION NINE HUNDRED AND SIXTY THOUSAND FOUR HUNDRED AND NINETY-FIVE
TEN SETS OF GASKETS REF. NINE MILLION EIGHT HUNDRED AND SIX THOUSAND FOUR HUNDRED AND SIXTY
TWENTY SETS OF R FOUR GASKETS
ONE POINT SIX ZERO METERS OF THREADED ROD THICKNESS SIX MILLIMETERS
FOUR HEXAGONAL NUTS
FOUR PACKETS OF ROUND-HEADED WOOD SCREWS THIRTY-FIVE BY FOUR MILLIMETERS
ONE PACKET OF ROUND-HEADED WOOD SCREWS FIFTY MILLIMETERS BY SIX
FOUR PACKETS OF SOLDERING STRIPS TWO POINT FIVE MILLIMETERS ;
ONE PACKET OF SUPER VIOLETTES THREE MILLIMETER SOLDERING STRIPS
TWO KILOS OF WASHABLE WHITE PAINT
TWO KILOS OF WASHABLE BLACK PAINT
ONE KILO OF WASHABLE RED PAINT
SIXTY SQUARE METERS OF PLEXIGLASS THICKNESS FIVE AND SIX MILLIMETERS
TWO SQUARE METERS OF PLEXIGLASS THICKNESS TWO CENTIMETERS
THREE HUNDRED AND SEVEN KILOS OF ACRILIC ALTUGLAS GLUE

Left, **Arman**
Accumulation Renault, 1974
Renault engine parts
(water pumps) screwed
on painted wooden panel
247 × 618 cm

Right, **Victor Vasarely**
Freg 1-2, 1968
Oil on canvas
180 × 180 cm

Renault corporate headquarters,
Quai du Point-du-Jour, 8th floor

an outpouring of numbers, which so obviously delights its author and which staggers the reader. It is the work of a kind of mechanical Gargantua. The poem perfectly expresses the fervid excitement that seems to have gripped Arman when given a free hand at Renault.

We can distinguish four main categories of works amongst this ensemble. In the first, the pieces are meticulously arranged. In the second, they occur in a loose display prepared to varying extents by the artist: the *Accumulation Renault n° 114*, made up of fan blades, and *n° 137*, consisting of cut-up cylinder heads, both belong in this category. These are paradoxical works in that, despite the raw industrial appearance of their components, they do exude a certain aestheticism. It is, indeed, something of a surprise to see heavy pieces of steel turn into decorative motifs, or engine blocks form surfaces as ornate as lace, and fragments of cylinder heads sketch friezes like the garlands of fruits and flowers painted by Renaissance masters on church ceilings. This category also includes the monochrome sprays or skeins of electrical wires.

Among the unarranged *Accumulations* we might mention *Accumulation n° 115*. It belongs to a series of three whose content is particularly significant, since it happens to be the company logo. However, looking at the disposition of the parts more closely, one realizes that here and there, Arman probably abetted the workings of chance with his own promptings. For example, on the right there is an almost perfectly aligned row of lozenges. Did the artist arrange this or did he simply accept a phenomenon that he had ample opportunity to observe, that is the tendency of objects to form their own compositions? Indeed, Arman often intervened precisely in order to remedy the effects of this auto-composition. Some objects (not so much the smaller ones, like nails or screws) need to be assisted because they tend to produce what Arman calls a *"negative system,"* either by excess of composition or excess of chaos. In such cases, he tells us, *"I assist the automatic arrangement of objects that tend to compose themselves or, on the contrary, I break it down. I take the initial result and I either lighten it or make it more emphatic."* The eight big accumulations under plexiglass in the Renault Collection – the only ones unnumbered – offer a very good example of this dialectic between the emancipation and the subjection of the object. The straight rows of Renault 4 headlights in one work answer the teeming mass of joints in the other. The organized lines of the ventilators – which objects are already very graphic in themselves – trace out an almost iterative motif in the third work, which contrasts with the jumble of little pipe tongs lost in the resin of the fourth. In another piece, the object literally dissolves in the overall effect: the mass of resin in the plexiglass box has gradually eaten away at the surface of the red paint covering each part. Coming to the work frontally, one has the disconcerting and fleeting sensation of standing before a large abstract painting.

The third group of works to have arisen from this collaborative venture is perhaps the most spectacular and original. These are the accumulations of coachwork parts which, according to Arman, have more to do with the craft of the sculptor. In this series we find, for example, *Accumulation Renault n° 152*, which Daniel Abadie, one of the most keen observers of Arman's work, appropriately judges to be *"closer to Minimalist sculpture than Pop Art or Nouveau Réalisme."* Anyone who has seen Arman's most recent exhibitions, and particularly the works he calls "cascades" (for example, *Spinal Cord*, 1996, an accumulation of armchairs), will be curious to note that he has continued to work in the direction inaugurated by these scaffoldings, whose rationality and power are heightened by their gradated colors and monochrome finish.

The fourth remarkable ensemble is that of the walls of accumulations, which are integrated into the building. It consists of two bas-reliefs six meters wide, which were fitted into Renault's corporate headquarters in early 1974. Thus, when Arman began working on them he had already gained much experience with the materials and the personnel with whom he would be working. Perhaps it is this intimate familiarity with his resources that explains his extraordinary mastery here. Consisting of sawn-off cylinder head boxes juxtaposed in a regular pattern on a black ground, these two works are incredibly alive yet perfectly serene. From a distance, the objects making up these frescoes seem to have no trace of individual existence or autonomy. We see neither the individual pieces nor an accumulation, but simply a large, homogenous surface evoking some monumental piece of silverwork glinting in the light. Only when we come closer, as one would to a painting to appreciate the finesse of the material or the dexterity of the painter, do the forms grow apart from each other and their outline become clear. These works prove the accumulative method's formidable capacity for transforming objects. Certainly the objets used by Arman are real enough, but when they merge in the overall mass of the wall, they create a globally uncertain image that verges on immateriality. Once again, here, Arman demonstrates that his work is not an exaltation of the object. In other words, the accumulations are not about setting off the qualities of the object. On the contrary, it is the object that serves to reveal to the gaze this abstract quality which so fascinates the artist: quantity.

Apart from the works belonging to these four ensembles, it is also worth singling out a series of slices of engines in plexiglass boxes, as well as a series done on the model of the *Allures d'objets* (Gaits of Objects) of the late fifties. In those days, Arman used all kinds of objects (shoes, ball bearings, bottles, etc.). For the paintings done during his collaboration with Renault, he marked the canvas at regular intervals by placing upon it an engine part dipped in paint.

While we can get an idea of what this adventure meant to Arman from the photographs taken at the time – if not always from the works themselves[3] – it is harder to imagine what it meant to its patron. François Mathey's preface in the catalogue to the Musée des Arts Décoratifs show indicates that the idea was driven by a certain utopian impulse characteristic of the period. Let us not forgot that in the wake of May 1968, changing the world meant above all changing human relations. Thus Mathey hailed the rapprochement of art and industry as something that would foster *"shared creation by artists and technicians."* The initiative benefited Arman in that it gave him an opportunity to try out various materials, products, and machines with the assistance of the company's specialists, but it was also supposed to benefit the company because it was crucial to *"the humanity of relations in the world of tomorrow, and to our very vision of this world."* Subsequent events (beginning with the death of the proletarian left activist Pierre Overnay in 1972) would reveal just how idealistic such hopes were. As for Arman, though, it is unlikely that he ever pursued any goal other than to progress in his art. That, perhaps, is what we call "the irony of history."

CATHERINE FRANCBLIN

3. A number of which have been destroyed or lost.

Bibliography and origin of the citations

Interview of Arman by Claude-Louis Renard, in the exhibition catalogue, *Arman, Accumulations Renault,* Union centrale des Arts décoratifs, Paris, 1969.

Interview of Arman by Daniel Abadie, in the exhibition catalogue, *Arman, Accumulations Renault, 1967-1970,* galerie Georges-Philippe Vallois, Paris, 1995.

J.D. 74

Jean Dubuffet

From *Hourloupe* to Castille: Dubuffet at Renault

Just as the press has a penchant for catastrophes and delayed trains, so the collective memory tends to reduce Jean Dubuffet's dealings with Renault to the law suit that brought them into years of conflict. It began when the *Salon d'été*, an environment commissioned from the artist for Renault's corporate headquarters, was razed before it could even be completed. It ended, on appeal, with the victory of artist over patron, a judgement that continues to set the precedent for the thorny issues of artistic rights. And yet, however regrettable this episode, it should not be allowed to overshadow the work Dubuffet had already done for Renault at the behest of Claude-Louis Renard, then (this was the sixties and seventies) director of a department for supporting art, the Service de Recherches, Art et Industrie. As a result of this initiative, Renault now holds what is in many respects an exemplary collection. It is true that the twenty-one pieces constituting Dubuffet's *Roman burlesque* and displayed in the hospitality rooms at 34, Quai du Point-du-Jour are not as well known as the *Group of Four Trees* made by the artist for Chase Manhattan Bank in New York, but (although the rooms are not open to the public), they are nonetheless there, right under the Parisians' noses, and attest to a model of boldness in a sphere where it is deemed appropriate to dismiss French companies as incapable of competing with their transatlantic counterparts. This ensemble, which only habit or linguistic indolence would describe as *decorative*, is the centerpiece of a larger collection that also features *Le mur bleu*, a large bas-relief from 1967, a polyester figure known as *Fiston la filoche*, the series *Paysages castillans*, and of course, the model for the very controversial *Salon d'été*.

As we know, Dubuffet's work is organized in major cycles and periods, which he went to pains to name himself, thus preempting the approximations that, for him, were the critics' stock in trade. The works at Renault belong to Dubuffet's second important period, a cycle covering some twelve years (from 1962 to 1974), which is now known under the name of "Hourloupe". Made in November 1973, the commission for both the decor of the hospitality rooms and the monumental edifice coincided with the end of this cycle and its most singular developments, which often still arouse resistance today. Some are put out by the fact that the *Roman burlesque* and *Paysages castillans* (which the artist himself described as the "swan song" of the Hourloupe cycle[1]) were not physically made by Dubuffet himself, but are enlargements

1. Letter to Claude-Louis Renard dated 25 October 1974. See below and note 16.

Le citadin, 1974
Vinyl on canvas
208 × 130 cm

made by assistants from projections of his small drawings. This logical development in the artist's methods can only be properly understood if we take the trouble to look at the origins and main stages of Hourloupe.

Alexander Graham Bell and Baron Bich

Like many other inventions, the Hourloupe resulted from the paradoxical meeting of two technologies: the telephone and the ballpoint pen. Both were conceived at the end of the nineteenth century, and neither was really popularized until after the Second World War. They came together on the note pads placed beside the phone where, in counterpoint to the conversation, the tip of the pen traced doodles whose sole meaning and purpose was to keep the free hand busy.

For Dubuffet, this encounter was particularly propitious to the occurrence of art. It took place where art was not expected or where one would never dream of naming it – *"it runs away immediately"*[2] when one does; it used instruments few would suspect of being implicated in the academic tuition of drawing (in the early sixties, use of the ballpoint was banned from all schools in favor of the traditional nib, aptly known as the "Sergeant-Major"); and it involved a certain lowering of one's mental guard. Like many others, Dubuffet had produced his share of telephone graffiti and, in July 1962, he decided to cut them out to see what they might yield. *"Having cut them out,"* recalls Max Loreau, *"he soon discovered that they started to change as soon as he put them against a black ground. They were empty of meaning, but pressed and crushed by the black, they were suddenly full of allusions that gave them an unexpected weight."*[3] In 1963 Noël Arnaud published twenty-six of these drawings and the portmanteau word "Hourloupe" was coined to christen the volume.

Certain aspects of these telephone doodles, and the way in which they liberate unexpected forms, are redolent of the automatic writing that André Breton originally sought to establish as the principle of Surrealist painting. However, their banal, ordinary, almost trivial character protects them from the seductions of fantasy, which inspired Surrealism. Formally, Dubuffet's instinctive drawings have two main characteristics: their colors, first of all, the alternating or synchronous play of red, blue, and black against the white of the paper; and, secondly, a structure of coarsely hatched cells divide up the sheet of paper like hedges on a tiny piece of farmland. Originally,

2. *"Art is a person in love with anonymity. As soon as it's unmasked, as soon as someone points the finger, it runs away. It leaves in its place a prize stooge wearing on its back a great placard marked ART, which everybody immediately showers with champagne, and which the lecturers lead from town to town with a ring through its nose."* Jean Dubuffet, "Crude Art Preferred to Cultural Art" ("L'art brut préféré aux arts culturels"), translated in Charles Harrison & Paul Wood (eds.), *Art in Theory 1900–1990* (Oxford: Blackwell, 1992), p. 595.

3. Max Loreau, *Jean Dubuffet, Délits, déportements, lieux de haut-jeu*, (Lausanne: Weber Editeur, 1971), p. 418.

the blue, red, and black represented the three colors of ink available in these inexpensive ballpoint pens (blue or black for the text, red for corrections – and then there were those pens that contained two or three colors which could be alternated using a spring mechanism that was very satisfying to activate . . .). The first Hourloupe paintings are not always limited to this range; some rather large and well-known paintings such as *La houle du virtuel*, *La vie de famille*, and *Pourlèche fiston* also use pink, green, and yellow, sometimes in bright hues. However, it became the almost exclusive norm for the works done after 1965, underlining the cerebral (or, as we would say nowadays, conceptual) character of the undertaking, as well as Dubuffet's determination to avoid the trap of prettiness. All the pieces in the Renault collection are based on this range, except for the *Paysages castillans*, which, with their curious blue-gray skies and light ocher ground, mark the end of the Hourloupe cycle.

These three colors are not neutral. Daniel Abadie sees the red and blue as a possible allusion to works on anatomy, where they are used to represent new and old blood. Indeed, is not Dubuffet very much an artist who makes new things from old, rich harmonies from such poor materials?[4] But, in the form of Azure, Gules, Argent, and Sable, blue, red, white, and black are also the favored colors of heraldry. After all, a coat of arms is nothing less than a form of pictorial writing, a coded pictogram designed to provide a forceful representation of purely abstract values: name, lineage and rank. The historian Michel Pastoureau has noted how these colors have remained present in our modern system of blazons, road signage, where they often accompany the most imperious symbols, those concerning interdiction and obligation.[5]

It is not a rare occurrence in the history of painting for artists to opt for a limited palette, what we might call "combat colours." This is obviously the case with Braque and Picasso's ochres and grays during the most innovative years of Cubism, 1910 and 1911, but there are plenty of other examples. The Hourloupe cycle was enlisted in a combat against an imposed and conventional vision of reality. And it is within this critical framework that the second innovation derived from the telephone doodle, the sort of skein of hatched cells that sometimes seems to overrun the canvas or sheet of paper, acquires its full meaning. It would be tempting to describe it as an alphabet of forms or a modular composition, but this would be something of mistake. The elements of the Hourloupe do not obey the economic logic of efficiency, which is that of the module as conceived by architects or geometric abstract

4. Daniel Abadie, "Réflexions aux couleurs de Jean Dubuffet," *Dubuffet*, proceedings of the symposium on Jean Dubuffet, (Paris: Edition du Jeu de Paume, 1992).

5. See his *Dictionnaire des couleurs de notre temps: symbolique et société*, (Paris: C. Bonneton, 1992).

Le vaisseau, 1971–1972
Acrylic on klégecell
292 × 385 cm

Le convoi, 1971–1972
Acrylic on klégecell
295 × 384 cm

Lice tapisse, 1971 – 1972
Acrylic on klégecell
293 × 390 cm

artists. Each of the elements is unique; assembled any old how, like a buhrstone wall, they seem to engender each other rather than take their place in a global project thought through in advance. If they do evoke architecture, it is more in the reference to urban growth than to the construction of a building. Although he was reluctant to admit to it, the urban phenomenon was no doubt very much on Dubuffet's mind when he started work on the Hourloupe. It was because he was growing weary of the natural sites of Provence, where he settled in 1955, that in 1961 – in other words, just before the Hourloupe – he went back to the city figures of his early years in the series *Paris circus.* At any rate, the town, when left to develop freely, was for Dubuffet an ideal figure of productive chaos. In a text entitled "Restore the Hydra's Million Heads,"[6] he argued vigorously against the plan-oriented urbanism of the architect and technocrat ("the disastrous one-headed hydra") and in favor of the harmony that results from the sum of differences, as exemplified by Arabian towns. *"My wish for the city is that it should be immense, uncountable, untellable . . . I think that this character requires that*

6. Jean Dubuffet, *Prospectus et tous écrits suivants*, texts selected and edited by Hubert Damisch, (Paris: Gallimard, 1995), pp. 25–27.

the town, instead of being a huge enlargement of a simple, logical figure, should be extremely composite, made up of an infinite number of disparate figures, teeming with contradictions like the world. In a word, chaotic. Chaos is the food relished by the stomach of thought."[7]

Dubuffet was also fascinated by the physical sciences (in 1978 he wrote to Robert Pinget: *"The only things that interrupt my reading of your books are works of microphysics."*[8]) and was hoping that in the Hourloupe he would be able to bring into painting our century's radically new insights into matter and the non-difference of time and space, rather than to stay with a vision inherited from Aristotle. Responding to Max Loreau, whose analyses rested

7. *Ibid.*

8. Letter to Robert Pinget, 1 August 1978, *Prospectus . . .*, op. cit., vol. IV, p. 375. Hubert Damisch, whose selection for this volume includes some of Dubuffet's reading notes, emphazises the artist's interest in works of popular science, especially on physics and cosmology: see vol. III, p. 390.

Château de vent souffle, 1971 – 1972
Acrylic on klégecell
298 × 332 cm

on the classical opposition of matter and form, he stated: *"In my paintings I strive to represent a world where the notion of the individuated, finished object is called into question, the object being treated as a temporary accident, like ripples on the water; fleeting folds in a moving drapery; while at the same time the undifferentiated continuum is seen as teeming with all kinds of temporary accidents, which have just as strong a claim to be considered as 'objects' as those accepted as such by common sense."*[9] It looks very much as if, after the fifties, when he set out to *"capture the imprint of the world,"* to celebrate the mineral and the vegetable, he now wanted to use the skein of cells that came into being one day at the tip of his Bic pen to generate not only all known and unknown forms, but also the space that contains them. Sites and figures regress to formlessness or, on the contrary, the formless becomes figure and site. Such might be one lapidary definition of the Hourloupe.

Sleeping in the Shadow of an Idea

In the early tentative stages of its emergence, the Hourloupe formed a rather abstract jumble. If we are able to make out figures and objects in the first drawings, then it is only with the assistance of their captions and that imaginative capacity that enables us to see faces and horses in the clouds. We need to spend a long time looking at and getting used to *Le principe dansant de l'Hourloupe, La houle du virtuel* or the superbly named *Banque des équivoques* before we can make out familiar features, and even then we can never be sure that they were put there on purpose.

In accordance with a law of productive paradox much valued by Dubuffet, it is precisely the unsuitability of the Hourloupe drawing style that makes the images deriving from it so precious. These began to appear in 1963 and 1964. *"For the moment I am making very 'Hourloupish' objects (the typewriter, the wheelbarrow, the bed, the fishing boat, the lamp and the scales, the provincial houses in Etaples). That is to say, I am going upstream towards the* Hourloupe, *taking it in the opposite direction; instead of starting off with indeterminate traces which end up delivering a wheelbarrow, I start off with the idea of making a wheelbarrow and I add my indeterminate traces. The truth is that I am making the current flow in both directions at the same time."*[10] This demiurgic vision gradually led Dubuffet to a dream worthy of Borges, that of a Hourloupean double, which would somehow supplant, or double up for reality – or what

9. *Prospectus . . .*, op. cit., vol. IV, p. 324. Dubuffet's reply was not made directly to Max Loreau. Rather, he challenged his interpretations in two letters to Gaëtan Picon, whom he congratulated on not taking *"the big heavy book"* (*op. cit.*, note 3) to the Île de Ré with him.

10. Letter to Jacques Berne, 1971, quoted in *Les Dubuffet de Jean Dubuffet*, donation by Jean Dubuffet to the Musée des Arts Décoratifs in 1967, (Paris: Union des Arts Décoratifs/Maeght Editeur, 1992), p. 176.

we perceive as such. One of the most tangible consequences of his pursuit of this dream is the desire to move into the third dimension. This ambition would find its own specific medium in expanded polystyrene, which is modern and surprising, light and free of sculptural history. This synthetic material is to clay and bronze more or less what the ballpoint of the early Hourloupe cycle was to the marten-hair brush. Even its name is marvellously apt for Dubuffet's project of a drawing that would suddenly acquire volume (an *expansion*). There was no need for the gouge, burin, or saw: the polystyrene would be worked with a Moulinex electric carving knife or thermal butter wire specially cobbled together by Lili Dubuffet's brother. A whole arsenal of strangely assorted objects emerged from this curious cottage industry: teapots, teacups, spoons, clocks, tables with carafes, bottles, or bread (was Dubuffet unconsciously referring to the Cubist still lifes, which, for a while, were similarly tempted by the third dimension? One thinks in particular of Picasso's *Verre d'absinthe* and Laurens's bas-reliefs), which, to use the artist's expression, go *"downstream"* or *"upstream"* along the current of the Hourloupe.

Renault has one of the key ensembles from this period, the *Mur bleu.* Dubuffet began work on this wall in 1967. Originally, it consisted of nineteen carefully numbered and separate elements, known simply as the *Eléments bleus,* which we know were cut from polystyrene between 6 June and 14 July 1967. Limited to blue, black, and white, they clearly belong to the family of works that went *downstream* along the current of the Hourloupe. One could, again for the sake of convenience, describe them as non figurative. Carved using the electric knife then cast in resin, they have raw surfaces whose rough texture catches color and light and each one has its own autonomous existence.

It was while he was producing this ensemble that Dubuffet first envisaged the hypothesis of building a global environment that would be, quite literally, *habitable.* At the time, he was unable to find the right formal solution, the binding agent that would have allowed him to assemble the elements in a grotto or igloo. It was not until 1970 that he opted for the so-called *Mur bleu* presentation, consisting of a bas-relief adorned with pilasters from which a kind of figure almost sticks out. *"This fellow,"* says Alexandre Vialatte, *"is the Seated One. He is very fine, a Mr. Average you might say, as seen waiting*

Fiston la filoche, 1966 – 1967
Transfer on polyester
154 × 61 × 37 cm

Site à l'homme assis, 1969
Polyester painted
with polyurethane
60 × 64 × 38 cm

in the drizzling rain for bus number 27 at the corner of Rue Glacière."[11] Fine, without a doubt, and surely disturbing too. This figure emerging surreptitiously from the wall is also a kind of Horla or a golem – but with an affable manner you would expect from your concierge.

Dubuffet was quick to spot the opportunity offered by the new materials now available (not only expanded polystyrene, but also all the varieties of synthetic resin) to extend his program of subverting conventional forms and techniques to architecture, a discipline supposedly bound by its rules. *"From birth onwards, we have all been constantly surrounded by level planes and rectilinear elements. We sleep in a parallelepipedal bedroom, in a rectangular bed and our furniture is the same . . . I was very curious about our capacity to escape from dwelling in these planar and rectilinear geometrical structures . . ."*[12] The *Salon d'été*, which he planned and began to build for Renault, is one of these attempts, not all of which were completed, to free architecture from the laws of geometry. These constructions were often commissions. Thus it was that for several years Dubuffet adopted a way of working that had been abandoned by most twentieth-century painters.

Even the architects of Art Nouveau, even Antonio Gaudi, for all their determination to free themselves of restrictive principles of construction, had of necessity to limit their use of curves and fanciful lines so as not to overtax the strength of brick, stone, concrete, and ceramics. While it did not abolish them, plastic pushed these technical limits back so far that Dubuffet could in a sense do whatever he liked. His architectural structures were not designed with a view to their scale – the models were freely shaped, occasionally enlarged to a habitable size by means of a pantograph. This instrument used by sculptors to make the transition from the rough model to monumental scale (Dubuffet was very taken with the transformative capacities of this apparatus) was a new addition to the architect's box of tools. Whether made either directly in resin or from concrete poured into the polystyrene

11. "Dans l'atelier de Jean Dubuffet, entretien avec Alexandre Vialatte," in *Prospectus . . ., op. cit.*, vol. IV, p. 32.

12. *Prospectus . . ., op. cit.*, vol. III, p. 516.

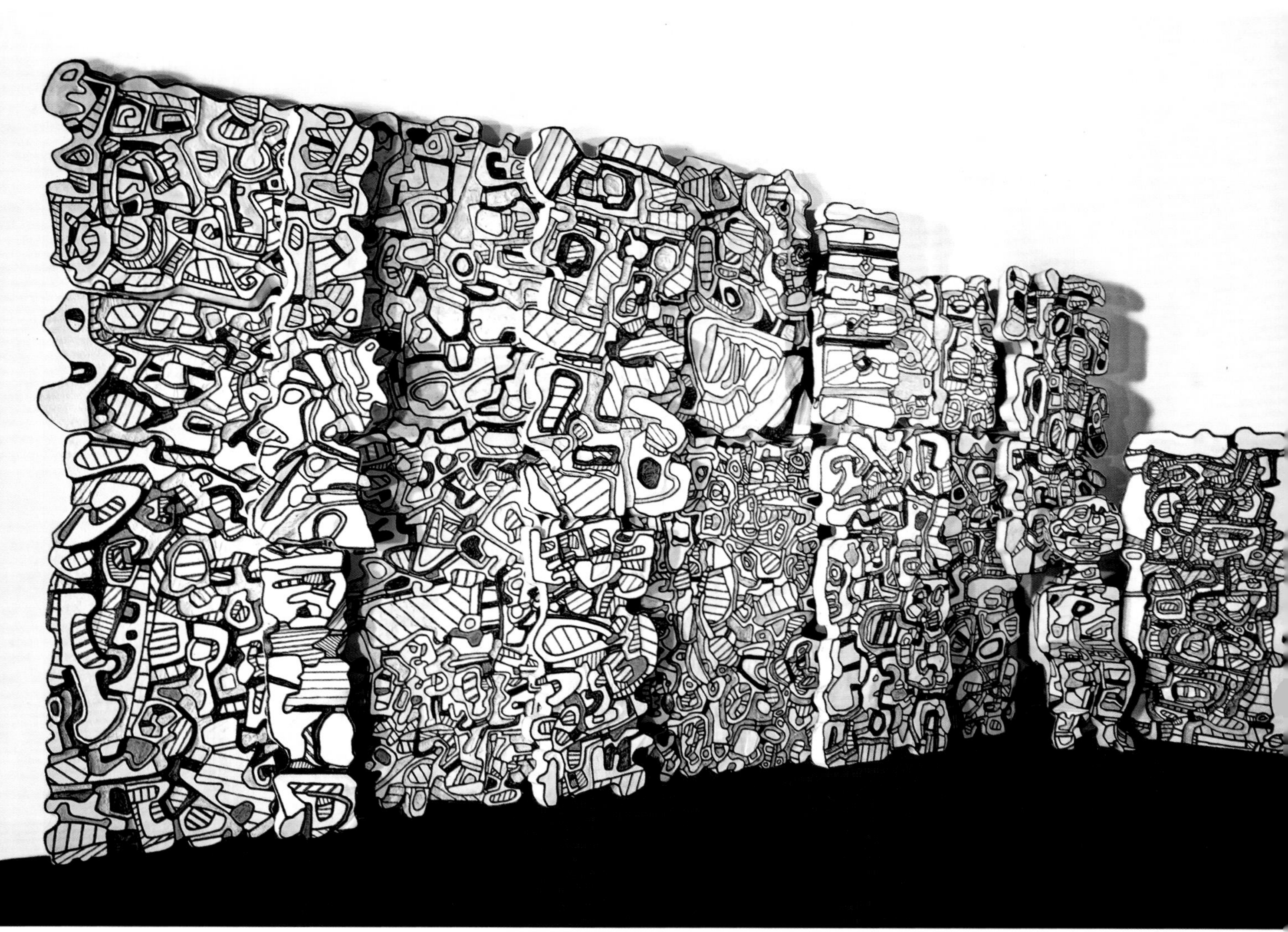

and reinforced with steel mesh, the forms he produced and forced to stand erect were a long way indeed from the logic of builders.

This no doubt explains the fact that these environments (or at least, those whose construction was completed, such as the *Jardin d'émail* in the Netherlands, the *Closerie Falbala* in Périgny-sur-Yerres, the *Jardin d'hiver* at the Musée National d'Art Moderne, and the *Tour aux figures* in Issy-les-Moulineaux) are still so alien to our understanding, which finds it very hard to accept what one might call *disharmony* in matters of architecture, even though it frequently admits its possible virtues in music, poetry, and painting. For the architect's follies, grotesques, and surprise gardens – to which Dubuffet's environments are often likened, and to which it is tempting to annex them – do not contradict architectural tradition; they are an integral part of it, just like the most noble buildings, and preserve the heroism attached to the mind's mastery of intractable matter, like that of a horse in dressage. Whereas what Dubuffet does here is radically transgressive. His overly docile material complies uncomplainingly to the caprices of what he calls the *mental landscape.* Devoid of virtue or morality, it confronts us with the meanders of the mind that we might rather not see. The three-dimensional world of the Hourloupe is not constructed, it is *secreted,* as Dubuffet once put it, just like the cocoon of an insect. If these edifices can be compared to anything else from the history of our century, then it is surely the *Merzbau,* the grotto that Kurt Schwitters built up in the thirties from accumulated layers in his own apartment. At the time, even Schwitters's supporters – among them Alexander Dorner, the talented curator of the museum in Hanover – had trouble seeing it as anything other than the formless work of a madman verging on the scatological. This may well explain the affair of the *Salon d'été*: instead of the expected garden suited to post-prandial promenades, Dubuffet produced a profoundly unsettling, no doubt uncomfortable space of the kind that would provoke some very strange reactions from both ordinary visitors and those more familiar with art. Confined to the flat surface of paintings, the products of the Hourloupe were still only images; the situation changes when they become sculptures, and then living spaces. *"The* Hourloupe *began with paintings on canvas, representations that were very much transpositions, mental reconstructions, simulacra of places and objects. After that I wanted to give these simulacra more materiality by building them in the third dimension. If you make a drawing*

Le mur bleu, 1967
Polyester painted with polyurethane
350 × 710 × 110 cm

Compagnonnage en site urbain,
1974
Vinyl on canvas
195 × 130 cm

showing a tree on paper or canvas – I mean, a mental representation of a tree, the ideational representation of a tree, it is interesting; but if, after that, you build this ideational representation in three dimensions and give it a body, and if you give it the dimensions of a real tree, in whose shade you can take shelter and which you can walk around, then the work is endowed with a very new effect upon the mind. Because if you take to the shade of a purely mental creation, which you have paradoxically endowed with a material body – if you constitute your mental creations in such a way as to actually inhabit them, to make them your surroundings and, in short, your world secreted by yourself, then what you get is the mind working in a closed circuit, with the mind feeding on its own fantasies instead of an environment provided by nature, an environment that is alien to it. But when I say provided by nature, I am distorting my ideas. Not for a moment do I believe in what is called nature, nor in the so-called reality that is attributed to it."[13]

Arid Castille

When you invent a space, it is natural to want to put something in it, to bring it to life. Dubuffet's involvement with architecture went hand in hand with a growing interest in theatre and performance. The outcome of this was *Coucou bazar*, a kind of ballet-cum-opera premiered at the Guggenheim in New York with "Hourlouped" sets and costumes. This new orientation

13. *Prospectus . . ., op. cit.*, vol. III, pp. 513–514.

afforded the artist a chance to develop new working methods, which themselves spawned new forms. Indeed, such was the magnitude of the *Coucou bazar* project that Dubuffet had to recruit a whole troupe of assistants, painters, boilermakers, and seamstresses for the preparatory phase in France. They were housed in the old munitions workshops in Vincennes, where Dubuffet

Paysage épisodique, 1974
Vinyl on canvas
203 × 130 cm

Le Roman burlesque, 1974
Paysage avec trois personnages dont l'un est assis
Vinyl paint on cut-out plywood
215 × 388 cm

Le Roman burlesque, 1974
Automobile
Vinyl paint on cut-out plywood
160 × 259 cm

Le Roman burlesque, 1974
Tour
Vinyl paint on cut-out plywood
233 × 94 cm

Le Roman burlesque, 1974
Cheval-jupon
Vinyl paint on cut-out plywood
171 × 219 cm

Le Roman burlesque, 1974
Site avec deux personnages dont l'un est couché
Vinyl paint on cut-out plywood
217 × 329 cm

Le Roman burlesque, 1974
Tour
Vinyl paint on cut-out plywood
239 × 109 cm

Le Roman burlesque, 1974
Développement horizontal
Vinyl paint on cut-out plywood
112 × 270 cm

whizzed around in a high-speed electrical chariot. For his sets he devised a series of two-dimensional elements that could be laid out to form several planes and moved around in space. These paintings or sets, which he called *praticables*, were made on large, irregular cut-out panels. The emancipation of Dubuffet's paintings from the rectangular format had begun in 1971. *Parade nuptiale,* a work in the Renault Collection, is among the most splendid of these "cut-outs" that dispensed with the picture frame and took the burgeoning, constructive momentum of the Hourloupe modules to its logical conclusion. If you consider that a form engenders itself by the juxtaposition of cells, then there is no reason why it should be contained in one frame rather than another, and the border of the painting will quite naturally coincide with the end of the motif. As we may recall, the telephone doodles, too, became *cut-outs.*

Coucou bazar and its pieces of scenery led directly to the *Roman burlesque.* Chronologically, the two projects are very close: the ballet-cum-opera was premiered in April 1973, and in November of the same year, Dubuffet accepted Claude-Louis Renard's invitation to work for Renault.

In the days that followed this proposition, Dubuffet came up with the idea for the punningly titled series *Roman de Renard.* Although in the end he took it no further, this project was accompanied by what is now a very valuable document, the *Traité du roman de Renard,* in which he expounds his working method for the benefit of Renault's service Recherches, Art et Industrie. It covers everything from the brand of felt pens, color samples, and details of the type of paper to be used to the actual process of composition. This process, a highly complex sequence of several phases of drawing, collage, and cutting, seems curiously restrictive. Yet, at the same time, these freely accepted constraints tell us a great deal about the stratagems used by Dubuffet in order to elude the traps of habit, to preserve the Hourloupe's capacity for innovation and, no doubt, to keep surprising himself with the creatures brought into being by his hands, free from censorship of the controlling, ratiocinative mind. The elements he eventually selected for enlargement, twenty-five in all, were chosen from another series of forty-seven preparatory drawings, which, it seems reasonable to assume, were made using similar methods but for which, unfortunately, the documentation is not as precise.

As one might expect, the origin of the commission did not influence the nature of the drawings. The clusters of Hourloupean cells develop at their own rhythm and, while it is true that we can at least make out the odd car, this was an object that took shape often enough in Dubuffet's other drawings, an object for which we can often observe a kind of amused attraction on the part of the artist (Dubuffet owned several cars, and among the texts published by Hubert Damisch in *Prospectus et tous écrits suivants* is a very droll letter to the road tax office[14]). The cut-outs of the *Roman burlesque* series are done in vinyl paint on laminated panels, using drawings enlarged to their definitive size by a technique of photographic projection identical to the one already tried out on the *praticables* of *Coucou bazar*. The space they were to occupy – the walls of the six hospitality rooms, which, at the artist's request, were painted a slightly bluish gray color – were treated as a general ground on which each panel floated freely, so that the overall impression given by the ensemble is one of a very light and delicately balanced composition that makes absolutely no compromises with the canons of decorative art. While this work obviously benefited from what Dubuffet had learned from theatre, it is also likely that when making the *Roman burlesque* he had in mind the metal wall he built at the back of his studio for trying out different combinations, using magnets to hold the elements in place and then gluing down the final configuration. *Roman burlesque* never yields to the predictable demands of monumental display: it neither glorifies the functions of its setting nor manifests much concern for the destiny of the car industry. It is housed in Renault's executive rooms rather like a swallow's nest under the beam of a veranda: it lives its life and ignores those around it, but we are happy to have it there.

As one would expect of a "burlesque" piece, this *roman* (novel, romance) has a rather light-hearted tone to it, but it is not uniformly joyous and frivolous, nor playful. Here and there, in the *Cortège funèbre* or *Tumulte à deux personnes*, a touch of gravity creeps in.

Ballet, architecture, and monumental sculpture introduced Dubuffet to a new experience, that of *delegating*. The architect-engineer who validated the building plans, the technician who cast the resin or concrete, the costume makers working in the huge shed at Vincennes – all were partners in the Hourloupean adventure. Handing the baton to a third party in this way was a perfectly normal thing to do: the random modules of the Hourloupe

14. *Prospectus . . ., op. cit.*, vol. IV, p. 200. I cannot resist the temptation of quoting it in full [the French term for the annual licence is "vignette"– *Trans.*]:

Paris, 12 November 1965

Dear Miss Licence,
Mademoiselle de la Vignette,
Mademoiselle des Vignettes et des Vignes Bonettes, my great misfortune is that I do not know your pretty proper name, but our friend Monsieur Blanc will pass on this message and, to help you feel like opening it, will offer you a drop of gin from Lambrechies. I am as you know a great consumer of licences and this year I need four, as follows:

Simca (Versailles) 13 CV 1957
839 EX 06
Simca (Chambord) 13 CV 1961
9539 LS 75
Renault (Rambler) 22 CV 1965
913 PK 06 this one will be a whopper
Citroën (I.D.) 11 CV 1963
224 PL 75

I would suggest that with your gracious little hands you place these four licences in an envelope with my address on with a slip of paper showing the sum it will cost me, including, of course, legitimate remuneration for your troubles, and in return, with all expediency, I will send you the requisite sum in the form you desire, by cheque for example, or by transfer to your Girocheque account, assuming of course that the postal service consider you a sufficiently reasonable young woman to open an account in your own name.

Le Roman burlesque, 1974
Tumulte à deux personnages
Vinyl paint on cut-out plywood
225 × 329 cm

Le Roman burlesque, 1974
Développement horizontal
Vinyl paint on cut-out plywood
99 × 242 cm

were bound to free themselves sooner or later from the strict register of easel painting, and its architectural developments were both predictable and logical. Just as no one would think to take umbrage if an architect failed to do the masonry on the walls he had planned, or if a fresco painter was helped by a horde of assistants, only a very narrow conception of the painter's art, inherited from the Romantic vision of the nineteenth century, could make us demand that the artist be the sole maker of his or her works. Dubuffet knew, however, that the taboo still remained almost absolute, and he confronted it head on in the *Paysages castillans*. His ambitions for this astonishing series

Le Roman burlesque, 1974
Trois personnages
Vinyl paint on cut-out plywood
232 × 362 cm
From left: 225 × 102;
228 × 94; 232 × 136 cm

Le Roman burlesque, 1974
Nuage
Vinyl paint on cut-out plywood
101 × 230 cm

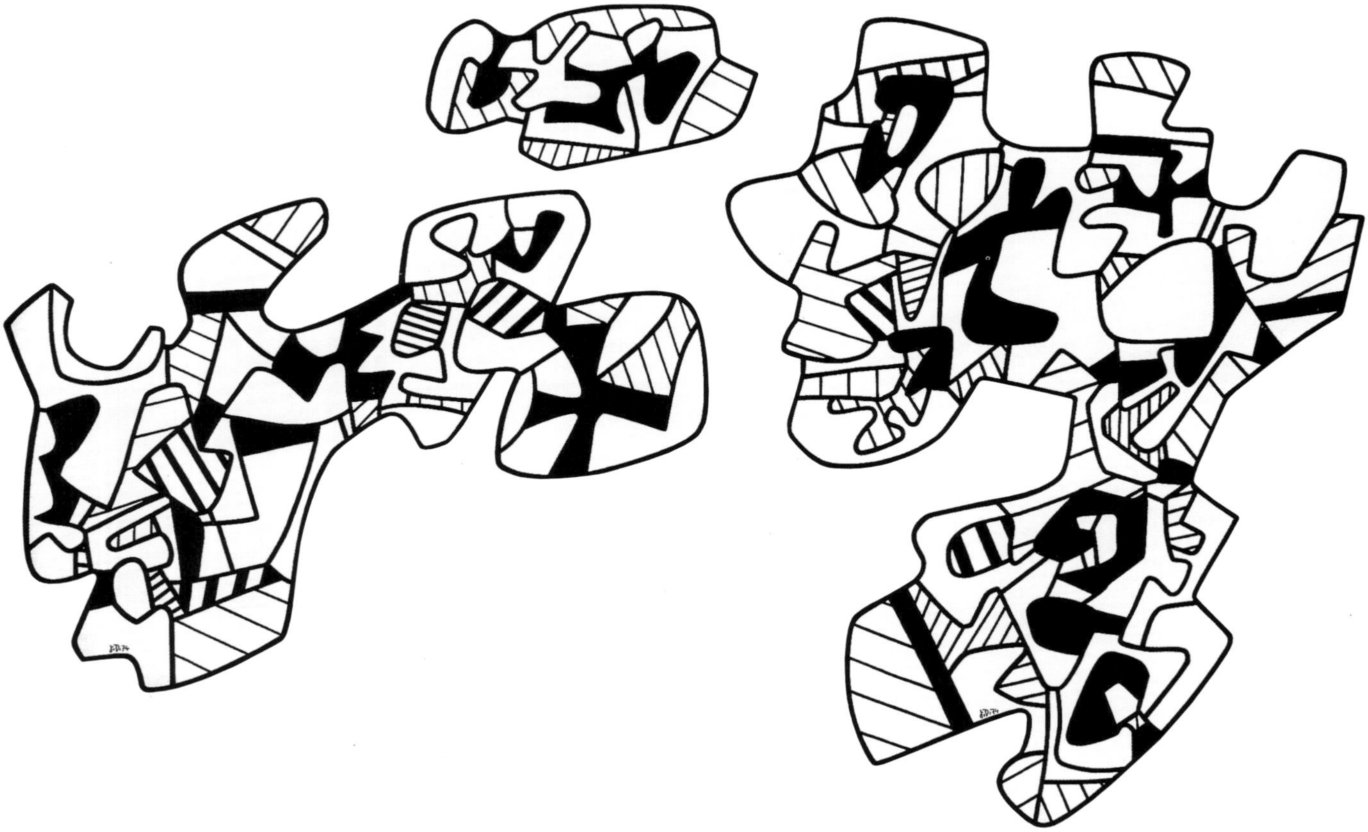

Le Roman burlesque, 1974
Cortège funèbre
Vinyl paint on cut-out plywood
230 × 368 cm

Le Roman burlesque, 1974
Décor funèbre
Vinyl paint on cut-out plywood
245 × 446 cm

Le Roman burlesque, 1974
Logologie
Vinyl paint on cut-out plywood
216 × 303 cm

Le Roman burlesque, 1974
Motif à l'homme couché
Vinyl paint on cut-out plywood
135 × 190 cm

Le Roman burlesque, 1974
Motif horizontal
Vinyl paint on cut-out plywood
99 × 188 cm

Le Roman burlesque, 1974
Grande parade
Vinyl paint on cut-out plywood
221 × 385 cm

were expressed in a letter to Claude-Louis Renard, where he presents it as the end of the Hourloupe cycle:

Paris, 24 October 1974

Dear Claude Renard,

I will be delighted to show you soon a series of forty-seven paintings on canvas, which are the swan song of my Hourloupe cycle. It began twelve years ago with canvases and now, after all kinds of variations that have taken it out of the frame for a good long period, it is returning to it. But, as you will see, it has changed considerably. After this, it will come to an end. The works that will occupy me from now on (they have already been started) use a very different key.

The paintings in question are obtained by tracing with a brush on the canvas, used as a screen, the enlarged image provided by the projector of drawings done on paper with a felt pen. The tracing is done by someone else's hand. All they are asked to do is to recreate the drawing as faithfully as possible, without adding

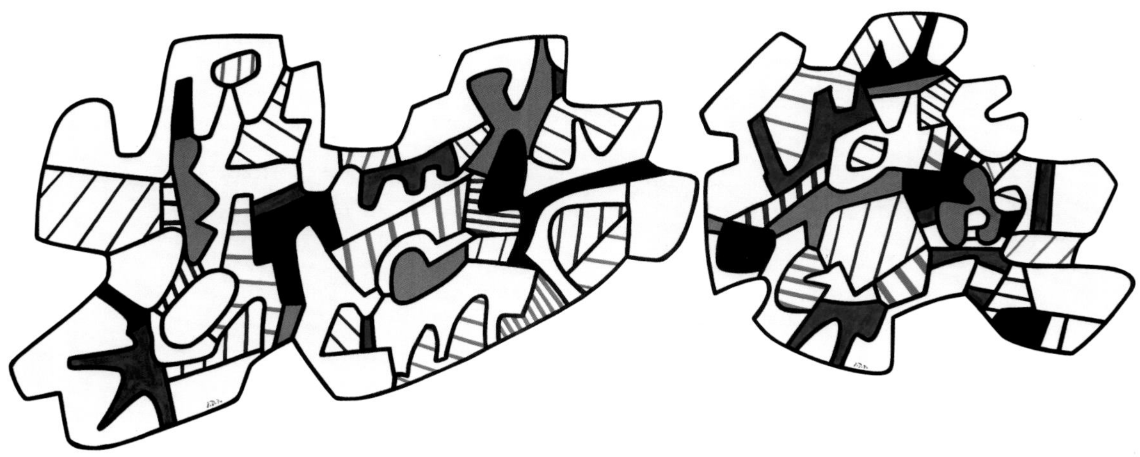

Le Roman burlesque, 1974
Nuages
Vinyl paint on cut-out plywood
152 × 364 cm

or interpreting, in order to perfectly reproduce the cursive style of the felt pen sliding over the paper. This is very particular, very different from the style of a direct improvisation with a brush on canvas. I think that these paintings owe a great deal of what makes up their very special language to this mode of execution in two successive stages (without my intervention in the second of these stages).

My drawings used for these enlargements have an average format of 50 × 32 centimeters. Each one shows a landscape, often with a figure, or sometimes two, who are sometimes drawn separately then cut out and added. Stuck into the middle of the site without precautions, I mean, without trying to avoid the effect of an abrupt ellipse or arbitrariness (this is one of the key factors in this whole business).

The first of these drawings use only black and white, hence a certain funereal quality. They date from last April.

Those that followed (June and July), to which I have given the name Paysages castillans *(for me, they evoke the aridity of Castille, where in fact I have never been) of which there are nine, are in black on yellow paper with only the sky*

Parade nuptiale, 1971–1972
Acrylic on canvas mounted on klégecell (detail)

Parade nuptiale, 1971 – 1972
Acrylic on canvas mounted on klégecell
164 × 487 cm

painted light blue where the odd cloud hangs. The figures that appear in them are sometimes white and sometimes colored blue and red.

In the most recent – the most numerous – the blue and red come in differently for the landscapes and the figures. These are the Sites tricolores.

The last of these drawings is from August 31. I have not made any others like it since then and I will not make any more. The episode is closed. The enlargements on canvas are under way; they will all be finished for Christmas.

Like all my works from before this Hourloupe cycle (and those connected with the performance Coucou bazar*), these paintings show networks of erratic traces that have the power to conjure up conjectural figures. Here, they are figures of territories and sites. They have this power for me, at any rate. I have no idea about other viewers. It depends, evidently, on your mood. Of course, the uncertainty of these works (their uncertain virtue) has not escaped me. But I very much like artistic productions to be uncertain. I don't mind it even if they are extremely so.*

The ambiguity that runs through all these paintings is due to the uncomfortable uncertainty as to whether they belong to the purely mental and immaterial register of the doodles with which they originated or to that of representations of the real physical world. I say uncomfortable because nothing is as frightening as the confusion between the imaginary and the real, and the idea that what we consider as real could well be only imaginary. In the end, though, one has to accept this. That is the orientation taken throughout the Hourloupe. Now that it is put back in the frame of the traditional rectangular painting (bearings are

102

Scène à l'invalide, 1974
Vinyl paint on polystyrene
50 × 85 × 14 cm

given by a skyline, a top and a bottom), which in our culture is so closely linked to the representation of a physical world that is held to be real, the parallels between this physical world and that of these fugacious fancies may perhaps be more immediately striking.

Lovers of painting will no doubt be frustrated to find here nothing in the way of rough textures, unexpected reprises of touch and improvisation, which were so highly prized in the recent past. I myself have been very fond of them, too. This has reached the point that many tend to see the deployment of all these accidents of execution, which please us so because they constantly reveal the hand of the maker, as being of the essence of painting. There is no hand of the maker here. Nothing but impersonal traces and cursory, flat coloring. A whiff of the timeless and the incorporeal, as is appropriate for sites taken from the world of dreams, where there is no flesh. Those with an appetite for painterly sweetmeats are invited here to a feast that is very likely to strike them as meager. But I would ask them to bring their thoughts to bear on this: that most of the time steps forward are achieved at the price of abandoning something that had thitherto seemed indispensable. Renunciation, impoverishment, these are methods that I believe in. However, I do not contest that it is tough to give things up, that the decision is a painful one when one is not sure what one will find in its stead – and even if one is sure. But if we do not bid farewell to what we loved, if we do not set out for new lands, all we can hope for is exhaustion and extinction.

Yours as ever,

Jean Dubuffet.[15]

The melancholy that emanates from this paean to renunciation (in which, true to form, Dubuffet proves himself a great writer) is surprisingly present in the works themselves, where the sienna and faded blue create a leaden quality of light redolent of De Chirico. The figures that wander over their surfaces are no more than skulls and bones, specters come to claim their due.

Chateau de vent souffle, 1971
Epoxy painted with polyurethane
94 × 110 × 50 cm

The letter to Claude-Louis Renard magnificently expresses the nature of these *Paysages castillans*: an act of mourning for the Hourloupe cycle and its familiar forms, not true mourning, perhaps, but something like muffled grief at forced severance. The series (of which Renault has five elements) openly proclaims the dimension of pathos to be found in whole sections of the Hourloupe, a cycle in which many prefer to see only playful bonhomie. We should remember that, while we, as incorrigible sceptics, tend to hear only *entourloupe* (trickery) or *looping*, for Dubuffet the assonance of the name evoked *hurler* (to cry or howl), *hululer* (to hoot, like an owl) and *le Horla* (subject of an uncanny tale by Maupassant).[16] *Fiston la filoche*, that harlequin bowed down by lassitude, who seems to be apologizing just for being there, is, as Alexandre Vialatte informs us, a self-portrait of the artist.[17] Dubuffet's saturnine side is greatly underestimated, even though it is present in several phases of his work, and sometimes deliberately underlined by the title – Here, the reference to an imaginary Castille as a paragon of desolation, and later, for his final works, the choice of the term *Non-Lieux*, which refers to a non-suit in legal proceedings. Dubuffet's muses sometimes have their disturbing side.

It may be a good idea to qualify this somewhat top-heavy historical account with an observation: Dubuffet never saw himself in historical terms, even less art-historical ones. Culture and its flag-wavers were his declared enemies, and the brotherhood of painters an alien universe. His statements are so wholehearted, his writing so compelling, persuasive, and musical, that many commentators choose to look no further, only venturing their parallels with learned culture in registers where there is no risk of their contradicting the painter's image of almost total autonomy. And yet we would not be slighting this virtuoso of anarchist thought and salutary suspicion if we refused simply to give him full discharge from insertion into history. It would, for example, be fascinating to set the Hourloupe in the context of other attempts made by painters since the nineteenth century to invent new codes for transcribing reality, and particularly by the systematic application of discrete units – Seurat's

15. This letter is published in *Prospectus . . ., op. cit.*, vol. III, pp. 397-400. It constituted the preface to the catalogue *Jean Dubuffet, Paysages castillans, Sites tricolores*, (Paris: Centre National d'Art et de Culture Georges-Pompidou, 1975), n.p.

16. Jean Dubuffet, "Biographie au pas de course," *Prospectus . . ., op. cit.*, vol. IV, p. 510.

17. Interview with Alexandre Vialatte, *Prospectus . . .*, op. cit., vol. IV, p. 32.

Territoire aux deux explorants,
1974
Vinyl on canvas
204 × 130 cm

pointillism, however remote it may seem from the Hourloupe, brings into a play a method that engenders new forms, new light, one related to the principle of ex-nihilo recreation professed by Dubuffet. And the latter was not the only one to be fascinated by the physical sciences: Kandinsky, Kupka, and Delaunay, to name but a few, felt a great nostalgia for times past, when an artist was also a man of science. More than the others, perhaps, Dubuffet was careful to ensure that this fascination did not result in the imitation of scientific imagery, whose products informed so-called biomorphic abstraction in painting. His whole strategy of deliberately forgetting what he had learned (*"the important thing with technique is not to master it"*[18]) was designed to put him in the position of one who does not imitate nature but becomes nature, transcribing from the depths something of its fascinating "continuum," participating in its dancing chaos. But even this radical attitude makes him a man of his age. One need only think of Picasso declaring that he did not work from nature, but like nature or, even more, of Paul Klee – no doubt the only artist whom Dubuffet would have accepted as a neighbor: *"The artist is a man; he is himself a piece of nature in the space of nature."*[19] Dubuffet seems worlds away from the formalist preoccupations which, until only recently, have shaped

18. *Ibid.*

19. Paul Klee, *On Modern Art.*

Paysage avec villa et personnage, 1974
Vinyl on canvas
195 × 130 cm

the history of modernity. And yet, how can we not compare the cut-outs of the *Roman burlesque* or the *Parade nuptiale* to the idea that the form of an abstract painting must derive from the motifs that compose it, as expressed by the American painter Frank Stella? Stella's *shaped canvases* and Dubuffet's *praticables* are more or less contemporaneous: the fact that the former marched under the somewhat austere banner of avant-gardist criticism and the latter in the ranks of a carefully nurtured personal mythology should not be allowed to hide the fact that they may share a common language. (Stella's most recent works, designed on a computer, confirm this kinship: like the Dubuffets of the seventies, they too went through a phase of mechanical execution and provoked similar reactions of refusal or enthusiasm).

The hardest task now facing historians of Dubuffet's work is probably that of escaping the tremendous fortress constituted by the artist's words and writings and looking at his painting from new, incongruous angles. While not forgetting the irrefutable axiom *Plu kifekler mouinkon nivoua*,[20] we would not be in danger of blinding ourselves if we explored this immense body of work with a modest torch.

DIDIER SEMIN

20. *Plu kifekler mouinkon nivoua* [plus qu'il fait clair, moins qu'on n'y voit: the lighter/clearer it is, the less one sees – *Trans.*], by Jan Dubufe, (Saint Maurice d'Etelan: L'Air du temps, 1950). (Reprint of the first three texts written by Dubuffet in the comical phonetic language he called *le jargon*).

Victor Vasarely

Vasarely or the Dream of Vision

The case of Vasarely provides an exemplary illustration of the vicissitudes of fortune, the vagaries and sudden reversals to which success and fame can be subject. For Vasarely was certainly famous, and perhaps that fame reached its saturation point. That fame touched the man himself, but also his works, which have been seen all over the world, entered the biggest public and private collections, and been linked with all the emblematic sites of contemporary activity (universities, social housing, bank and company headquarters, etc.), thus helping to provide a visual counterpart to the three "glorious" decades of postwar prosperity enjoyed by the West. Vasarely's fame also extended to the general public, which contributed to his success (and perhaps his decline) with its undiscriminating acceptance of the "byproducts" of his formal inventions, popularized and thus banalized by fashion and the consumer industry.[1] But if the judgements now levelled at Vasarely are unjustifiably and excessively harsh, there can be no question of trying to rebuild the pedestal on which the young Fifth Republic and the voluntarist Pompidou regime placed this artist as a beacon of the modernity to which the whole of society was exhorted to convert. A more interesting way of reassessing Vasarely today would be to try to understand the important and singular position he occupied (and with him, the whole tendency of Op and Kinetic art) in a kind of revealing historical marginality. Vasarely was an heir to the great Constructivist tradition (he trained at Sandor Bortnyik's Mühely, an attempt to acclimatize the teaching of the German Bauhaus, where Bortnyik himself had studied, to Budapest), but his work was also, in a way, a perversion of that tradition. A perversion inasmuch as it opened a very different world of meanings, one that was a long way from "classic" Constructivism. For whereas the latter manifests an effort to achieve total conscious control over the world, which the artist shapes and builds in keeping with a reasoned, calculated plan, making frank and literal use of plastic elements; Vasarely used an incredibly varied and inventive range of illusionistic procedures to demonstrate the impossibility of grasping appearance, the traps of vision, the incessant metamorphoses of the world, and its continuous flux. From this point of view, Vasarely's art does indeed constitute a kind of aberration in the most eloquent sense of the word, as defined by Jurgis Baltrusaïtis,[2] and does so in spite of its proclaimed scientific approach, its rational methods of design and construction – in spite of its apparent certitudes,

The author would like to offer heartfelt thanks to all those who helped him prepare this study by offering advice and giving him access to important documents, in particular Jean-Pierre and Michèle Vasarely, Denise René, and Catherine Gallois.

1. See the significant illustrations to the articles by Otto Hahn, "Vasarely, le père de l'Op," *L'Express* (Paris: 30 May–5 June 1966), pp. 80-82, and Gérard Blanchard, "L'Op art à Prisunic," *Opus international*, no. 1 (Paris: April 1967), pp. 90–92.

2. In optics or astronomy, the word "aberration" designates the phenomenon whereby one sees things that are not actually there. With anamorphosis, they "give rise to legends of forms in the domain of vision and to legends of myth in the domain of the mind. They all partake of the same reasoned and poetical mechanism." J. Baltrusaïtis, *Anamorphoses ou Thaumaturgus opticus* (Paris: Flammarion), 1984, p. 2.

CTA 102, 1965
Oil on canvas (detail)
170 × 170 cm

which, up to now, have been the exclusive focus of all the studies and nearly all the commentaries on his work.

Vasarely's art really begins with the end of the forties, at a time when the triumph of abstract art prompted the new generation of artists to reject what, abetted by success, were becoming no more than facile tricks and hackneyed techniques, adopted by the many imitators who crowded the walls of the Salon des Réalités Nouvelles. Vasarely realized that it was not enough for art to be abstract if it was still using the same recipes as figurative art, those based on composition, the equilibrium of forms, and the harmony of tonal relations. *"Abstract painting today,"* he stated, *"is still tied to the old world, to old painting, by a shared technique and formal presentation which hold it back and make its conquests equivocal ones."* [3] And yet, in his initial efforts to overcome what he saw as the fundamental inadequacy of a certain form of abstract art, the artist sought inspiration in renewed contact with the most concrete forms of visual reality.

Thus, behind the three major cycles around which much of Vasarely's work in the fifties was articulated,[4] we can detect the subjacent structures of a de-hierarchized reality, which the artist explored with an acute sense of both its dominant rhythms and its most insignificant manifestations. From contemplation of the pebbles and objects carried by the ebb and flow of the tides came the smooth forms that fill the works of the *Belle-Isle* cycle with their bulging edges and rounded corners; the network of cracks that form on the ceramic tiles of the métro stations inspired the contours of the foliated blocks of color in the *Denfert* series; and, in the *Gordes* series, broken lines and acute angles translate the crystalline mineral forms of the eponymous Luberon village on its rocky outcrop. Each of these cycles of works attains a high level of perfection in the use of certain aspects of the abstract tradition. *Belle-Isle* is a fifties prolongation of interwar biomorphism, particularly that of Jean Arp, and without a doubt one of its finest flowers. *Denfert* and *Gordes* are still attached to the space of Cubism, a space that is almost flat, just deep enough to slide in – one atop or under the other – planes delimited by lines of fracture that are alternatively straight or curved. Without fundamentally renewing the language of abstraction, the great value of these works was nevertheless that they gave Vasarely a chance to define the kernel of a poetics of creation, which would

3. Vasarely in Marcel Joray (ed.), *Vasarely I*, (Neuchâtel: Editions du Griffon, 1965), p. 14. At about the same time, Jesús Rafael Soto made the same observation: "When I arrived in Paris [1950], all the art was made with forms that reminded me of those I had used to make portraits of landscapes. Including the geometrical artists who, it seemed to me, were still not abstract artists. I saw compositions of lozenges, triangles, polyhedra, a whole series of elements which had in fact been suggested by figurative reality, and I was sure that figurative painting used for its internal composition the same system as so-called abstract painting. For me, it was not abstraction, but the simplification of figurative art." "Téoría de Jesús Soto," *El Minero*, 1967, quoted in A. Pierre, "Chronologie," *Jesús Rafael Soto*, (cat.), (Paris: Galerie National du Jeu de Paume, 1997), p. 180.

4. It is more appropriate to speak of "cycles" or "series" than the more commonly used "period," a term which may be taken to suggest a succession in time. Here, the cycles developed concurrently and sometimes even interpenetrated.

Gordium PS positif, 1951
Oil on canvas
195 × 160 cm

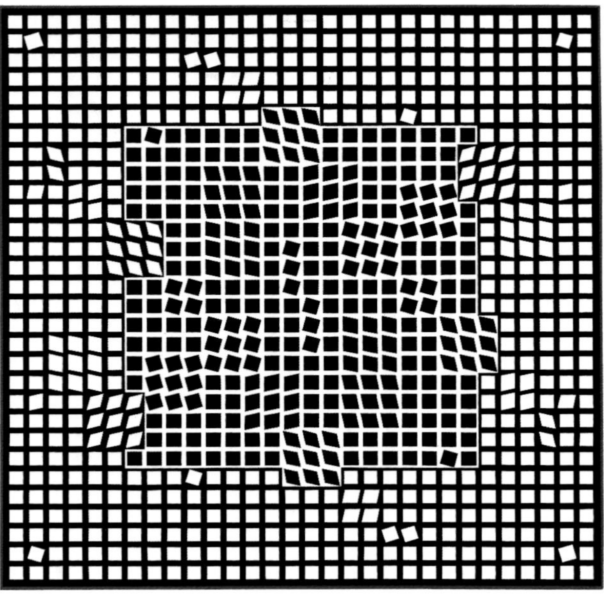

Tlinko 22, 1955
Oil on canvas
190 × 190 cm

never cease to inform the exploration of his fundamental obsessions: perpetual genesis and metamorphosis, the instability and mutability of structures, and the deceptiveness and reversibility of appearances. What Vasarely was stating here, and striving to express in visual language, was a conception of the world dominated by this awareness of transformation, by the sense of a prevailing sameness within universal movement and change.

In speaking about *Belle-Isle*, he formulated in 1952 one of the first declarations of faith in what he called his "unitary philosophy." By studying pebbles, driftwood, and sea-smoothed fragments of glass, he could gain access to *"the internal geometry of nature."*[5] Their forms were also those of the wash and eddies of water amidst rocks, of morning clouds, of the setting sun flattened at its extremities, so that what was manifest in the ovoids and ellipsoids of the series was *"the secret link between places and objects, between the different elements, between the planets."*[6] Their roundness, their dynamic curves held the trace and memory of the *"one swirling medium"*[7] from which they all emerged, that place of primordial genesis where all things and beings become different. Often interlocking or radiating from a shared center, as in *Inguiniel (Belle-Isle)* (1947–1955, Musée de Gordes), they suggest processes of parthenogenesis, the analysis of growth patterns.

From pebbles, Vasarely went to cosmic reverie. This meeting of incompatible scales also explains his fascination with crackled earthenware, a strange, modern variant on Leonardo da Vinci's interest in the pulverulent walls where he discovered new imaginary landscapes. *"Some were vertical and they suggested the ruins of once great cities – there was something ghostly about them. The others,*

5. *Vasarely I, op. cit.*, p. 19.

6. Jean-Louis Ferrier, *Entretiens avec Victor Vasarely*, (Paris: Belfond, 1969), p. 20.

7. *Vasarely I, op. cit.*, p. 19.

Tonk, 1954
Oil on canvas
168 × 100 cm

the horizontal ones, looked like hallucinatory landscapes . . . To me this was matter offering proof of a common law that controls the whole universe, right down to its most seemingly random accidents. I was renewing the experience of Belle-Isle, where I had sensed that all the beaches in the world obey one and the same cosmic rhythm."[8] *"These great landscapes were like so many metamorphoses: to my imagination, the tiniest crack due to a break at the level of the molecular structure was like a big geosyncline, or something even greater . . ."*[9] Later, Vasarely would speak of the *"considerable broadening of the idea of nature"*[10] in his representations influenced by the concepts and objects of contemporary science. Vasarely's responsiveness to both the infinitely big and the infinitely small goes back to this formative period of his sensibility when *"the myth of the infallible human scale of the Renaissance and of the reference to named objects was already beginning to wobble."*[11] While man remained *"this highly differentiated complex of perpetually youthful matter,"* he was no longer the measure of all things; he participated in the whole in which he was immersed, neither more nor less than the elementary particles of which he was constituted. *"Whatever the number of sources of energy or processes of diversification, of genesis, of mutations in the expanse of physical things, whatever the quality of things and beings at so many levels of life, of instinct, of sensibility or intelligence, the immense fabric of the world is all woven of the same weft."*[12]

Soon, he was combining the visionary landscapes inspired by the crackling of *Denfert* with his concrete experience of the Luberon, which fascinated him both by its mass and *"by the perpetual transformations wrought in it by the light."*[13] The ambiguity of form and mass due to the play of light and shade is indeed the subject of the works in the *Cristal-Gordes* cycle. In its attempt to grasp the organization of the vertical motif constituted by the village on the tiers of rock, the eye follows first the solid land marks, then the diagonal of a gable, and the edge of a wall before, suddenly, focusing on the immaterial separation of light and shade, which, under the southern sun, is as clear-cut as architecture. In a first series of drawings made in 1948, this produced a combination of broken lines and sharp angles. This later recurs in paintings such as *Garam* (1949, Musée de Gordes), in which the color arbitrarily separates planes that interlocked in the artist's original perception wherein the violence of the light made it impossible to determine the precise location of the forms and masses. *"Southern towns and villages*

8. *Entretiens, op. cit.*, pp. 40-41.

9. *Vasarely I, op. cit.*, p. 10.

10. *Entretiens, op. cit.*, p. 61.

11. *Vasarely I, op. cit.*, p. 10.

12. Vasarely, "Ce que devrait être la critique d'art," *Entretiens, op. cit.*, p. 165.

13. *Entretiens, op. cit.*, p. 40.

devoured by an implacable sun revealed to me a contradictory perspective. The eye can never identify what a shadow or bit of wall belong to: full and empty spaces merge, forms and ground alternate. A triangle is attached now to a lozenge on the left, now to a trapeze on the right, a square jumps up higher or teeters downwards . . . Thus identifiable objects are transformed into abstractions . . . and take on a life of their own."[14] Rather than following the architectural logic of the motif, transformative perception becomes caught up with the play of appearances, which threatens to undermine the stability of the real.

The play of shadow and light is also that of black and white, whose reversibility is also something Vasarely experienced in a very concrete way. Observing the intense brightness that entered his house in Gordes through a small, sharp-edged square window, he realized that, seen at the same moment from outside, its shape formed a black square against the burning hot white wall. This concomitant and simultaneous existence of the black square and the white square, the two extremes of the absolute in Malevich's painting, would later be brought together in the alternating positive and negative of Vasarely's *Hommage à Malévitch* (1953, private collection), and in many other dual compositions in which a single canvas organized in terms of axial or central symmetries contains positive and negative versions of the same motif (*Algenib 2*, 1956, Renault collection). The use of black and white, whose possibilities Vasarely systematically exploited during the fifties and early sixties, was not just a visual game; it served to demonstrate the reversibility of the real and thus radically question the appearances of the world.

For reality does indeed flicker uncertainly here. The eye has nothing to hold on to: aggressed by the sharp contrast of black against white, pushed to the limits of what is physiologically bearable, it is confronted not with the solidity of forms but with their dissolution in a luminous optical vibration. The surface is no longer the neutral and passive receptacle of forms, but a beating, pulsing whole to which no motif seems able to adhere. The viewer is carried into an optically unstable, moving environment and abandons any sense of orientation. Vasarely struggles in vain to fix his surface. To this end, he makes frequent use of the grid, which is eminently a figure of the certainty, of the logical organization and grasp of the real to which reason might lay claim. But the regularity of these grids is invariably broken up, their all too fine order modified and disrupted. Luminous spots of fluctuating intensity appear at all the intersections and dissolve the structure, as in

14. *Vasarely I, op. cit.*, p. 29.

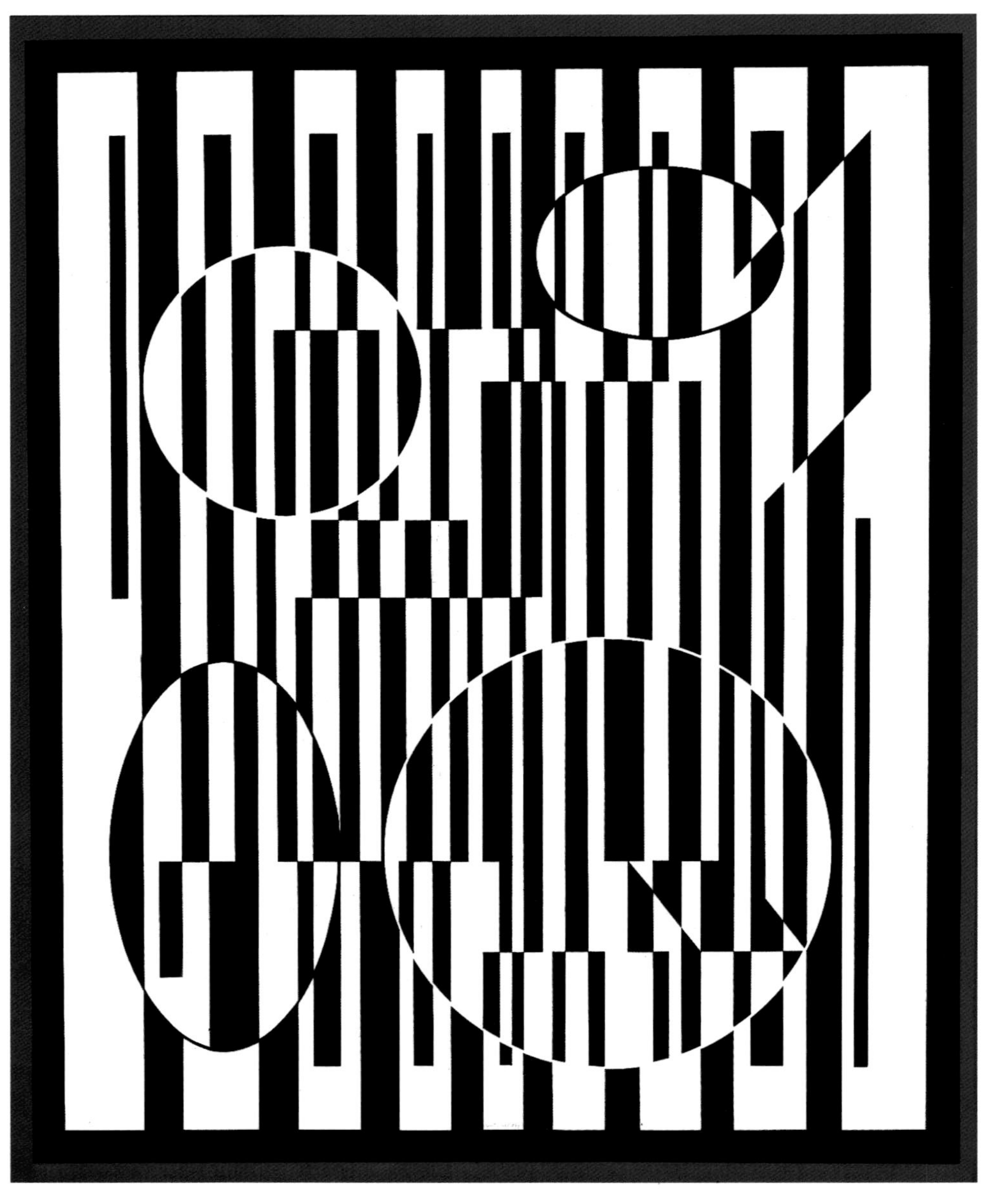

Yanina II, 1956
Oil on canvas
148 × 120 cm

Unova (1960, Renault collection). On other occasions, it is the effect of interference between several staggered grids that makes the whole surface vibrate, as in the "deep works" presented at the 1955 show *Le Mouvement* at the Galerie Denise René. Elsewhere, the spatial ambiguity is created by a sudden modification of the modules in a limited part of the grid, as in *Supernovae* (1959–61, Tate Gallery, London) and *Métagalaxie* (1959–61, private collection), which contains a light and a dark pole, respectively created by regular contraction and dilation of the basic module. Elsewhere (*Yanina 2*, 1956), reserves and spaces, cut from the overall structure and breaking its continuity, prompt viewers to see forms that exist only in their own tricked perception. In the *Tlinko* series (*Tlinko*, 1956, Renault collection), the squares of an impeccable modular grid suddenly start pivoting about their axis and come to rest on their tip, while others stretch into lozenge shapes. The round forms of the *Bételgeuse* paintings (*Bételgeuse*, 1957, private collection) undergo the same process, turning into ever finer ellipses. Whenever this phenomenon occurs, the surface seems to be caught up in an accelerating movement, which overthrows the usual static order of the grid.

This passage from square to lozenge (a square seen in perspective) or from circle to ellipse (a circle seen in perspective) is determined by the simple equation, which posits that

lozenge = square + space + movement + time

or, in the same way, that

ellipse = circle + space + movement + time.

All the parameters of this equation reveal a dynamic conception of creation. But this represents only one aspect of Vasarely's metaphoric imagination, according to which all forms are contained within each other and are perpetually self-generating, like natural organisms: *"Planar geometry,"* explains the artist, *"starts with an infinitesimal point and describes a straight line, which is the first of the dimensions. This line breaks three times at an angle of 90 degrees, at equal distances, producing the square or plane in two dimensions, the place of the plastic phenomenon known as painting . . . Let us turn the square about an axis, starting with the central one. The plane attains space, three dimensions, changes in appearance, becomes a rectangle, grows thinner, then disappears into a line. Now let us turn the square about its diagonal axis: it transmutes into a lozenge, its section is the triangle, which, as it too moves, becomes pointed, different . . . Let us trim the four corners of the square:*

we obtain an octagon. Then repeat the operation until we have a circle, which, when it undergoes all the previous manipulations, gives us the ellipse and all the other curvilinear forms imaginable. With distance providing scale, we thus have the whole range of forms of the same species, from the smallest to the biggest . . . Malevich's square, the beginning and end of the plastic adventure of the plane, transcends its destiny." [15] Considered in this light, Vasarely's geometry need no longer be seen as the attribute of a rigidly scientific approach; it is a relativist geometry that is constantly modified by the movement and forces of which it is the momentary result.

Although at certain periods Vasarely stepped up his efforts to gain the fullest possible control over his art, these were never sufficient to resist the free play of the plastic elements, to prevent them from living their own life. We can observe this when, starting in 1960, he developed and used a rigorous plastic alphabet consisting of a series of modular square units containing elementary forms presented against different shades, thus affording an infinite number of permutations. Vasarely used this system to compose the first works in what he called "planetary folklore" (*Orion-or*, 1965, private collection). They evince a corpuscular conception of painting and the organization of the picture plane – one harking back to Seurat and Mondrian's *Boogie-Woogie* paintings. This had been revived somewhat in the early fifties by a number of "point-ist" painters such as Soto, Valera, and Nurking, harking back to Seurat and Mondrian's different shades and thus affording an infinite number of permutations. Vasarely used this system of matter-energy. These intensely colored, flickering works by Vasarely offer further proof, by default and despite the rigor of the method and its overtly normative intentions, of the impossibility of anchoring anything stable and durable on the surface of a canvas.

From 1965 onwards, in combination with the units of the plastic alphabet, the modular grid makes it possible to control the gradations of lighting with great precision, and to have these variations play over the entire surface. From square to square, and in every direction along the grid, the darkening or lightening of the shades follows a perfectly predictable and measured development. Once again though, the remarkable rigor of the system nonetheless engenders a series of elusive and contradictory phenomena that defy our perceptual habits. Thus, on the surface of a given work we are aware of mutually incompatible centers of luminosity implying a multiplicity of light sources. These may coexist in clearly separated quadrants

15. *Vasarely I, op. cit.*, p. 32.

166 Sirs-Kek, 1953
Oil on canvas
75 × 116 cm

Algenib II, 1956
Oil on canvas
152 × 81 cm

(*Freg 1-2*, 1965, Renault collection) or in contrast, merge their discordant effects (*Zoeld-KZ*, 1967–73, private collection). In the perfectly regular grid of the *CTA 102* paintings (*CTA 102*, 1965, Renault collection), the gradation of the metallic tones leads the gaze towards the work's geometrical center, from which there emanates a unique white light. In this illusory opening, *"the eye loses itself, and the visual screen sets up a kind of perceptual dream"* [16] whose power of enchantment is magnified by the scale of the canvas.

For Vasarely, this opening into optical infinity was another way of escaping human scale and gaining access to cosmic supradimensions. *"The unapproach-*

16. *Entretiens, op. cit.*, p. 56.

Unova, 1960
Oil on canvas
155 × 141 cm

able: stars and the invisible, atoms, all come out of these compositions . . It is no longer a matter of taking inspiration from things or beings, whether present or remembered, but of inventing worlds, which, up to now, eluded investigation by the senses – the worlds of biochemistry, waves, fields, relativity." [17] Here, the poetic-scientific imagination informing Vasarely's work for several years now, in which extravagant flights of fancy vie with rational appearance, attains a true summit. It is expressed through titles in which the Hungarian words and names found at random in the geographical atlases hitherto used by the artist are replaced by references to "signals of the worlds," "metagalaxies," the "noise of quasars," and the "beating of pulsars." Indeed, *CTA 102* is a reference to the distant radio sources that astronomers started detecting in 1965. This may all seem like an aberration, like science fiction, but it is part of the sweeping meditation that Vasarely sought to articulate in his art, touching on the origins and destiny of the universe and on the processes determining its incessant metamorphoses.

As contemporary equivalents of sfumato and chiaroscuro in pre-modern painting, Vasarely's light effects are, like their predecessors, the privileged agent of these metamorphoses. Their fluctuating ambiguous presence means that everything is constantly liable to change and threatened with disappearance, only to be reborn with a different but always indeterminate appearance.

17. *Vasarely I, op. cit.*, p. 57.

B. 4 Kerman 2, 1952
Oil on canvas
32 × 42 cm

18. *"Much more disturbing is the problem of the staircase, which, after an undeniable succession of steps, brings you back to the floor you have just left."* G. de Pawlowski, *Voyage au pays de la quatrième dimension* (1923), quoted in Jean Clair, *Marcel Duchamp ou le grand fictif* (Paris: Editions Galilée, 1975), p. 42. In a way, Vasarely provides a convincing visual image for the project formulated by Duchamp in the notes to *La Boîte verte*, which Claire quotes on this page, i.e., to show, simultaneously, what is *"above and below the volumes."*

C. 14 Basilian 4, 1953
Oil on canvas
38 × 35 cm

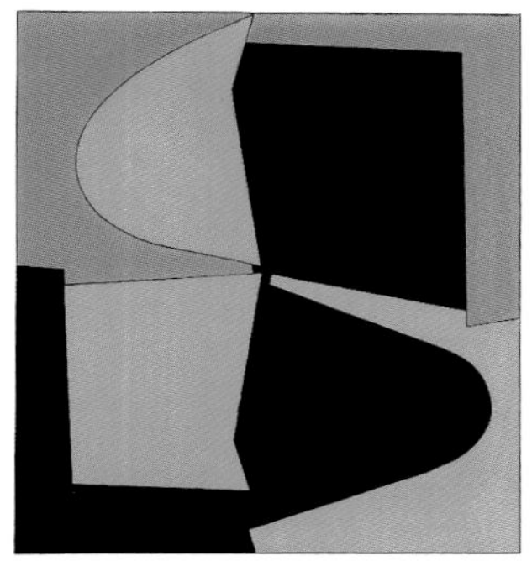

To these artifices, the artist adds those of a baroque geometry drawing on all the resources of perspectives that Baltrusaïtis would have described as "depraved" and which engender the most baffling forms of spatial illusion and visual enigma. Work after work, Vasarely mapped out the shifting ground of an imaginary world à la Borges. Since 1964 he had been using axonometry to build small modular units in three dimensions – cubes, and mainly "Kepler cubes," which are a specific variety of axonometric cube. Formed by dividing a hexagon into three equal lozenges, the Kepler cube can be read as either a salient volume with its edge pointing towards the eye of the beholder, or as a hollow volume, whose lines of construction give access to an illusory depth. This ambiguity is exploited by Vasarely, who deploys this illusion at the levels of the corpuscular unit, as well as of the overall motif and the painting itself. Vasarely uses these cubes to build Pirandellian architectures where there is no sense of gravity, where all the information provided by the unreliable spatial coordinates is liable to be called into question (*Kepler-Gestalt*, 1968, private collection). Incompatible perspectives cause volumes that seem to belong to different spaces to meet and merge (*Basq*, 1973, Renault collection); space itself becomes reversible and, in the batting of an eyelid, switches from concave to convex, from seeming hollowness to apparent plenitude, and deceptive clues given by the light only reinforce these illusions. Significantly renewing the Mannerist themes of mirrors and reflections, these "impossible objects," as the gestaltists call them, create visual paradoxes that are always varied and stimulating. These kinds of visual paradoxes in the literary descriptions of Gaston de Pawlowksi[18] delighted Marcel Duchamp as examples of the disconcerting ease with which the eye can be tricked and proof of the lie upon which "retinal" – necessarily retinal – painting is founded. In the same way, we can trace a line of descent running from one "depraved" perspectivist to the other, from Duchamp's roto-reliefs and attempts at "precision optics," to the younger artist's *Vonal* series (begun in 1966), in which concentric square or circular waves draw the gaze into endless corridors and spirals, like visual screw threads.

The expanding or regressing structures created by the systematic deformation of the work's modular structures, whether based on the square, the hexagon, or the octagon, all exemplify the way Vasarely abused or perverted perspective. In them, he renewed the experiments of the fifties in which, already, he had begun playing with deformed checker patterns and

Basq, 1973
Oil on canvas
158 × 117 cm

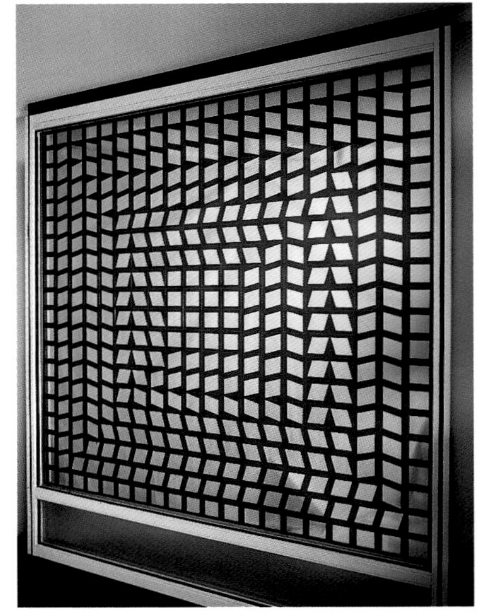

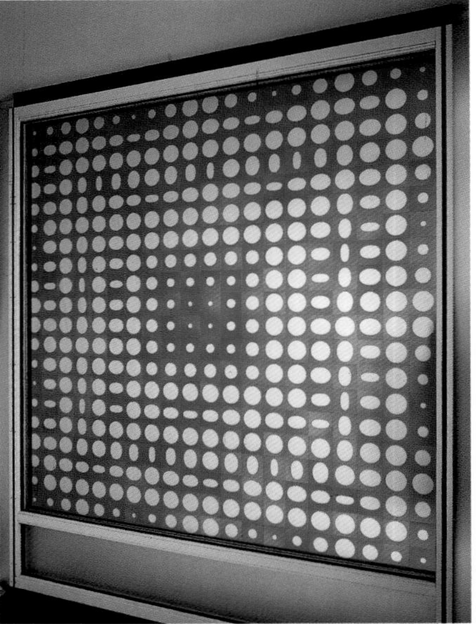

Tau-ceti négatif, 1974
Silk-screen on aluminum
200 × 200 cm

Betelgeuse négatif, 1974
Silk-screen on aluminum
200 × 200 cm

Novae régressif-progressif, 1974
Silk-screen on aluminum
200 × 200 cm

networks of fine black lines whose regular inflections suggested relief, as if there were forms growing beneath the surface (*Vega*, 1957, private collection). The later *Vega* works (1969) stand as immediate descendants of the first efforts. These *"breathing surfaces,"* as Vasarely called them, show grids that are stretched to breaking point: a huge bubble forms on the surface, stretches the forms and makes the light stream over its rounded contours (*Véga bleu*, 1970, Renault collection). *"They seem to be breathing heavily, like Pulsars born of a gigantic explosion that happened fifteen billion years ago. I myself am convinced that this birth is continuous, that it has no end and that it constitutes the very structure of the universe."* [19] The plane blisters, palpitates, burgeons; it offers yet another image of those geneses that remained so fascinating to the artist. In accordance with a constant of metamorphic thought, Vasarely seems to endow his cosmos with exuberant life, likening it to a kind of giant animal. In some of the more complex compositions, where the swellings of the plane are combined with the shrinking of a grid that seems to be sucked down into unfathomable depths, the viewer has the impression of being faced with a double movement, the diastole and systole of this enormous organism (*Boo*, 1978, private collection).

19. *Entretiens, op. cit.*, p. 80

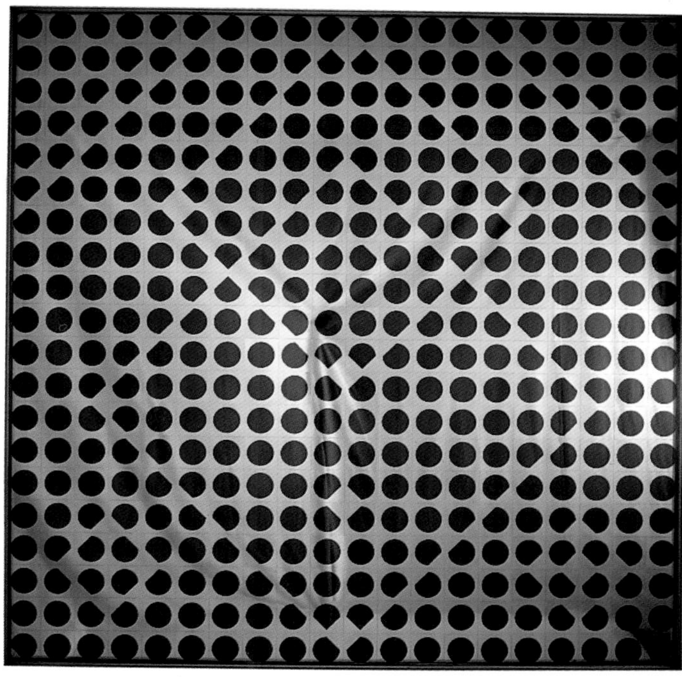

Andromède positif, 1974
Silk-screen on aluminum
200 × 200 cm

Surely, not since the Mannerist and Baroque periods had anyone developed so many deceptive devices, so many perspectives of all kinds, from the most orthodox to the most denatured atmospheric perspectives and chiaroscuros. The art of Vasarely, along with the most significant of Op art, dismantles like a vulgar machine all the essential operations of painting and reveals their fundamental illusions. It is the tension between the rigor of the method and the extreme illusion it serves to produce that is unsettling. The artifice and the means used by the artifice are always exhibited to the eyes of the viewer, who can verify the exactitude of the progressions and permutations and check the accuracy of the conceptions and calculations ordering the deformations that come into being before their eyes. And yet the viewer is always taken in. *"Monstrous images"* is what Vasarely called his compositions,[20] perhaps without suspecting that the same term was used in the Enlightenment to describe anamorphic images.[21] Like these, Vasarely's images prove that it is not only the sleep of reason, but also its excesses and the fact of taking certain logics to their absurd extreme that brings forth monsters. Also like them, they are the expression of a fundamental doubt about the appearances of the world, one that draws on a scientific culture and imagination that can only be made to yield unstable, elusive, mobile, and multidimensional images.

20. In M. Joray (ed.), *Vasarely II* (Neuchâtel: Editions du Griffon, 1973), n.p.

21. See the article "Anamorphose" in Diderot and d'Alembert's *Encyclopédie*, quoted in Baltrusaïtis, *op. cit.*, p. 116.

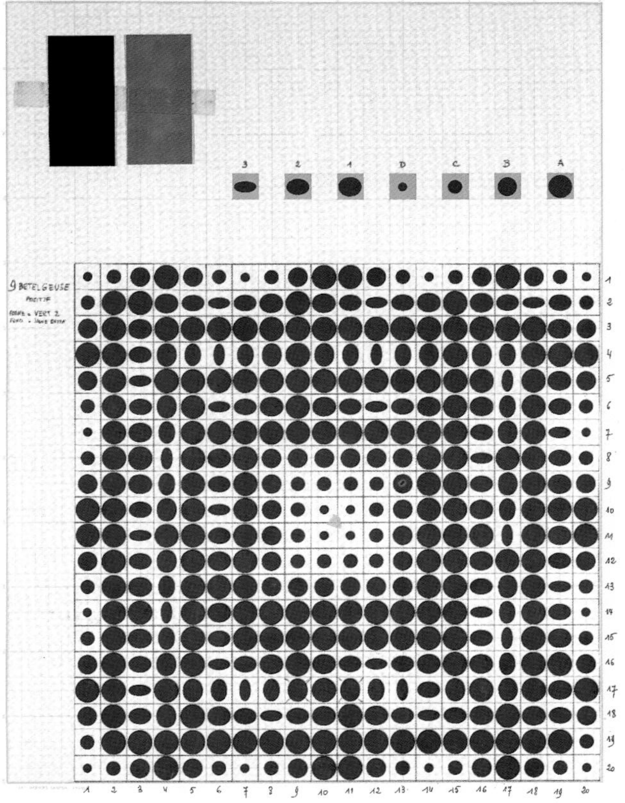

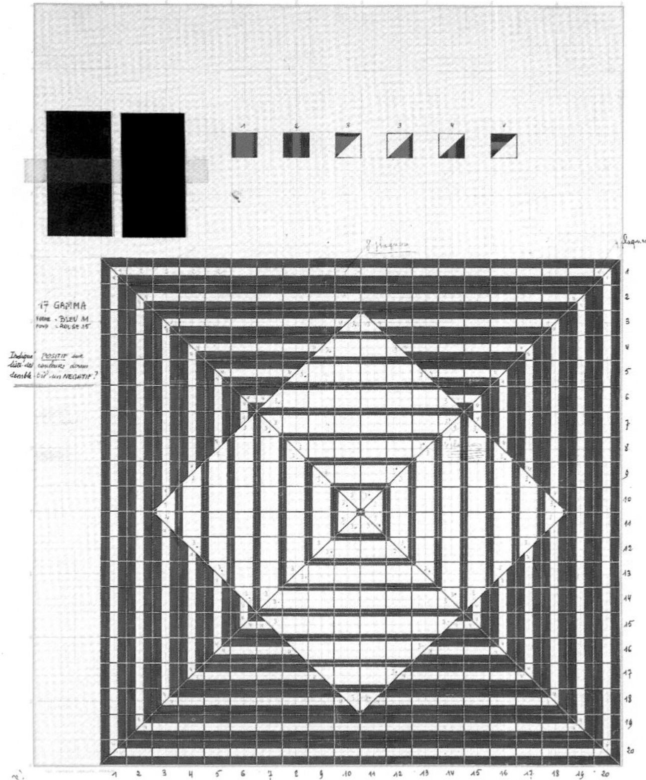

Preliminary studies on paper for the series of silk-screens on aluminum, 1973

Constantly referring to the concepts of contemporary science, as to a *"new source of poetry,"* [22] of which art would provide the intuitive equivalent, Vasarely forged a conception of the universe for which, now and again, he found expressions. Take for instance Diderot's answer to the question "What is this world?" in his *Lettre sur les aveugles* (1749): *"A compound subject to revolutions, all of which indicate a continual tendency toward destruction; a quick succession of beings who follow on, jostle each other, and disappear; a fleeting symmetry, a momentary order."* This *"fleeting symmetry,"* this *"momentary order"* are very much those of Vasarely's own *perpetuum mobile*, caught up in the universal flux, those of a body of work, which can in its entirety be considered as one of the most magnificent recurrences of the transformative vision that endures through time and space.[23]

ARNAULD PIERRE

22. *Vasarely I*, *op. cit.*, p. 74.

23. On this subject, see Michel Jeanneret's very inspiring book, *Perpetuum mobile, métamorphoses des corps et des œuvres de Vinci à Montaigne* (Paris: Macula, 1997).

Jesús Rafael Soto
Through Soto

This is the leitmotiv of my work. Space-time precedes form and, given this fact, we can say with some authority that form is nothing more than a kind of space.

J. R. SOTO

Among the works commissioned and acquired by Renault, the ensemble of pieces by Soto is remarkable both in nature and in scale. More than all the others, his intervention is structurally tied to its sponsor because it is bound up with the overall architectural project into which it is placed, and was necessarily projected and conceived simultaneously with the construction of the Renault building. This is an integrated work in the fullest sense of the word, for the commission and, even more, the actual proposal (which of course went beyond the original limits) are wholly engaged with the architectonic reality of the building. Indeed, the art-architecture relation remains significant even today. From a contemporary viewpoint, one cannot fail to note how the period determines the building: the regular spacing of its round-cornered windows and its aluminum cladding help create a very "seventies" smoothness – which is not a criticism for a building inaugurated in 1975. In contrast, it seems difficult indeed to reduce Soto's interventions to their moment, to assimilate them to the language of a period. Despite the powerful presence of the architectural parameters, Soto's "grande écriture" (large handwriting), his hanging volumes, and even the wall covering, all retain their power of emancipation with regard to any hastily compiled stylistic catalogues, and do so in spite of the shared materials (aluminum) and the fact that the intervention was expected to function on a decorative level. This indeed was the challenge facing Soto at the outset. For the patron – and the working documents leave no room for ambiguity on this point – the demands made on the artist reflected what was a classic and predictable remit, given the nature and function of the site of his intervention, that is, the lobby. More particularly, it is the lobby of the headquarters of a corporation, which, given its position between the poles of technological excellence and the laws of the market, between industrial importance and the authority of a national publicly-owned industry, was necessarily concerned with symbolic significance. The symbolic function of thresholds, pediments, entrances, steps, halls, and other details recurs throughout the history of architecture. The question was, how would Soto cope with the commission? He was

Progression, 1974 (detail)
Wood and metal
Renault corporate headquarters, Quai du Point-du-Jour, staff restaurant

Following pages:
Grande Écriture, 1974 (partial view)
Metal, nylon filament, and wood
Renault corporate headquarters, Quai du Point-du-Jour, lobby

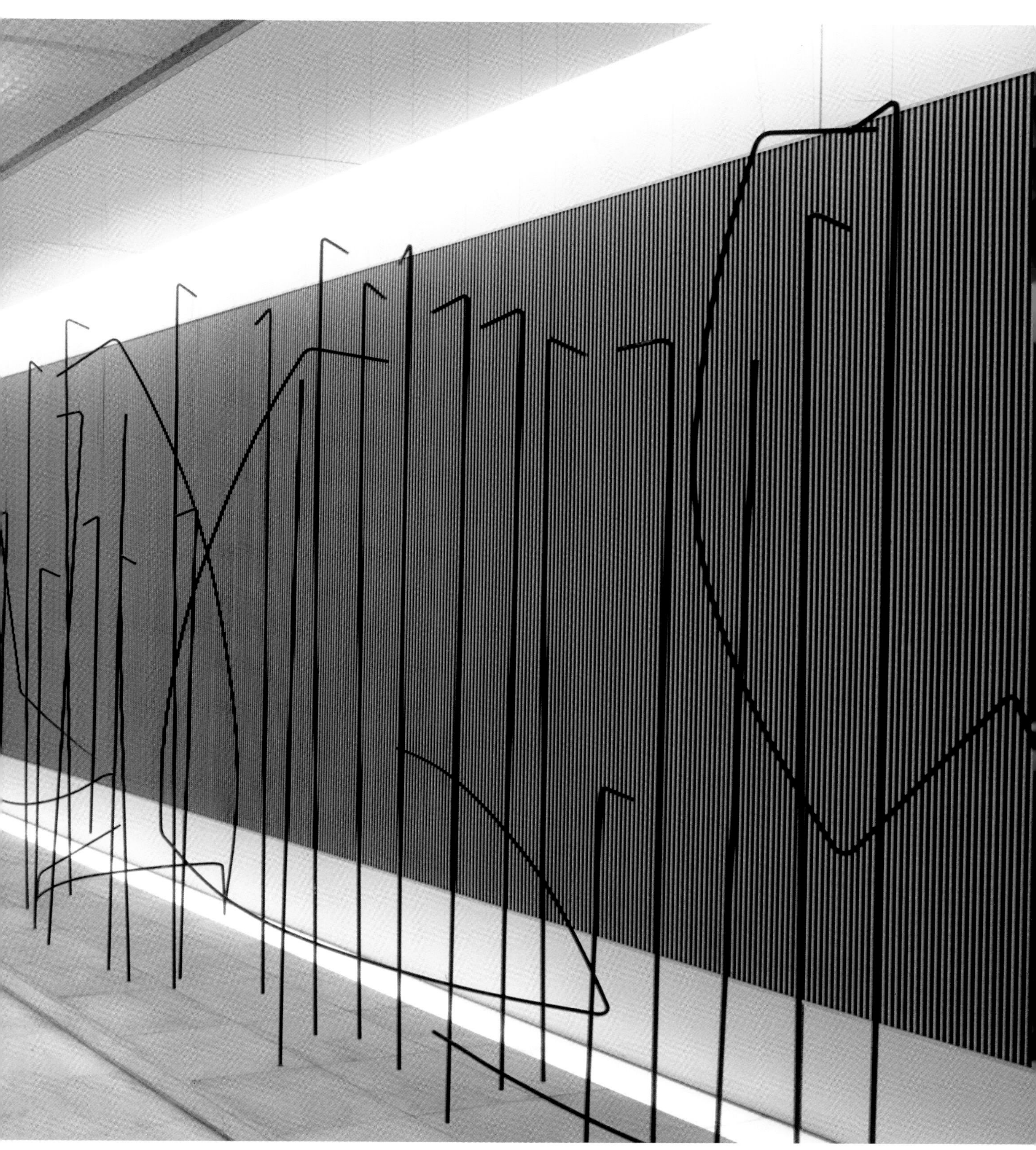

« Carrés vibrants », 1974
(partial view)
Renault corporate headquarters, Quai du Point-du-Jour, lobby, central aisle, 1974

certainly well aware of its implications – he who, as a sixteen year old in his native Venezuela, had painted signs and cinema posters and who, before Boulogne, had already worked on integrated environments.[1] No doubt the power and authority of Soto's response are due to the fact that he did not answer the question directly, but followed the concerns of his own aesthetic engagement rather than the logic of ideological service. The architecture of the time, whose modernism was fortunately without appetite for pomp and grandiloquence, and more responsive to a machine-like or even democratic regularity of construction than to hierarchical orders, meant that Soto could quickly free himself of the symbolic dimension of his mission. However, the functionality of the space entrusted to him was worth pondering, and it was this dimension that initially inspired him to embark on a project that was fully coherent with his artistic investigations. As a place for the egalitarian experience of transit, of passing through, the lobby is a place of movement. It articulates many of the issues at stake in the artist's own work, in which the movement of the viewer has a motor function. Yet, while it is true that here Soto had a "captive audience," he had no desire to enclose he viewer either symbolically or visually. This indeed is one of the characteristics of the project, due primarily to the fact that Soto uses a multiplicity of formal and material vocabularies. This stylistic variety helps define the decisive features of the proposition, which – although stemming from the logic of the environment, from a response to a global and necessarily closed architectural space – wholly avoids not only the monumentalism that

1. In 1957, for the *Kinetic Structure* in Caracas and then, in 1958, at Expo 67 in Montreal, in 1969 for UNESCO in Paris, and for several others during the seventies. Among the many realizations that followed, people in France are particularly familiar with the *Volume virtuel*, 1979, in the Centre Georges Pompidou.

Renault corporate headquarters, Quai du Point-du-Jour, lobby, central aisle, 1974

the scale of the intervention might have given cause to fear, but also the authority of the all-encompassing.

The Dynamic of the Relation to the Viewer

The intervention consists of several units, which are difficult to separate with any precision because they form a whole but not a real continuity. In all, the ensemble covers some 4,000 square meters. Only the fact that the regular vertical lines on the aluminum in one of the two spaces are repeated on specially printed gray formica in the other space discreetly suggests a principle of connection between two neighboring but architecturally very different areas. This includes the lobby, which provides access to all the other buildings, as well as the company restaurant, which is located behind the lobby. Soto's response to the variety of functions defined by the architectural program was to create several moments by using different vocabularies – which he had already tried out elsewhere, in most cases separately – and not a global solution, which would inevitably be more obtrusive. From the double security doors to the cladding of the walls, from the furniture to the rods on the ceiling, he combined no less than four different plastic languages – and, if we include the tables and the long vitrine at the other end of the room, on the opposite wall, as well as the yellow and white kinetic wall, two or even three more in the restaurant. Whether the elements used are massive and solid, or hanging, mobile pieces, each of these moments derives in its own way from Soto's highly distinctive graphic-rhythmic style.

The sliding security doors area is an adaptation of the spatially ambiguous cubes used in *Rome Cube*, a work shown in Amsterdam in 1969, which was not penetrable. There is nothing oppressive here about the effect of being surrounded, especially since the spatial ambiguity results from the juxtaposition of lines and transparent areas, which allow the gaze to penetrate the volume before the body can do so. The effective integration of Soto's signs into the internal architecture is thus clearly stated at the point of entry.

The ceiling is occupied by a more complex volume that cannot be grasped at first glance. This is constituted by a sequence of rods of increasing length. This ceiling was conceived to express a silent but powerful relation to the function of the setting. Notwithstanding the eighteen-odd metric tons

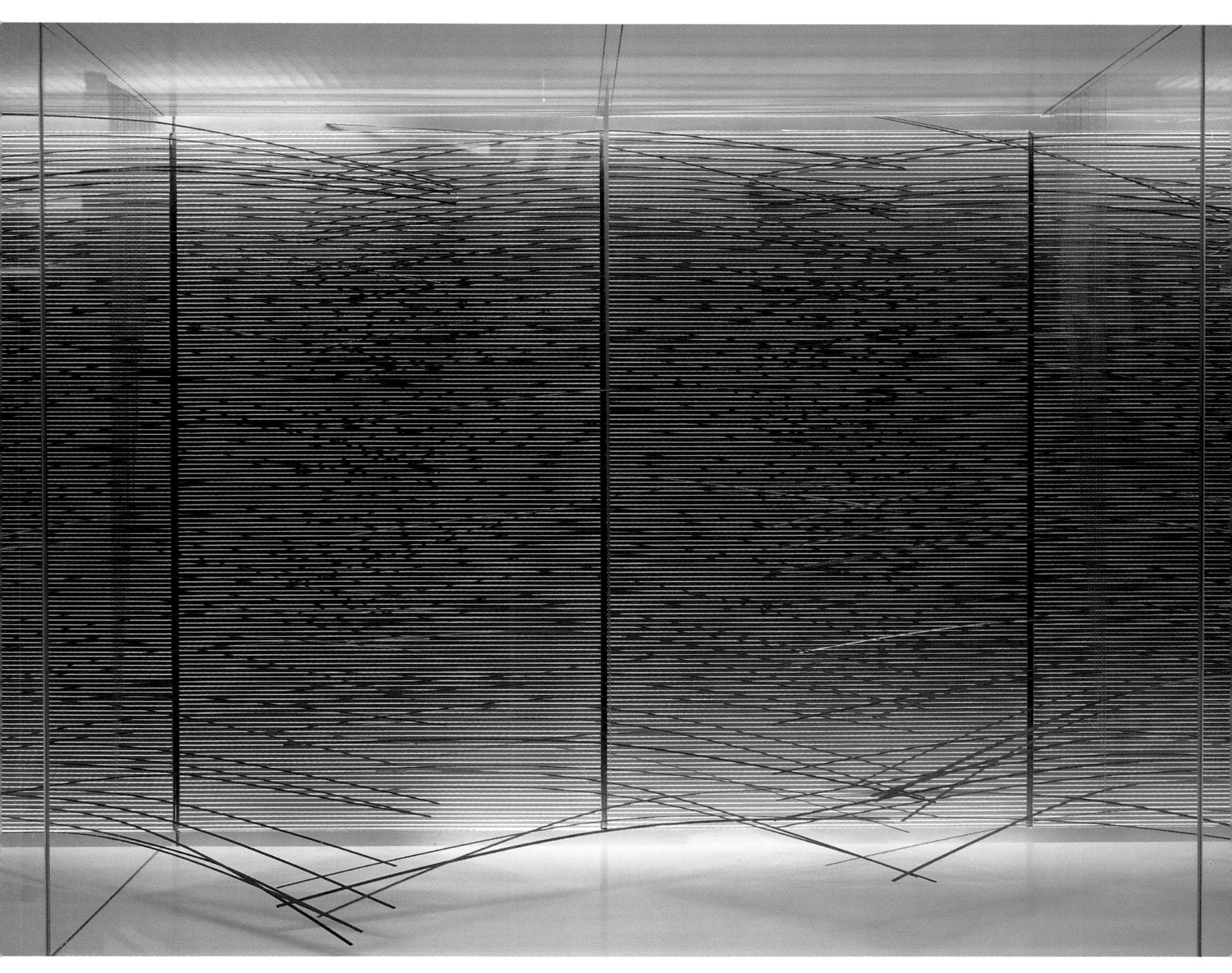

Vibration, 1974 (partial view)
Wood and metal
Renault corporate headquarters, Quai du Point-du-Jour,
staff restaurant

of its 250,000 elements, it produces a sensation of lightness. This is how Soto imparts a sense of meaning and direction to the three aisles defined by the two pillar-like blocs that occupy the space, forming the core of the building. In the central area, the plane constituted by the rods rises so that the volume appears to expand toward the rear wall. The visual effect is one of attraction, encouraging movement into the building. In contrast, the progressive movement to each side goes in the opposite direction, with the volume expanding toward the exit. Thus the ceiling organizes the movement through the space, respecting the flow from the sliding panels of the security doors to the frontal wall. These elements are enough to make us aware that the basic architectural plan is one of a temple or church, constituted by a central aisle with side aisles running alongside it, separated by thick pillars, and coming to a halt at the retable, represented here by the "grande écriture" – which indeed is a very sizeable thirty meters in length.

Soto's "écritures" form a series whose first formulations date back to 1958, when he made a mural for the World Exposition in Brussels. This piece in turn pursued the explorations undertaken in an earlier work, *Vibrations* (1957). The appearance of the different "écritures" varied in accordance with the graphic elements that were hung in the foreground, and the vibrations set up by their superimposition over the vertical lines that make up their ground. Here, the black rods initially worked out using a model seem to be organized in relation to a quasi-circle laid out almost in the center of the lobby. Of course, this *quasi* and *almost* are important, for geometry and symmetry are never more than suggested. The complexity of the lines evokes the intertwining of plants as much as it does calligraphy (although Soto was always wary of references to nature). The artificial backlighting heightens the feeling of vibration.

In the center of the lobby is a reception desk, now surmounted by aluminum structures, which inevitably break up the original continuity of the space and weaken the effect of the work's integration, although it is still easy enough to imagine its initial role. Most importantly, the two cores of the building support a series of "vibratory squares" typical of Soto's research – he achieves an effect of separate, floating planes by placing square-shaped colored surfaces against a striped ground. As in the seminal works of 1953 (for example, *Two Squares in Space*, 1953, Soto Foundation collection, Ciudad Bolívar), the regularity of the squares, the contrasts and the shadows make the skin of the architectural mass breathe, and thus make it seem lighter.

From Volume to Plane

By virtue of both their scale and design, the two works on the restaurant side do not play on the space in the same way as a global whole, nor on the same perceptual disparities. The long vitrine can be seen by those sitting at tables, its suspended rods in front of (again) a striped ground producing a shimmering watery surface. At the back of the large dining room stands a kinetic wall with hanging yellow and white rods. It is highly integrated into the form of the wall, in which it occupies a recess. Although it seems modest in scale compared to some of the artist's other kinetic walls (*Vibrating Wall*, 1966, Rome), it nonetheless creates an opening at the end of this restaurant space marked out by the regularity of the tables, acting as an elliptical, horizontal echo of the squares in the lobby. In formal terms, the two ensembles are linked by the uniform line pattern used on all the restaurant walls. For a while, Soto thought of adapting the principle of the ceiling of metal rods for the eating area. For economic reasons, however, and with the artist's agreement, a standard system of overhead lighting was preferred. Still, it does contain elements of the artist's favored grid pattern.

Looking beyond their apparent diversity, these propositions share a common feature that, although discreet, does much to keep this ensemble from authoritarianism. This is especially obvious in comparison to many other monumental or environmental propositions by Soto and is bound up with the relation of these real volumes to the plane, in the sense of the picture plane. For, if we consider them carefully, even though they are constituted in a relation to the three dimensions of architecture, each of these moments – with the notable but discreet exception of the ceiling which, as we have seen, constitutes a volume – can be read as planes, and, precisely, *in* the plane of the wall, that is to say, in a reference to their architectonic role. The vibrant squares appear to be flush because, although they stand free of the wall, they are also set in recesses of this same wall. The "écriture" is beheld frontally from the virtual screen marked out by the small step on the floor, since the linear grid recedes or hovers in a nowhere space defined by the vibration of the superposed graphic elements.

Vibration, 1974
Wood and metal
Renault corporate headquarters,
Quai du Point-du-Jour,
staff restaurant

From the other side of the wall, however, the screen ceases to be virtual. Here, vibrant hanging rods run along the dining room wall behind a glass case divided up into two parts. Here again, depth is kept behind the plane of the wall, the unity of which is not broken because the glass is flush with its surface, while, as we have seen, the yellow and white kinetic wall fills a recess. It is true that Soto often stated he was a painter, not a sculptor, even when using three-dimensional elements. Here, in any case, the question of depth and the plane is approached in several different ways, leaving none of the walls untouched, or at least always disrupting their planar inertia.

In fact, the paradox of this work on real space is due to the fact that the vocabularies it employs are more those of painting, or at least of the picture plane, than of sculpture: it makes no incursions into living space, into the area of circulation. This recession into the wall, this holding back within the plane, are further extended, or given a new twist, in the radical reversal that Soto effects with regard to the logic of the environment. Not only can the works be read as planes receding into plane, but they never occupy peripheral spaces. On the contrary, they repeat, and dematerialize, and occupy only the constructive volumes (cores, pillars, blank walls). They leave free

Progression, 1974
Wood and metal
Renault corporate headquarters,
Quai du Point-du-Jour,
staff restaurant

all the walls with windows and the points where light comes into the interior, and are thus never seen against the light. They are installed only on the central, outward-facing walls, as if the intervention had been undertaken in a centripetal movement. Natural light is thus free to penetrate the space, to enter even its blind spots. This particular economy concentrates, as if by inversion, the building's power of self-revelation, setting up a vibration only between the parts that are architecturally the heaviest, the fullest. Thus, far from a systematic encircling, the inscription of each moment of the project seems to have been guided by a critical structural awareness of the building – this is one cause of the arrangement's non-systemic efficiency.

The continuing legibility of Soto's intervention, and its pertinence, afford a useful lever for gaining a historical purchase on the whole field of artistic practices grounded in fifties modernism, and for confirming that in their successful moments, as Frank Popper wrote in 1988, *"the work of the kinetic artists in the fifties has contributed to a number of the developments of the last thirty years, and in particular to the dematerialization of the art object, the integration of art into architecture and the environment, and the encouragement of viewer participation."* Popper then adds: *"The introduction*

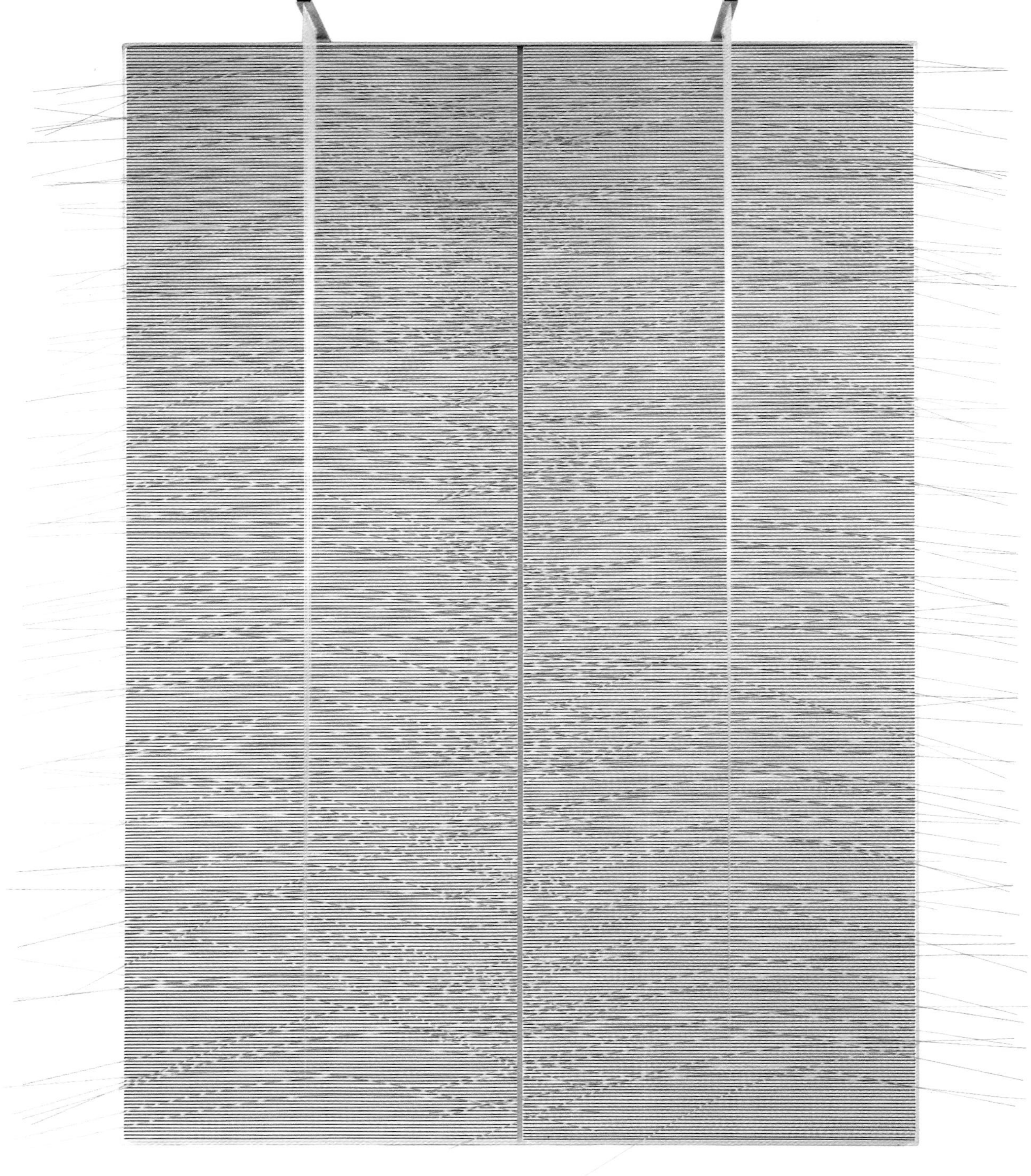

Gran Amarillo, 1974
Wood and metal
202 × 142 × 42 cm

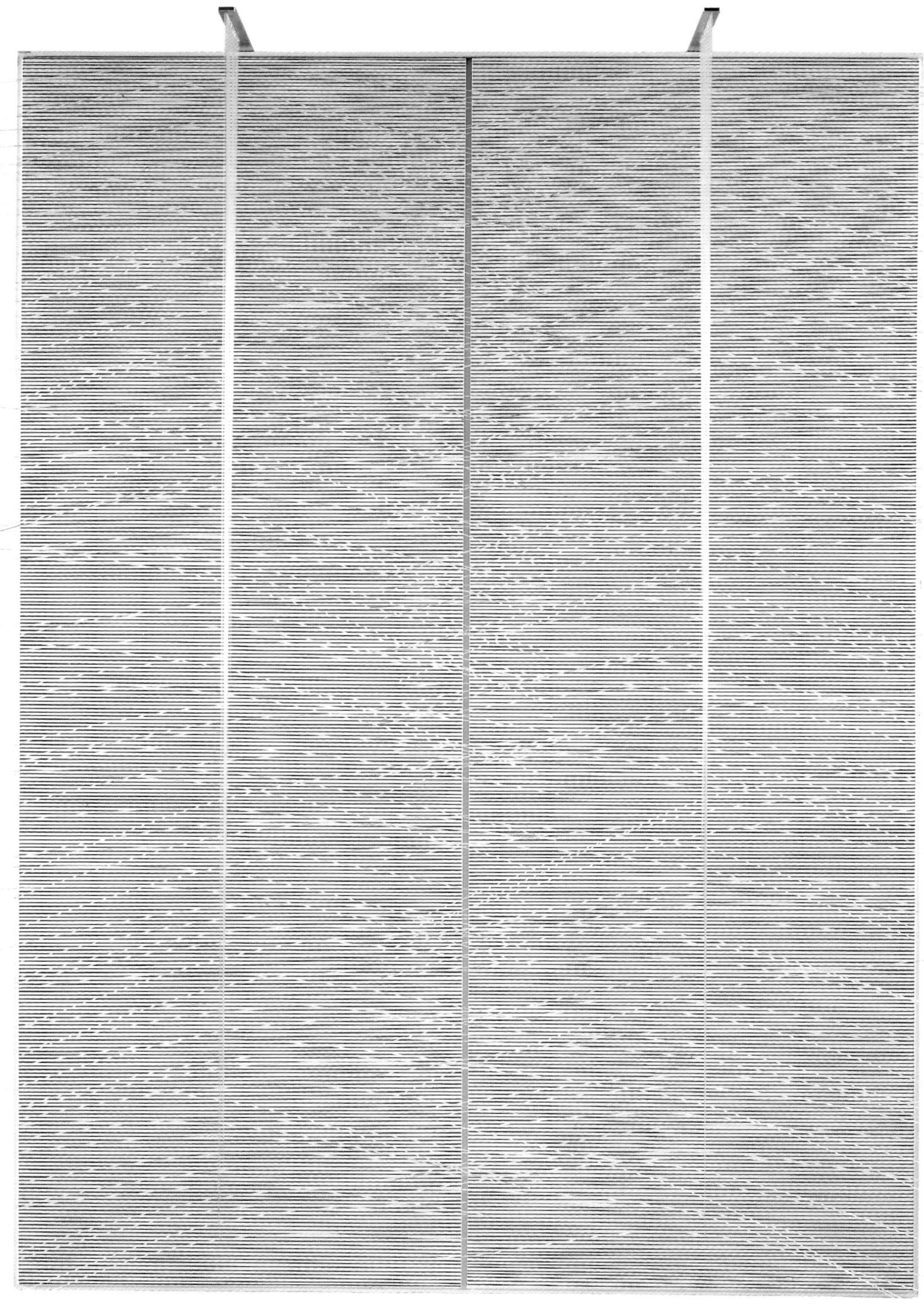

Gran Blanco, 1974
Wood and metal
202 × 142 × 42 cm

of movement and space into abstract works and their resulting dematerialization can be credited with breaking down the barriers between the traditional categories of painting and sculpture. But these factors also played a role in the strengthening of links between visual research and scientific and technological research that occurred at that time." [2] All of which very much applies to the encounter between Soto and Renault at the turn of the seventies. Above all, the continuing rightness and pertinence of his proposition give good reason for going back to other propositions made at the time,[3] and for rereading the theoretical issues addressed in kinetic art and constructive abstraction, for which the *relational* dimension is above all inscribed in the experience of the work itself – as indeed it is in the still active current of Concrete Art. Some have called these movements "the last avant-garde," and it is true that their modernist intentions and liberating ambitions have opened a fertile critical field, all the more so because their positions were deeply thought out and solidly argued. This was certainly the case with Soto's appetite for European modernism when he arrived in Paris in 1950. However, this is not quite to say that kinetic explorations are just as necessary today as they were then, even if the questions they addressed continue to show their relevance, if not their topicality, when it comes to certain much-canvassed themes such as the decorative and the conception of the aesthetic experience. One proof of this, as I see it, is the regularity with which these themes have been the subject of theoretical enquiries and exhibitions.[4]

Without fearing the opprobrium of the modernists and the negative connotations of the word itself, Soto's work touches on the decorative dimension in a *functional* manner. The Renault lobby reminds us of this in that it takes into account a real concrete space, a space considered as a material and not as a void to be filled. The fear of mere padding implied by the pejorative use of the word "decorative" becomes meaningless from a viewpoint such as his, founded as it is on the sensation of the density of space and on a vision of art as a permanent reactivation of that sensation through phenomena of vibration, through all kinds of optical and luminous vibrations. The confrontation with architecture occurs on just such a basis, in the search for what, writing in 1957, the Venezuelan architect Villanueva described as a *"new attitude which, like the Baroque era, would free internal*

2. Frank Popper, *Les Années 1950* (cat.), (Paris: Centre Georges-Pompidou, 1988), p. 197.

3. As indeed Arnauld Pierre suggests we should in the catalogue to the recent Soto retrospective in Paris (Paris: Galerie Nationale du Jeu de Paume, 1997), p. 30.

4. In 1998 the question of the decorative in art was raised by a number of exhibitions such as the one at the museum in Villeneuve d'Ascq (autumn, cat.), and was at the center of a number of reflections by abstract painters (for example, Richard Kalina, "The Uncomfortable Armchair: Abstraction and Decoration" (1996), translated in *Tableau: nouveaux territoires* (Valence: Editions de l'Ecole des Beaux-Arts, 1997). At the same time the propositions of the Groupe de Recherche d'Art Visuel (GRAV) were reconsidered as an alternative to the traditional exhibition for their idea of the relation to the viewer, by the retrospective at Le Magasin, Grenoble (summer, cat.). Between 1960 and 1968 the members of GRAV (Horacio Garcia Rossi, Julio Le Parc, François Morellet, Francisco Sobrino, Joël Stein, and Yvaral) pursued the developments towards a participatory, spatial abstraction since the exhibition *Le Mouvement*, at the Galerie Denise René in 1953 and at the Salon des Réalités Nouvelles in the fifties.

space from any static vision."[5] Posited anew, outside the historicist heritage, the question of the decorative does indeed seem to be shifted here towards a pragmatic approach that cannot be reduced to the superstitious taxonomy brandished, for example, by the enemies of Minimal Art, of "literalism" and of the theatricality of poor materials – an approach that gives onto a much more positive, critical, and theoretical outlook.

Both essential corollary and theoretical issue, the movement of the viewer is wrested from the sublimatory and static spheres of old European idealism and "reactivated" in the present experience of the work.[6] Soto's approach to this process is radical, especially in his penetrable sculptures, in which the experiential space of the viewer and the volume of the work coincide so that the sensorial experience switches constantly between the visible and the tactile. These works are about touching as well as seeing. It is a twofold process, involving both the anthropological ambitions of Soto's art and the classic reversal of microcosm and macrocosm about the pivot that is the modern subject's "experience of the world." The lobby of the Renault corporate headquarters, which is by its very function penetrable, has simply inflected towards construction, and not deviated from the project of the open work, which runs through all modern art and which, even now, maintains its potential for new metamorphoses.

CHRISTOPHE DOMINO

5. Quoted in the chronology of the Soto retrospective at the Galerie Nationale du Jeu de Paume, *op. cit.*, p. 186.

6. The ultimately rather banal idea of the importance of experience was dignified by an usage that only a certain North American philosophical tradition could pull off – a tradition which underpinned much innovative art in the United States during the thirties. One of its main proponents was the philosopher John Dewey, the author of *Art as Experience* (1934, reprint New York: Perigee Books, 1980).

Jean Tinguely

Requiem for a Dead Leaf

"The return almost to conventional sculpture."

JEAN TINGUELY

R*equiem for a Dead Leaf* is the name of the elegant work eleven meters long and three meters high made by Jean Tinguely for the Swiss Pavilion at Expo 67 in Montreal. The artist responded to the commission with a monumental sculpture. However, unlike *Eureka*, a compact, autonomous machine made three years earlier for the Schweizerische Landesausstellung in Lausanne, this is a transparent, expansive, and airy relief, which takes up a very large piece of wall and, illuminated by several light sources, can be seen glowing from a considerable distance. At the time, this imposing and soberly beautiful piece of machinery surprised Tinguely connoisseurs, accustomed as they were to the noisy and aggressive machines of the early sixties, made of scrap and all kinds of weird and wonderful found objects. The title refers to an orchestral and choral composition, implying that the work is to be heard as well as seen, yet this "mass for the dead" is conducted in silence. The machine is almost mute: all one can hear is a discreet constant humming. The atmosphere is solemn but not sorrowful. The serene yet dynamic movement of the machine evokes life more than it does death. It is full of vigor, and it seems astonishing that the tiny white leaf relegated to the bottom right-hand corner should be at the origin of this impressive ballet. This "dead leaf" turns, dances, and seems to impart its own movement to the dark machine. It is the director of a brilliant polyphonic performance.

In *Requiem*, the sculptor's creative method had undergone a metamorphosis, but of what kind?

In the sixties, Tinguely was extremely active on the international scene. His capacity for work and his energy seemed limitless. Ever since 1960, when he made his huge self-destroying machine *Homage to New York* out of spare parts and objects found in local dumps, he had been producing his works in makeshift studios. For each new exhibition, he created new kinds of machines made of junk and materials found *in situ*. Thus the machine that burst into flames in the garden of the Museum of Modern Art, destroying itself in a unique and spectacular action, was made up of different kinds of wheels of American origin, taken from bicycles, prams, carts, and scooters. When producing this work, Tinguely also learned the technique of electrical welding. The monumentality of this elegant assemblage of rods,

Requiem pour une feuille morte, 1967 (detail)
Painted steel and various elements

levers, axles, belts, and bearings, make it an early precursor of the big machines and meta-harmonies to come. It contains the seeds of the formal vocabulary that would shape Tinguely's future output.

At the time, Tinguely found it fairly easy to obtain scrap iron and junk, and the proximity of his studio meant that transport costs were minimal. Moreover, these found objects usually struck a chord with viewers since they were always familiar objects taken from the everyday life of the particular place. Tinguely's art during this period was in tune with the spirit of the American avant-garde, as represented by the work of his friends Robert Rauschenberg, Jasper Johns, Larry Rivers, and Claes Oldenburg. He was on a roll, quick to assimilate changes in his environment and to exploit whatever creative opportunities they afforded. From 1961 to 1964 Tinguely was constantly on the move, working tirelessly, and gaining new insights and perspectives, both technical and expressive. Still, however conducive to artistic daring, to an imaginative emancipation from traditional norms and concepts, the American avant-garde scene was not without its pitfalls: there was always the risk of diluting one's artistic intensity, of lapsing into the facile use of banal everyday objects.

The evolution of Tinguely's machines over these years can be read in his letters, like this one written in 1962 from Seattle to Franz Meyer, back in Basel: *"I am over in 'half-Alaska' for a few days to build* Narwa, *a furiously fast maxi-machine which will at last inject a little order into the chaos of my art and – how shall I say? – give it balance. But in NY I now have a studio (40 meters long!) and I am working like mad there, making one radio relief after another; they are rather handsome."* Clearly, Tinguely was striving to clarify and order his formal language.

In 1963, returning to Los Angeles after a trip to Tokyo, he told Meyer about the exhibition he was preparing for the Dwan Gallery: *"I am now making a Giant & Co. sculpture – black as Hell, not very big, but powerful machines packed together so densely that it scorpions and slices with devilish precision. It is terrible and superhuman and sometimes at the same time silent (that's the best): anyway, I am trying to turn it out with a bit of 'clarity.' I have a big studio here and marvellous machines and iron and axles and volts galore, ball bearings, etc. . . . So there's nothing to stop me from working on complicated things. It is the idiots who are tough. In spite of the mildness of the*

Montréal, 1966
Study for *Requiem*
Ink on paper
25 × 60 cm

Pacific, I have managed to serve up what I started in Japan in a real mean, hissing kind of way."

Such statements indicate a major change in the way Tinguely conceived his machines. He was now painting these in a uniform black, thereby focusing the gaze on the formal aesthetic aspects of the sculpture and not, as in the first *Balouba* or *Char* sculptures, on the unexpected assemblage of identifiable found objects from which they are made. Thus coated, the rusty iron components of the machines take on a new mechanical reality, an unprecedented and sometimes disturbing autonomy. I am thinking of *Hong Kong*, *Samouraï*, and *Bandini*, the works that Tinguely alludes to in the letter quoted above. The forms and structures of these machines are evident and simple and their dimensions are human. Saws, spirals, and other attributes signal their dangerous, aggressive nature. Their greater solidity endows them with a more pronounced sculptural presence and their simple, clearly defined movements are more assertive. Such were the qualities of the works Tinguely had just made when, the same year, he was commissioned to produce a monumental sculpture for the Schweizerische Landesausstellung in Lausanne.

Requiem pour une feuille morte, 1967
Painted steel and various elements
305 × 1105 × 80 cm

Tinguely worked on this commission in the winter of 1963–64, creating a huge, compact, painted in black, sculpture which he entitled *Eureka.* It featured a system of levers that made it possible to vary its dimensions. As Tinguely explained, *"It grows; it goes up and comes down . . . this dome, this arm comes out and goes back in, this tube moves up and down, there are blades that move up and down. It grows bigger, it gets shorter, shrinks, increases."* About the paint, he remarked that *"in a way, the black ensures that the contraption has formal homogeneity. This is a return to sculpture – I mean almost to conventional sculpture . . . in its physical aspect. Again, movement creates the unexpected . . . movement remains a phenomenon that is not as 'classical' as all that . . . The black is a way of making the found object disappear – it is the anti–Nouveau Réaliste gesture par excellence – no more Nouveau Réalisme – no more found objects."*[1]

1. Interview with Alain Jouffroy, *L'Œil,* no. 316 (April 1966).

When making this piece, Tinguely gained precious technical experience and considerable self-confidence in assembling and using countervailing mobile structures. It was also an opportunity to observe the reactions

Requiem, Bascule V, Eos VIII, at the Tinguely Museum, Basel

Eos XII, 1967
Painted steel and various elements
178 × 188 × 76 cm

of a large audience. *"Is this or is it not art?"* wondered the Swiss. Nonetheless, this congenial contraption, which tips its lid in greeting, succeeded in winning the hearts of visitors, to the extent that it became a popular meeting point at the exhibition.

Eos VIII, 1966
Painted steel and various elements
180 × 220 × 120 cm

Bascule V, 1967
Painted steel and various elements
90 × 200 × 50 cm

Another thing that Tinguely had learned from his familiarity with the American avant-garde was the suggestive power of junk and consumer objects, which he exploited in his impish tiny machines. He now knew that more rigorous forms could fascinate the public as well. The magic lay in the use of perceptible and recognizable movements and noises and in the interplay of elements going up and down, forward and back, spinning and shifting to the hubbub of the machine. Public familiarity with machines and mechanics played an important role here. Many drew a parallel with Chaplin's *Modern Times* (1936). However, when the exhibition was closed, no public space came forward to accommodate the work. And so the machine was left in storage for a while with a Zurich collector before being "provisionally" placed outside the Zürichhorn Casino, where it still stands today. Ironically though, *Eureka* was the work chosen by the jury as the chief example of Tinguely's work when he obtained the official commission for the Swiss Pavilion at Expo 67 in Montreal.

Tinguely had already been selected to represent his country once before, at the 1965 São Paulo Biennial. Among the works he sent to Brazil were new black-painted versions of *Eos* and *Bascule no. 5*. The machinery in these works was solid, fully functional but nonproductive. The underlying social satire was evident, as was its target – industrial society. Yet, as Tinguely's remarks make clear, the pieces also had a certain gravity: *"For me their back and forth motion had something of the spirit of Sisyphus, the idea of being condemned to keep doing the same thing over and over again. Granted, they are free, granted they are joyous; but they are also without hope. They are doomed, in a kind of limited space, to keep making the same movement, always the same movement."*[2]

The jury awarded Tinguely a merit prize but, as he wrote to Franz Meyer, he was disappointed: *"I have sent that pathetic 'innovation prize' back to the Biennial: I do not need any 'encouragement.'"* Success, though, was slow to come. At the end of 1965, when his work featured in the touring

2. *Ibid.*

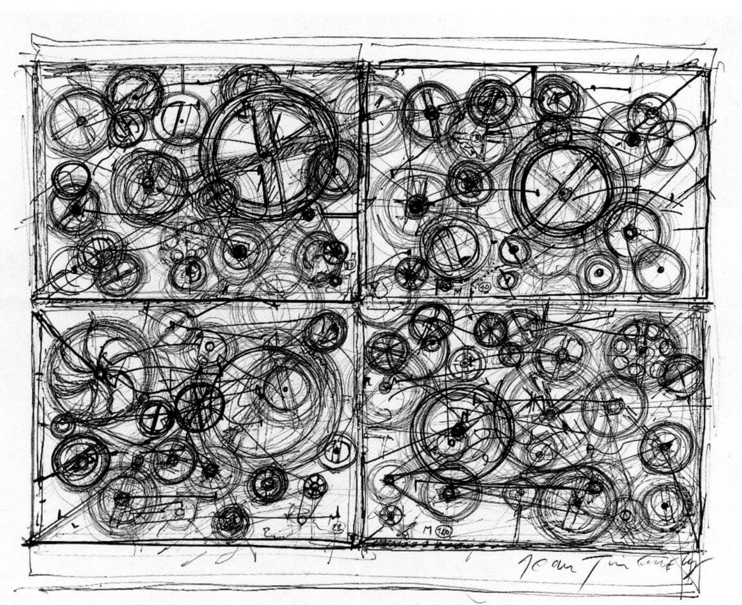

Untitled, undated
Pencil and pastel on paper
78 × 52 cm

Untitled, undated
Ink on paper
70 × 84 cm

show *Two Kinetic Sculptors* at the Jewish Museum in New York, Tinguely even came under fire from the critics. According to Pontus Hulten, *The New York Times* accused him of peddling pastiches whereas it described his companion in arms, Nicolas Schöffer, as an *inventor*. Tinguely was forty and beginning to hanker after recognition. After all these years he wanted to taste the success he believed he deserved. Caustic and horrific, the *Dissecting Machine* made in 1965 for the New York exhibition and then acquired by the Menil collection in Houston, shows how the artist was gathering up his energy and aggression, as if now there was nothing that could stop him. This cruel and barbaric work shows the limbs of a dismembered woman threatened by the disorderly thrusting of saws, drills, pliers, and other instruments of torture. The nightmarish motions of the machine are an unmistakable image of the pitiless, brutal reality of life. This work is diametrically opposed to the playful humor of other works from the same period such as *Pop, Hop, Op & Co*, a kind of satire on Disney-style romanticism and the excesses engendered by the artistic trends of the age. It also contrasts with those Sisyphean machines relentlessly performing their useless actions.

By the mid-sixties, Tinguely had fully developed his language as a sculptor of iron and a mechanic of dreams, achieving a remarkable diversity of expressive forms. He used junk not only to attain satirical or Dadaist-type effects, but also to draw attention to its own played-out beauty. These objects, which seem to inspire his creative imagination, exude a distinctive poetry. However, it was the kinetic dimension that proved most congenial to Tinguely's artistic imagination. Exploiting the dynamic power of electrical motors, he gradually moved away from the direct use of readymades and scrap metal covered with rust and the stigmata of wear, and began to search for more eloquent architectonic forms. The black paint transformed industrial products, motors, and parts into components of equivalent visual significance. The surprising effect of their cohabitation and presentation resulted in a new mechanical reality, a homogenous aesthetic form. The assemblages were now more solid, more simple, their movements clearer and more autonomous. Yet the new machines were just as wacky as their predecessors. The different variants of *Bascules* even had their own unpredictable dynamic, engendered by the somewhat anarchic play of movements and countermovements. On occasions, the momentum built up by these rocking movements even caused the works to suddenly slip off their supports. The repetitiveness of their direction made them even more intelligible and insistent. Where once Tinguely's machines squandered their energy in spectacular displays, they now enacted a playful but constant movement with both strength and reserve. Even when stationary, their expressive sculptural forms were eye-catching, presaging a new monumentality.

This context helps us appreciate the importance of the big relief *Requiem for a Dead Leaf.* It confirms the extent to which Tinguely's machines were made for an audience: it is in their nature to attract the viewer, to encourage spontaneous participation. The first major collective creations, such as *Dylaby* (1962) in Amsterdam, or in Stockholm, the huge walk-in sculpture *Hon* (1966), reflect this concern. Tinguely also invented a new kind of machine, the *Rotozazas,* which made a direct appeal to the viewer, haphazardly throwing out balloons and then catching them again. Another machine simply kept breaking the plates that were fed to it by an industrial-style conveyor belt. Systematic destruction replaces production and active participation takes the place of passive contemplation. Tinguely was only a step away from live performance.

In spring 1966 the choreographer Roland Petit asked Tinguely, Niki de Saint-Phalle, and Martial Raysse to design sets for his new ballet, *Eloge de la folie,* at the Théâtre des Champs-Elysées. Tinguely came up with a stage curtain in the form of a flat machine. Returning to the principle of his earlier meta-mechanical devices, with their fine wire wheels and colored metal dancing in a circular pattern, Tinguely cut out a set of large flat wheels from wooden boards, painted them black and had them spin in front of a backlit white curtain. A dancer sitting on a bicycle-like structure pedalled to set the mechanism in motion, causing driving belts to roll balls around. This ingenious stage device gave a new expressive twist to the artist's characteristic themes and motifs. The lighting evoked the world of shadow theatre while conveying an impression of weightlessness. Tinguely had already expressed an interest in cast shadows, notably in a letter in which he told Pontus Hulten that *"I am going to get the shadows of the machines working too with three or four cinema spotlights."* Here, he took the experiment a step further.

In the same year, Tinguely started work on the *Requiem for a Dead Leaf* for the exhibition in Montreal. Drawing on the theatrical experience gained from *Eloge de la folie*, he built a ready-to-dismantle relief that took up the whole wall of his studio in Soisy-sur-Ecole.

He cut out wheels in various forms and sizes from wooden boards, painting them black and arranging them in a rhythmic sequence on a long frame divided into compartments. Sometimes overlapping, sometimes juxtaposed, the circular forms created an open set of geometric figures. Numerous preparatory sketches indicate Tinguely's efforts to create a mixture of equilibrium and tension that would also allow for a considerable degree of movement. In his copious notes and drawings, Tinguely worked through the various material and technical problems involved in endowing his sculptures with motion and developed the formal solutions corresponding to what he was after. *"I draw . . . in order to find a connection between form, its appearance, and movements."*[3] In *Requiem*, Tinguely was particularly concerned with the harmony of these movements. He defined the speed of rotation for each element in the relief before integrating the data into the general choreography. This approach implied not only a global vision of the different rhythms animating the machine, but also the creation of the right technical conditions needed for such a large range of rotary and lever movements. Classical mechanics offered only a limited number of variations. As he later remarked: *"Having found the solutions corresponding to the necessary speeds – because, sometimes, within these movements, you have to find different rhythms and different speeds – I had to get them to coexist. I was therefore looking for a harmony of speeds . . . It had to be harmonious because ultimately I had only a limited number of possible motors. I had only a certain number of organs, which, from a mechanical point of view, it was possible to assemble, and with which I could obtain a given number of movements."*[4]

This is particularly true for *Requiem*, which is entirely driven by a single electric motor mounted behind a circular form in the third compartment from the left. Tinguely organized the sequence and speeds of the spinning wheels by means of an ingenious system of driving belts, sometimes crossing them over to slow down an overly rapid movement or to change the direction of the rotation. The resulting ballet is both solemn and

3. *Jean Tinguely, Dessins et gravures pour les sculptures*, cat. exhib. cabinet des Estampes, musée d'Art et d'Histoire, Geneva, 1976, p. 9.

4. *Ibid.*, p. 10.

Jean Tinguely, Paris, 1968

majestic. Facetious countermovements, superposed contrariwise rotations and unexpected lever movements show the subtlety with which Tinguely defined the rhythm of his work. The motor conducts this orchestra of wheels so as to move the little white leaf fixed at the extreme right-hand side of the frame. It begins to spin to the right, then to the left, as if it were being brought back to life.

In his studio, Tinguely lit his work from above and behind, thus obtaining the kind of Chinese shadow-play effects he had previously achieved on stage. The black thus became a uniform mass whose materiality was lightened by the rotating movements. Subsequently, when the work was exhibited in larger spaces, Tingely placed it on a platform, a kind of plinth covered with black panels, which allowed him to shine hidden spotlights on it from underneath and thus to heighten the backlighting effect and increase the work's intensity and the mysterious aura of its radiance. Later, he extended the scope of his relief by adding three autonomous black sculptures with outward-reaching open arms. Standing before the *Requiem* like altar boys, they seem to be presenting the dance of the wheels.

The title, *Requiem for a Dead Leaf*, sounds like something from a poem by Paul Eluard or Robert Desnos. By an ironic coincidence, the work was presented at Expo 67 just below a set of precision telescopes, which are brilliant apparatus designed to enlarge and transform the viewer's perceptual field.

The idea of taking otherwise insignificant or banal objects as the starting point for artistic creation is central to the ambivalence of Tinguely's work. His machines are satirical, devoid of function or economic utility, but they also have the power to touch us deeply, to awaken associations and trigger emotional reflexes. Their poetic power is signalled by their titles. As to whether these machines are works of art – a question Tinguely often had to face – it becomes irrelevant here. As Tinguely told John Sweeney in 1965: *"For me, the machine is above all an instrument that enables me to be poetic. If you respect the machine, if you enter into the game with the machine, then perhaps you will be able to make a truly joyous machine. By joyous, I mean free."* He was, in Sweeney's words, *"an artist . . . [a] creator of majestic toys, of poetic machines – machines which by their very essence belong to the world of imagination."* [5] The great black mechanism,

5. In the exhibition catalogue *Tinguely, Sculptures*, The Museum of Fine Arts, Houston, Texas, 1965, n.p.

Requiem, very much belongs to this poetic world and announces, through its design and powerful expressiveness, the meta-harmonies to come. Its multicolored wooden wheels – which were originally moulds for casting steel – would later make it possible for the artist to work on an even more monumental scale without incurring problems of construction or weight. In sculptures such as *Fata Morgana* (1985), the mechanical noises were gradually refined into distinct sounds. These would mark a new high point in his work.

MARGRIT HAHNLOSER-INGOLD

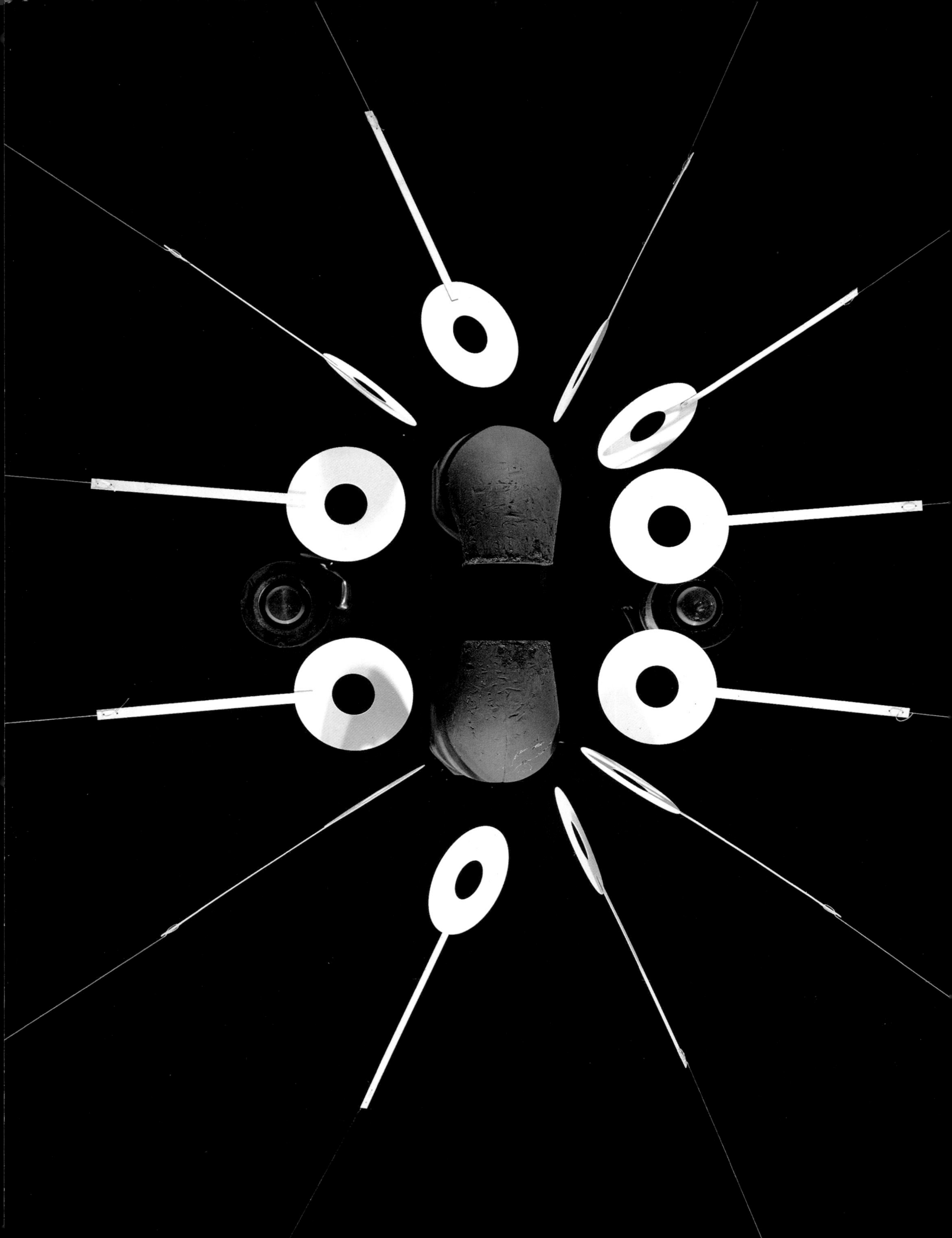

Takis

In Praise of Magnetic Fields

The sculptor is a person who works on matter to bring out and make visible its spirit, intelligence, and splendour.[1]

TAKIS, 1964

When he came to France in 1955, Takis broke immediately with the anthropomorphism of his previous works and embarked on a series of experiments that would lead him to start using magnetism as an invisible force – one capable of occupying the space traditionally allotted to sculpture. In his autobiography, *Estafilades*, the artist tells how, when leaving his native Greece, he suddenly became aware of the extent to which the universe of technology had overrun the postwar world, whether in the form of a signalization system in a railway station or radar at an airport. *"The lights of the monsters lit up and went out, rails, tunnels, a jungle of iron . . . Man makes for his own use tunnels, ways out, symbols to escape from death."*[2] A few pages later, we read: *"Ah, if only I could use an instrument like radar to capture the music of the beyond! . . . If, as it rotated, this object could pick up sounds and transmit them, that would have delighted my fancy."*[3] In fact, the kinetic possibilities afforded by magnetic fields soon became the basis of a sculptural practice to which, working deductively, Takis would add the use of cathode ray lamps and the light produced by electrons, as well as the sound waves emitted by the activity of magnets.

In the early sixties, Takis developed a project whose visual concerns were subordinated to a focus on the potential energy contained in matter. This practice naturally ran in harness with a universalist intellectual vision that set out to reveal, as Nicolas Calas very pertinently emphasizes, *"the secret forces of nature, in order to express man's Dionysian dimension."* Calas continues: *"Destiny seems to have decided that it would fall to a Greek sculptor to electromagnetically unite Thales's discovery with Pythagoras's conviction that heavenly bodies produce sounds."*[4] Indeed, for while Takis does make use of a number of scientific facts from the modern world of machines, he also knows how to reconcile these with the rigor and concision of a creative mind deeply marked by the founding mythical and cultural heritage of the oldest Mediterranean civilizations. For an artist who holds Daedalus to be the greatest artist of all time and who readily alludes to the role of Apollo as, in Plato's words, *"he who moves the heavenly bodies together,"* Greece, is

1. Luce Hoctin, "Takis, Conversation dans l'atelier", *L'Œil*, no. 119 (Paris, November 1964).

2. Takis, *Estafilades*, (Paris: Julliard, 1961), pp. 132–133.

3. *Ibid.*

4. Elena and Nicolas Calas, *Takis* (Paris: Editions Galilée, 1984), p. 23. In the sixth century BC, the Ionian philosopher Thales of Miletus knew that amber (electron in Greek) has the capacity to attract smaller bodies.

Untitled, 1974 (detail)
Screws, coils, graphite, and magnets fixed on a painted wood panel
Renault corporate headquarters, Quai du Point-du-Jour, corridor between the cafeteria and the elevators

an obvious point of reference. But so too is Egypt where, for some years now, he has become a regular visitor: the Egypt of the pyramid builders, the land of funerary rites that sought to replenish the soul with vital energy, the land of the goddess Isis, sovereign of the magical world. In an interview with Takis, Félix Guattari pointed out the paradox of his approach, *"its dimensions of hypermodernity and, at the same time, its primitive dimensions, those of a man who emotionally and cognitively inhabits the entire history of humanity."*[5]

These are the ideas we need to bear in mind when analyzing the work integrated into Renault's old corporate headquarters at 34, Quai du Point-du-Jour, commissioned at the time of construction. To these we will add two other major ensembles commissioned at a later stage, the "telelights" and "musical sculptures," insofar as these are perfectly representative of the fundamental explorations conducted by Takis and their place in the history of contemporary sculpture.[6]

Magnetic Paintings

"Magnetic paintings," "telelights" or "magnetic walls" – a variety of names are used for these large, almost invariably monochrome surfaces upon which one or several magnets, sometimes apparent, sometimes hidden, irresistibly attract or maintain in a state of levitation objects of which some are found, others, made by the artist. Here, two large black paintings face each other across a corridor in the Renault building on Quai du Point-du-Jour. Each of them is constituted by a diptych whose center is a magnet surrounded by gears from industrial machines. From these gears emerge wires. Attached to the ends of these wires are small white oval spatula shapes with a hole in the center and they float several centimeters above the support. The contrast between their lightness and the density and rootedness of the magnet, the choice of the monochrome, the form of each object, the organization of space in terms of a double network of diagonals (the visible diagonals of the sustaining wires and the invisible diagonals running through the position of the viewer due to the opposing positions of the magnets on either side of the corridor) – everything here is remarkably concise and simplified to the extreme. Indeed, it is only through this kind of rigorous formal economy that the artist can reveal the processes at work here. The invisible forces hold together these surprising small white metal objects

5. Interview by Félix Guattari in *Takis* (exhibition catalogue) (Paris: Galerie Nationale du Jeu de Paume, 1993), pp. 268–269.

6. The two magnetic pieces are still in place in one of the corridors of the Renault building. The two others, *Télélumière* and the set of *Sculptures musicales*, were sold back to the artist in 1985 and are now managed by the Fonds Jean Hamon.

Télélumière, 1963 – 1967
Mixed media

like loose particles adrift in the cosmos. *"I attempted,"* Takis wrote to Alexandre Iolas, *"to treat, guide, and dominate magnetic force itself in its properties of real communication: the space-communication of objects on this planet."*[7] Alain Jouffroy was the first critic to understand the aesthetic revolution implied by such a practice: " . . . *it is no longer the apparent subject that constitutes the emotional center of the work, but the energy it captures . . . the invisible is not only symbolized by the forms of sculpture, but participates materially in locating them in space. It is not a question of myth, therefore . . . but of the materialization of the presence of invisible energy by the visible object.*"[8] By systematically experimenting with magnetism, Takis has undeniably written a new chapter in the history of contemporary sculpture. His initial ambition was to go beyond Gonzalez, who, by twisting pieces of iron, obtained only graphic forms, but he has also gone well beyond the Russian Constructivists, who rejected the idea of the sculpture as an inert mass and sought to make space exist as an entity in itself. While Takis has often spoken of his debt to Giacometti and Calder, for whom movement was fundamentally related to space, he is also among those artists who have situated their projects within the overtly acknowledged inheritance of Marcel Duchamp. Indeed, two of his works are declared homages: the magnetic painting entitled *Jeu d'échec*, in 1961, and, in 1968, *The Perpetual Moving Bicycle Wheel of Marcel Duchamp*, which incorporated the object famously used by Duchamp himself. Introduced into the world of art in 1913 by the father of modernity, this external, incongruous (Duchamp called it *anartistic*) object, which turns on itself and seems to have its own motion, obliges viewers to radically change their attitudes towards the work of art.

By making systematic use of magnetism, Takis was going beyond the spatial domain of simple three-dimensionality. Saturating the empty space with invisible forces, he began to explore all the possibilities offered by this discovery in reliefs, sculptures, and environments. He even beat the Russians by five months in the race to put a man in space (again, this being a Greek artist, one thinks again of Daedalus and Icarus): in 1960, at the Galerie Iris Clert, a young English poet, Sinclair Belles, positioned between two magnets, was able to float free of gravity for a few seconds, long enough to say: "I am a sculpture."

7. Takis, letter to Alexandre Iolas, dated 1961, in *Takis* (exhibition catalogue), Galerie Alexandre Iolas, Paris, 1971. Translated in Muriel Emmanuel's (ed.), *Contemporary Artists* (London: St. Martin's Press, 1983), p. 921.

8. Alain, "Le télémagnétisme de Takis," *Takis* (exhibition catalogue), Galerie Alexandre Iolas, Paris, 1964.

Telelights

Takis started introducing colored light into his works at the beginning of the sixties. His first *Signaux lumineux* (Light signals) were green, yellow, blue, and red. Blinking atop their long thin stems, they are a symbolic representation of the modern technological landscape, which the artist had experienced as a kind of revelation at the Calais railway station. Takis soon began combining light and magnetism. As he has since remarked, *"capturing light and playing on light-color always seemed a way of adding an extra boost of energy."*[9] The "telelights" consist of one or more mercury vapor lamps whose light comes from the collision of the negative and positive electrons generated by the electrodes. As the heat increases or diminishes, so the color modulates: *"This is how the colours blue, green, and sometimes mauve occur. This is what exists in the void, that is to say, in the space above our atmosphere. It is the sky that becomes green when the sun is vertical and becomes mauve when its rays weaken at sunset. It is the void in miniature. It is the void, immensity, terrifying Ades."*[10] From the single cathode ray lamps of the first "telelights" through to the complex and sophisticated installations of recent years, Takis is thus paying an implicit and somewhat nostalgic homage to "the fairy of electricity" and all its apparatus, now threatened with extinction by ubiquitous electronics. While Takis of course sees himself as a sculptor, he has repeatedly claimed to be entirely dependent on the specific properties of matter and to give both functional and technological priority to the objects he chooses and sets in space – the primary goal of his work being to create that electrical atmosphere, which brings a permanently renewed energy. The large "telelight" made in 1982 is significant in this respect. It could be compared to a majestic votive altar whose every component, surrounded by corner irons, seems to be there to celebrate the central cathode ray lamp, which, with its head, its very short torso, and its raised stumps, could so easily be presiding over some magic, secret ritual – like Isis. This universal goddess, whose cult endured throughout antiquity, was the mistress of the three worlds: the heavens, the earth, and the underworld. This, as Takis is aware, makes her eminently qualified to grasp the attracted and warring elements. The dominant central figure, she is surrounded here by a whole array of apparatus: commutators, junction cables, burnt-out fuses, small warning light bulbs, ammeters, pressure gauges, and other devices recuperated from our modern technological

9. "Takis, hier et aujourd'hui", interview with Maïten Bouisset, *Takis* (exhibition catalogue), Galerie Renos Xippas, Paris, 1993.

10. "Réponse de Takis", *Opus International*, Paris, December, 1972.

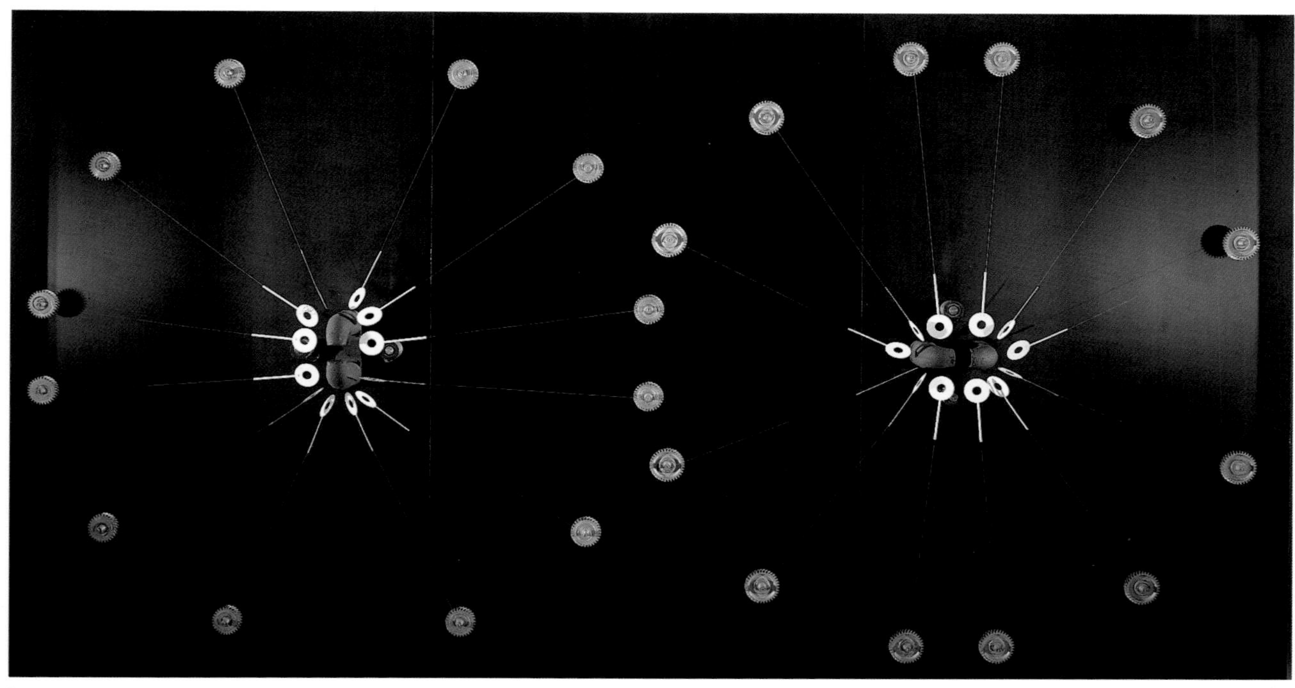

Untitled, 1974
Nuts, coils, graphite,
and magnets fixed on a painted
wood panel
171 × 318 × 2 cm
Renault corporate headquarters,
Quai du Point-du-Jour, corridor
between the cafeteria and
the elevators

universe and turned away from their primary function; they now symbolize the energy potential that science masters and that has an inexhaustible capacity for engendering metamorphosis. By making perceptible the conditions for the appearance of a magnetic field in the "telelights," Takis spectacularly draws attention to space and energy as the principles of a sculpture that exists solely in the conditions of their manifestation. Here, as throughout his work, the function creates the aesthetic, that poetic order in which each of the terms required by the intended demonstration asserts its own existence.

The Musical Sculptures

A long steel needle hanging from a vertical cable moves imperceptibly across large white monochrome panels – it is pulled by magnetic attraction so that it strikes a piano wire. Takis's "musical sculptures" are at once minimal

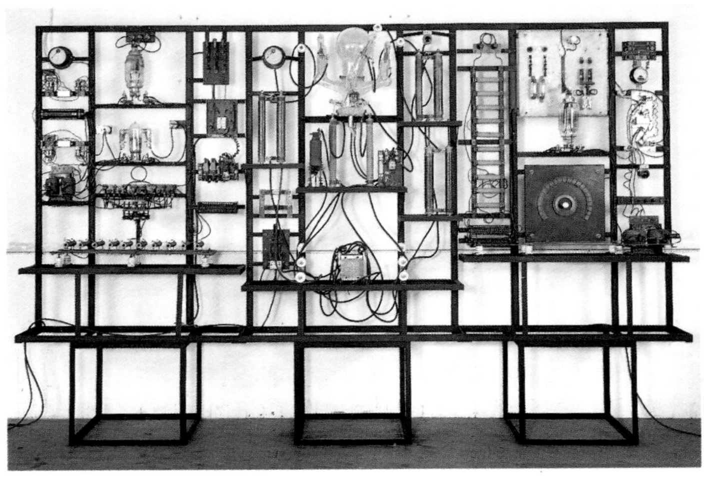

Télélumière (relief), 1982
Mixed media
180 × 360 × 30 cm

reliefs hung on a wall and the unexpected instruments in an unsettling concert. A whole set of electromagnets hidden under the panels draw the needles into their invisible web of forces, making them hit the stretched wires alone, in unison or off the beat, producing sound vibrations that may go from inaudible to the most strident contrasts. While music already played a part in the "telesculptures" and "telelights," there it did so only in the form of an almost inaudible rustle, one which inspired William Burroughs to observe that: *"In Takis's electromagnetic fields, you can hear metal thinking."* [11]
The sound produced by the electromagnets was first amplified in 1964 with the collaboration of the composer Earl Brown, in a work entitled *The Sound of the Void*. Shown in the New York exhibition *For Eyes & Ears*, this piece established the basic principle of the musical works that would appear two years later. It was, said Takis, a homage to Apollo: *"No more darkness for the Greeks, Apollo gave them music. At any moment, at any instant, they could communicate, so I thought that I could not sleep any more unless I gave music, music from magnetic waves."* [12]

By introducing invisible magnetic waves as an acoustic presence in space, Takis fulfilled his most ardent desire as a sculptor – the dream, inspired by radar, of capturing the music of the spheres. By revealing the musicality of magnetic space, this invisible phenomenon, which is nevertheless the sole subject of the sculpture, he spectacularly widened that "space-communication," which was central to his ideas. To his large white wooden panels, Takis has since added huge gongs, large metal tubes, and big wooden beams upon which electromagnets come clashing down.[13]

The space of communication intended by the artist can also be the spectacular space of the imposing installations that the artist has devised in museums all around the world ever since his first discoveries. His is

11. William Burroughs, *Takis*, poem in exhibition catalogue, Galleria Schwarz, Milan, 1962.

12. "The Takis Dialogues," *Eight Artists, Eight Attitudes, Eight Greeks* (exhibition catalogue), ICA, London, 1975, p. 86.

13. These, incidentally, were used at Easter as a means of communication by the monks on Patmos, whom the Turks had prohibited the ringing of bells.

a theatrical space suited to Greek tragedy, or so it is tempting to say, knowing that the artist designed the set and music for Sophocles's *Electra* at the theatre in Epidaurus. For Nicolas Calas, *"the aleatory series of sounds struck up by Takis's electromagnetic orchestra, correspond to the song of the chorus at the altar of Dionysus: Aeschylus heightened the antagonisms personified by each of the actors to the detriment of the chorus's unity. The heart of democracy beats faster when, in the name of memory, the citizenry is divided between those who are attached to the past and those who grow away from it."*[14] Now living back in Greece, Takis refuses to be just a purveyor of works for museums and collectors. He is an artist for whom the social space has a real meaning – a fact attested, as elsewhere, by the two magnetic walls that are the daily companions of all those who work at Renault, management and technicians alike. Going beyond the simple visual reality and aestheticizing function of art, Takis enfolds the viewer in a web of tensions and forces that subtly make themselves felt as so many particles of a world charged with energy. He is also a public-spirited citizen of Athens. As an artist, he is currently working on an environment to signal from afar the presence of the future Museum of Modern and Contemporary Art to be built for the Greek capital by I. M. Pei. As a citizen moved by the calamities of the modern world and, more specifically, reacting to the multitude of fires that have ravaged his country in recent years, he has developed an electronic signalling system linked to a pump, which should serve not only to set off the alarm, but also to automatically extinguish the fires in remote and inaccessible areas. The whole system is powered by solar energy. Takis has baptized his invention "Sun Against Fire." Knowing Takis, this could be another way of referring to Apollo, the luminous deity who makes the other gods dance to the sound of his lyre: Apollo who epitomizes the Greek genius.

MAÏTEN BOUISSET

14. *Op. cit.*, note 4, p. 237.

Simon Hantaï

Hantaï's Luminous Walls

How do you transform the nave of a church into a meeting room? A dining room into a church? Idiotic as they may seem, these are questions that have cropped up with some regularity and with major consequences throughout twentieth-century art. Lydia Delectorskaya explained how Matisse wanted to "crown" his career by working on a *"public place that was intended and accessible for all men. He would have liked to devote himself to a room for cultural gatherings."*[1] In the end, the result of this desire was the chapel of Notre-Dame-du-Rosaire in Vence, which he worked on from 1948 to 1951. Matisse considered it his masterpiece, and it is without a doubt the greatest masterpiece among all the buildings dedicated to the Roman Catholic religion during our century. In 1958 Mark Rothko was commissioned to make a cycle of paintings for a restaurant in the Seagram Building in New York. Having completed these works, he finally refused to have them installed in a luxury restaurant. His reasons continue to be debated. In 1961 and 1962 he painted five canvases for a meeting room at Harvard University. In the end, the works were used as the décor for a dining room, with disastrous consequences for their fragile materials. From 1965 to 1967, as the result of a commission, the artist was finally able to paint what he considered the culmination of his quest: the Saint Thomas University chapel in Houston (now known as the Rothko Chapel).[2]

Simon Hantaï also received commissions for several works of sacred art, including the project for an altar in the Parisian church of Saint-Germain-l'Auxerrois (circa 1978), and at the beginning of the eighties the suggestion was made at the Ministry of Culture that he might make some stained glass windows for the cathedral in Nevers, an idea that the artist never took up.[3] To this day, the largest decorative ensemble executed and installed by the artist is the one done in 1977 at Rueil-Malmaison, where Renault commissioned him to produce works for four walls, two in the company restaurant on the first floor and two in the cafeteria on the ground floor.

The parallels made above are not intended to suggest that restaurants can function as the churches of a secularized society. That said, we may note that, in the first floor room at least, the positioning of the works – a green panel and an orange panel, both facing a large and luminous glass wall – is the same as that chosen by Matisse for his ceramic panels in Vence. Matisse described his work for the chapel as *"juggling with and balancing two forces, the color of the stained glass on the right side and the black and white all along the left side."*[4]

1. Lydia Delectorskaya, quoted in Louis Aragon's, "Que l'un fût de la chapelle . . .," *Henri Matisse, roman* (Paris: Gallimard, 1971), vol. II, p. 222.

2. On the construction of this chapel and what led up to it, see Susan J. Barnes, *The Rothko Chapel: An Act of Faith, A Rothko Chapel Book* (Austin: University of Texas Press, 1989).

3. This information was provided by the artist himself and Mr. Jean Fournier in the course of numerous conversations between December 1997 and June 1998. I would like to thank them (and all the staff at the gallery) for their generosity and patience.

4. Henri Matisse, letter to Henri Laurens, 4 November 1949, reproduced in *Ecrits et Propos sur l'art*, edited by Dominique Fourcade (Paris: Hermann, 1972), p. 261.

Silk-screen on Formica, 1977 (detail)
Rueil-Malmaison technical center, staff restaurant

Hantaï proceeded in a similar way, except that he adapted to the distinct, less vivid light of the Île de France, and that he used only color, thus refusing to separate color and drawing, the better to balance or oppose, color (art) and light (nature). The important thing about this comparison is, first of all, that it allows us to underline the fact that in both cases the effect of these works goes beyond aesthetic pleasure, even if this plays a very important role in the decorative project. Like all of Hantaï's works, and I think in particular the silk-screens he made after 1969, this ensemble is thus a veritable knot of contradictions.

When the commission was issued, Hantaï was without doubt one of the best known figures in postwar French art (in 1976 there was a retrospective of his work, which also signalled the future closure of the Musée National d'Art Moderne at the Palais de Tokyo and its transferal to the Pompidou Center). Hantaï came to France from Hungary in 1949. Initially close to the Surrealists and then, around 1957, connected to the public performances of Georges Mathieu, he has, from the late fifties onwards, occupied a very singular position that has made him a rather isolated figure within his generation, but also an important reference point for younger artists – notably Buren and Parmentier and all those who had links, either close or remote, with the Supports-Surfaces group. From 1968 to 1971 he painted a series of paintings entitled *Etudes* and initially subtitled *À Pierre Reverdy*, some of which were silk-screened for various uses such as catalogue covers, exhibition posters, and ornamental panels in a variety of materials; and notably exhibited in the context of public commissions for the school in Trappes (begun in 1969) and the French Pavilion at the Hebraic University of Jerusalem (in 1972). The panels at Rueil were based on the same principle and used similar motifs, but with a greater degree of formal complexity.

It would appear that at first Hantaï thought of multiplying the motifs, in particular by making silk-screen versions of more recent paintings such as the *Tabulas* (which constitute the bulk of the painter's output since 1974) or an unnamed series painted around 1973 (obtained by making small, highly spaced knots, which, against the white ground, form a kind of pattern of small, circular forms with uneven outlines). Indeed, studio photographs dated May 1977 show silk-screens of a number of different motifs done on paper and hung on the walls. Among these can be seen the study for the green wall in Rueil. In any case, we know that the artist hesitated for several months,

Silk-screen on Formica, 1977
Rueil-Malmaison technical center, staff restaurant, west wall

as a letter dated 20 July 1977 explains that *"on the first floor the work* Les bourgeons *will be replaced by* Feuillages, *modulated in panels of 560 × 560."*[5] In the end, he chose to use similar motifs, all taken from the *Etudes* series (referred to as *Feuillages* in the letter), limited to forty-five kinds of square panels, on the basis of photographs of several paintings (at least three medium-sized works, i.e., with sides of between 1 and 1.5 meters), and belonging to both of the two categories into which this series is customarily divided: works in which the white forms are open and sparse, and those in which they are tightly packed and profuse. Transferred by silk-screening onto large sheets of paper (for the studies), and then onto Formica panels, these motifs were then divided up into small squares, which allowed for a considerable variety of permutations, like a jigsaw puzzle allowing both maximum unity and maximum variation. The forty-five basic squares were used to make several hundred combinations.

Thus, only motifs taken from the *Etudes* were used, and the emphasis was on simplicity, since the only changes were the result of choosing two different sizes for the modules (30 × 30 cm for the two ground floor panels, and 60 × 60 cm for those above) and four colors to set off against the white in monochrome panels (blue and yellow downstairs, green and orange upstairs).

5. Letter from the Galerie Jean Fournier to the SERI (Renault Engineering), duplicate kept in the gallery archives.

Silk-screen on Formica, 1977
Rueil-Malmaison technical center, cafeteria

The more varied solutions, which had originally been considered, were abandoned. Gone are the margins around the squares (although proofs do exists with white margins), the borders around each panel (although various borders were tried out[6]), and the polychromy (although Hantaï did at least try out bichrome works, reworking the principle of the panel in Jerusalem in which blue squares alternate with black).

Given this desire for decorative unity, there was a risk of transforming the silk-screen motif into a repeated motif. This would have meant failure of a kind for a painter who was always fighting against the presence of images in his painting, and who, to that end, invented the technique of folding. Instead of painting a figure on a ground, this technique consists in folding a loose canvas, covering the visible parts with paint and then stretching it out so that the motif – which is nothing more than the mark of the artist's work – is defined by the random effects of the folding, as made visible by the areas left white. Already, the risk of this repetition was greater in the *Etudes* than in any other series. For the first time, these works ensured that there was a real reversal, the image being formed by that which was not painted, and that

6. Could it be that the decision not to use these borders had something to do with the argument given by Dominique Fourcade, a close friend of Hantaï's, to the effect that Matisse must have given up the idea of a border for his 1911 *Intérieur aux aubergines*, judging it to be redundant. (Cf. D. Fourcade, "Rêver à trois aubergines", *Critique*, no. 324, May 1974, p. 467-489).

which was painted becoming a kind of ground, in an unstable relationship (*"Now, it's not what I paint that counts but what I don't paint – it's the white. The painting has become flat."*[7]) But they also gave rise to forms that the spectator might tend to identify with natural objects – birds or leaves (as indicated by the terms of the letter of 20 July 1977).[8]

Here, the continuity of the motif and its legibility are broken up by the fact of being cut into small, homologous squares, then being placed, not in such a way as to restore the image as in a puzzle but, more subtly, to let this image occur elusively. And indeed, it would be irremediably damaging and would cause a rigidity due to the simple coldness of abstract decision if the artist had made an external choice between the two antithetical solutions: no image at all or one and only one real image. As set down on the hand-drawn tables of 11 September 1977,[9] the positions of the forty-five forms were chosen in order to leave room for randomness and discontinuity, while at the same time engendering certain effects of unity. Thus, on each panel and with no apparent logic, we may find a connection between the forms on one square and the next – in accordance with the photographic image at the outset – and sometimes breaks; sometimes symmetry and asymmetry; sometimes an absence of definable connections.

The chief virtue of this method chosen by the artist for the decoration at Rueil is the way it underlines depersonalization. Designed for an almost public place, for the gaze of men and women whose identity could not be

Silk-screen on Formica, 1977
Rueil-Malmaison technical center, cafeteria

7. Simon Hantaï quoted by Geneviève Bonnefoi, *Hantaï*, (Centre d'Art Contemporain de l'Abbaye de Beaulieu, 1973), p. 24.

8. In this regard, the Surrealist phase was crucial. What Hantaï had to say about the image was said there and then, with, as Benjamin Péret noted in 1953, considerable potential for metamorphosis: *"A bone becomes a beating wing, a scrap of newspaper a questioning or threatening eye."* Here, the relation is no longer one of metamorphosis, even if Hantaï does sometimes retain that modality, as for example when he compares the *Tabulas* to his mother's folded apron. By now, Hantaï has put the world of images behind him almost for good. This makes him both the precursor of an entire generation and a perceptive admirer of Matisse and the Abstract Expressionists. We speak of motifs only for simplicity's sake, even if the gaze may pretend to see images in order to avoid doing the work that the painting demands in return. As if going backwards, the work rediscovers the motifs of artists who had only a very limited interest in the motif for its own sake: Owen, Matisse . . .

9. Archives of the Galerie Jean Fournier.

Silk-screen on Formica, 1977 (detail)
Rueil-Malmaison technical center, staff restaurant, east wall

known in advance (in contrast, Matisse knew he was speaking first of all to Dominican nuns, and Rothko to the Catholic faithful), the panels in Rueil express the utopian quest for an art that would take place on its own, without the agency of an active subjectivity. Dominique Fourcade states that the method of folding corresponds to a change in the artist's position: "How far it is, the time of Matisse when it was only a matter of cutting out one's tongue! The problem is to have nothing in one's hands, to put oneself in the situation of painting with one's hands tied behind one's back. It is now a question of painting with your eyes poked out. That is why Hantaï makes folds." [10] The images chosen here avoid composition, and therefore the image, and therefore premeditation. As for the use of silk-screen printing, it provides an extra degree of anonymity because the image comes from a photograph taken by a professional, because its concrete presence implies the intervention of a craftsman, and because, finally, its installation on the wall is the job of a workman – in a word, because all the technical aspects are delegated to people other than the artist. This attitude includes effects of chance due to the fact that the original photographs may have different parallaxes from the source photographs, and because the silk-screen may move between images.

We come here to a profound contradiction because this depersonalization works in two contradictory modes. On one hand, it makes the first appearance of the work a kind of ornamentation that is more or less pleasing, with pretty effects of color and line, in a magnificent visual proliferation (even if aspects of this may now be considered unfashionable in their evocation of the Pompidou years – for example, in the use of the color orange and of formica). On the other hand, this condition is necessary if the people in the rooms with the panels are not to stop short at identifying the image or the subjectivity that produced it, and instead absorb what is offered to their gaze without any feeling of separation, giving a free reign to their sensorial perceptions (they can get on quietly with their food, without being consciously aware of anything, it doesn't matter and the work certainly is not hostile).

This clearly chimes with Matisse's definition of the decorative function: *"The point is to channel the viewer's mind so that it rests on the painting yet is able think about something quite different from the particular object you set out to paint: to hold one's attention without deadening it . . . The mind must not analyze, that is arraigning the mind and not freeing it . . . ideally, the viewer will,*

10. Dominique Fourcade, "Un coup de pinceau c'est la pensée", *Hantaï* (cat.) (Paris: Musée National d'Art Moderne, 1976), n.p.

Silk-screen on Formica, 1977
Rueil-Malmaison technical center, staff restaurant, east wall

without being aware of it, let himself be caught up by the mechanism of the painting." [11] In Rueil, by virtue of the pared-down technique and the choice of abstraction, the work has a specific power to hold the attention that sets it apart. The whites do not so much draw motifs as empty the images of their substance.

The first function of the panels is to assemble a community: the employees of one of the world's most dynamic companies. The second, which is harder to detect, is one of negation. Subtraction is an active emptiness. It is in this sense that a dining room can become a church since, to quote the artist: *"In the East, throughout Christianity and also outside it, in revolt or in atheism, what is needed is always the same kind of emptying, of impoverishment, of denuding of being."* [12]

ERIC de CHASSEY

11. Henri Matisse, statements reported by Georges Duthuit in *Ecrits sur Matisse*, edited by Rémi Labrusse, (Paris: Ecole Nationale Supérieure des Beaux-Arts, 1992), p. 294.

12. Simon Hantaï, "Entretiens et témoignages sur l'œuvre peinte de Henri Michaux," *Cahiers de l'Herne*, no. 8 (1966).

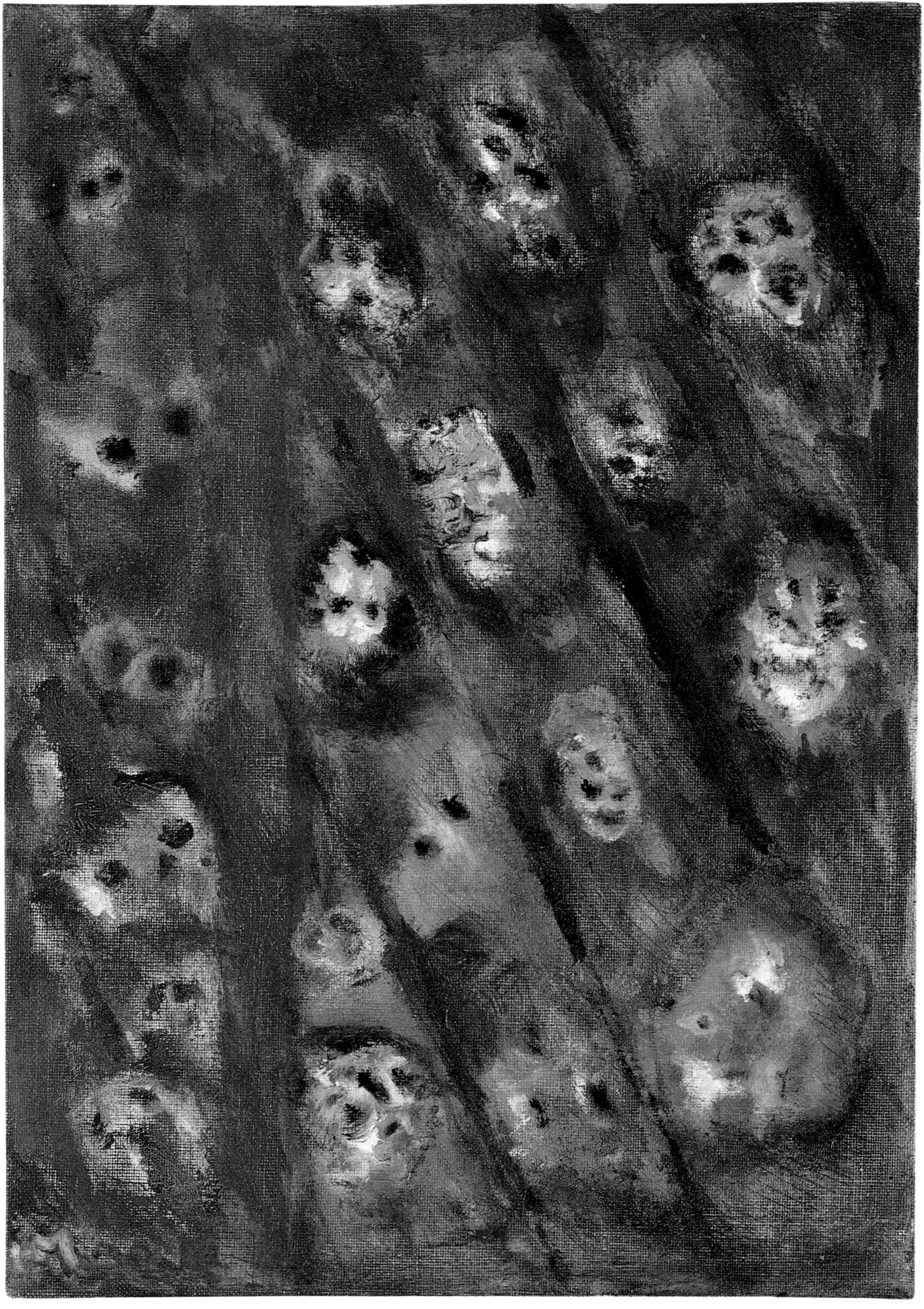

Michaux

Michaux Here and Now

Whereas most institutional collections, or collections that have become institutional, have sought to represent the different phases of Michaux's art, the works held by Renault make no attempt to "manufacture a continuity" tending to prove that past history should be founded in the present. At first glance, the ensemble is indeed surprising for, curiously enough, it gives pride of place to the oil paintings rather than focus on the productions for which Michaux's work usually draws attention and is thought "remarkable." I am referring of course to the inks.

Here then, the choice that is proposed ignores questions of artistic evolution, as if Michaux had ceased to believe in history, as if the notion of time itself were abolished, leaving only the contiguity of events. For this, there appear to be two main explanations. For one thing, the works are totally at one with the spirit of the Renault collection, which, in the eighties, was built up very much in the here and now, in a kind of urgency, rather than gradually as an individual collector might proceed. For another, the works were chosen in the presence of the artist and even if Michaux's reserve and discretion at such moments were legendary, the selection still cannot have been made without the artist influencing it in some way.[1] One can easily imagine that, having returned to painting after such a long absence – some forty years of pictorial practice – he would have wanted to illustrate this reconciliation with a series of small paintings, full as he was of the joy of rediscovering this recalcitrant medium. We know that Michaux had been allergic to varnish and turps ever since the war, that he disliked the stickiness of oils, and that in his attempts to *"extricate himself"*[2] he found he could use naphtha as a binder, without this provoking any adverse reactions from his skin.

The oil paintings, representing ten of the thirty works in the collection, show the artist's eye at its day work, in the rhythm of immediate production. This rare and thus very strange proportion, casts a new light on his work and makes the collection highly original. The presence of these oils does indeed signify a successful reappropriation, an acceptance of painting. Michaux was moving *Towards (a) culmination.*[3] *"With painting, I have made myself a new life,"* he wrote when he made his first paintings in 1939. In 1983, the same words would have been just as appropriate, fully justified by his new choice, which revealed that, perhaps for the first time, Michaux was at one with himself.

1. Henri Michaux and Claude-Louis Renard met at the Galerie du Point Cardinal in the company of Jean Hugues (who was hardly involved).

2. The expression is from Jean-Michel Maulpoix, in *Michaux, Passager clandestin* (Paris: Editions Champ Vallon, 1984).

3. These words appear on the final page of *Saisir* (Montpellier: Editions Fata Morgana, 1979).

Composition, 1983
Oil on Pavatex
35 × 26 cm

Composition, 1981
Watercolor, ink and gouache on paper
63 × 45 cm

Such a form of self-acknowledgement is exceptional here, for it goes against a way of doing of things based on refusal and opposition, an ingrained distrust and hostility towards conventions and proprieties. Contrary to divine reason, Michaux asserted himself in a refusal to paint expressed from the beginning in his early black paintings, which can be read as anti-paintings or paintings that are resolutely against. Now, refusing to pander to our habits, our established idea of the painter and his painting, Michaux was going back to this "infirmity," effecting a reconciliation.

During these last few years of his life, Michaux condensed the vocabulary of his already explored yet constantly renewed alphabet, continually surprising himself with his *Properties* as he reworked, recycled, and even wore them out: for he was always asking the same eternal questions.

Yielding to Painting

The series of small oils is remarkable for the heightening and intensification of Michaux's characteristically teeming occupation of the pictorial space. The vision suggested here is both intimate and distant, like the simultaneous

Composition, 1967–68
Acrylic on paper
72 × 91 cm

representation of a cellular microcosm and an aerial view. In their structure, these oils inevitably recall the period of the first works done on mescaline (1954–57), in which the furrow typical of this drug's effect runs across the canvas and transforms the world. The oblique axis transcribes the terrible impression of an unstable, subsiding medium, the metaphor of a chaotic inner world swarming with acutely febrile entities, again and as ever a *"space within,"* a transitional space that is at once "*oppressive and open.*"[4] Often identifiable, these elements draw on the vocabulary of the representation of roughly treated living bodies, evoking the universe of Bosch or, more generally, classical representations of a supernatural world. Here we see heads, often half-formed, gnome or tadpole-like creatures, ghosts, forgotten apparitions and formless silhouettes ducking and weaving, fugitive runners in a frantic, chaotic, and panic-stricken race. The use of white, which exacerbates the effect of the muted yet violent colors, *"led by orange colors,"* lightens and illuminates the representation, like regularly placed torches in some concentration camp universe. This light from within the painting would heighten its mysteriousness, in the manner of Georges de la Tour's paintings,

4. Jacques Dupin, "Henri Michaux," *Repères*, no. 66, Galerie Lelong, Paris, 1990.

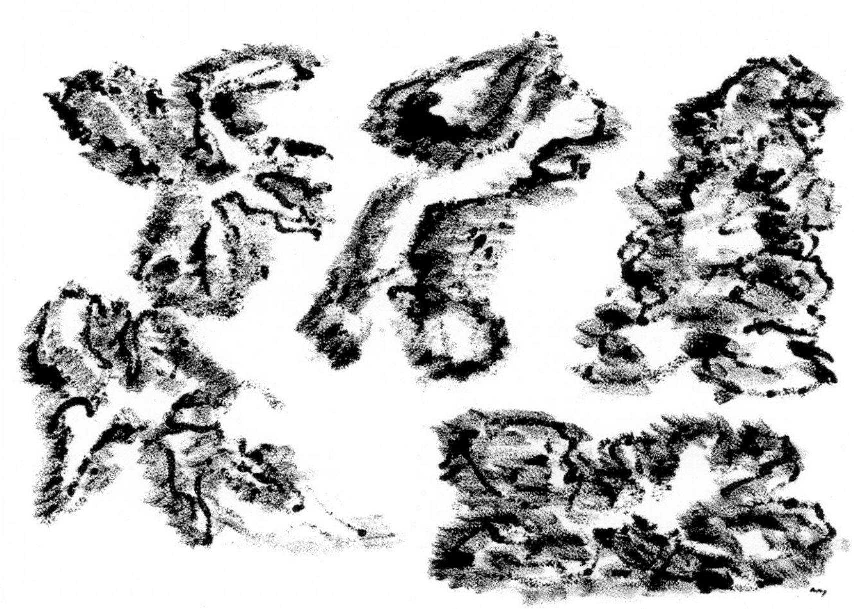

Composition, 1967–68
Acrylic on paper
72 × 92 cm

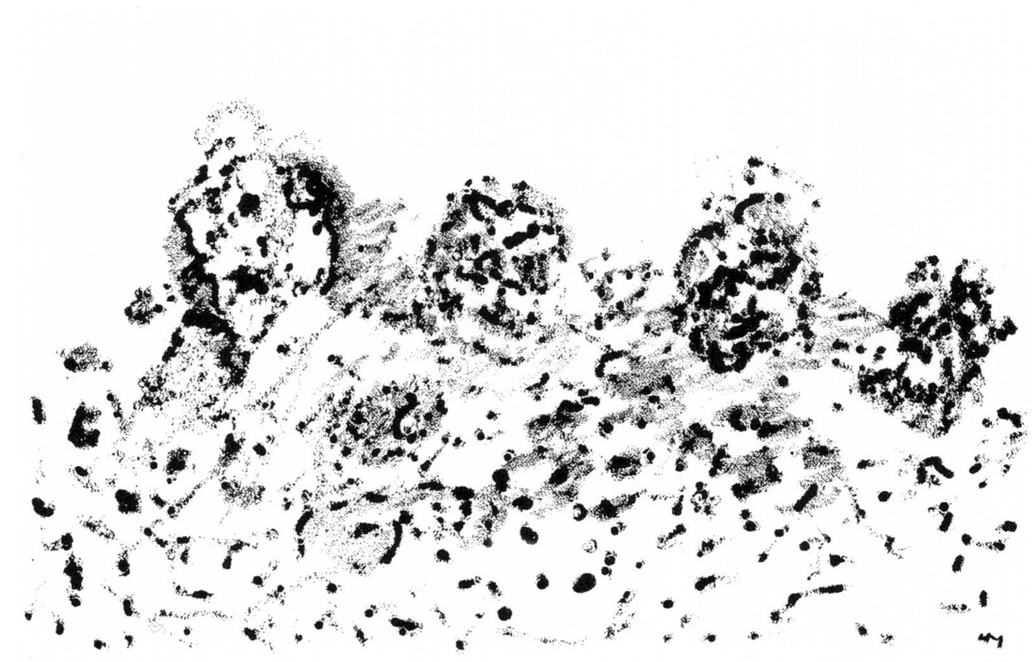

were the image not so blurred. For the fluid oil, used in flat patches and never in slow-to-dry impasto, rules out fixed shots or freeze frames. It contributes physically to the effect of liquidity but cannot be allowed to slow down our impression of a repetitive dynamic, of a discontinuous movement of oblique traces, like selected extracts from a continuum, which convert the paintings into fragments from a larger whole thrown into a hostile environment. Nothing can be allowed to distract Michaux from his quest for constant movement, as if he were seeking to convince himself that *"what [he] most appreciates in painting is cinema."* And so the paintings stick to the intimate size of the sheet of paper. Economy of means is the rule, perhaps the only rule. The easy to handle format and the banality or even the vulgarity of the support – a lawn finish cardboard known as *cartoil* or *Pavatex*, often used by Sunday painters loath to run the risk of wasting a canvas – attest to Michaux's concern not to become weighed down and thus to be able to change his means of expression from one moment to another. The tools and instruments remain modest, capable of responding at once to his desires, to the thrusts from *far-off inside*, to the urges of the unrestrained gesture, and to project, capture, and grasp impressions only to lose them in the very moment of their appearance. In his painting, Michaux puts himself in the situation of one who is ready to get out the moment he has entered, as if to avoid a trap. The point is to go fast. Speed, here again, is the law. The titles of his texts – *Passages, Par la voie des rythmes, Mouvements, Emergences-résurgences* – allude very clearly to his insistence on a tempo immediately suited to the process of painting. His *"confessions"* are only *"of the moment,"* in a brief leap, a flash, a snapshot: *"Before and behind, it is eclipsed at once, it can't wait an instant; that is why my properties are always absolutely bare of everything."* The figures, the apparitions, the enigmatic heads or, elsewhere, the lines, the blots, the signs, are *"drawn from inertia by flux and fragmentation in swells of rage."*

Composition, 1974
Acrylic on paper
76 × 107 cm

Composition, 1968
Acrylic on paper
71 × 90 cm

In these late works, the surface is peopled with all the things that have emerged since Michaux decided to free his hand from words, which are too slow and unsuitable as servants of a rational discourse, in order to plumb the depths that are *"free of the clutter of markers and ancestors,"*[5] as if in an exercise of liberation. As he noted in his autobiographical fragment: *"I paint to de-condition myself."*

5. Nicolas Cendo, "L'épuisante nécessité," (cat.) *Henri Michaux*, Musée Cantini, Marseille; IVAM Valencia; Musée Rath, Geneva, 1993, pp. 42–45.

Composition, 1967
Ink and acrylic on paper
50 × 65 cm

Composition, 1967–68
Ink and acrylic on paper
50 × 65 cm

The Flow of Water

Among the several watercolors and gouaches in the collection, two, dated 1981, refer directly back to Michaux's first attempts in this medium after the war. On the page, a fortuitous recurrent "motif" bordering on realist representation *"springs up with no particular intention,"* echoing an observation made by the artist in "Thinking on the Phenomenon of Art," a chapter in the book *Passages* that he wrote in 1946: *"If you scribble away mechanically, faces are almost bound to appear on the paper."*

The instinctive gesture of random drawing recalls the Surrealist advocacy of the artistic use of automatism. In the 1924 manifesto, André Breton declared: *"Surrealism = Psychic automatism in its pure state . . . Dictated by thought, in the absence of any control exercised by reason."* But Michaux shied away from such injunctions. For him, the war years were not only marked by events that threw a whole generation of artists, the heirs of a collapsing humanist culture, into disarray, but also by a more personal tragedy, the sudden death of his wife after appalling suffering. The postwar years were a time for thinking on human nature after the loss of the guidelines and values of the past. A visionary and seer, Michaux wrote: *"What are all these faces? Are they other? From what depths do they come? Are they not simply the consciousness of my thinking head?"* Clearly, he was not alone in his thoughts; the forties saw the emergence of an art that was *other*, seeking to recover a lost primitive state, a certain idea of man and his origins. As if in echo, Bram van Velde attempted to define the subject of his art in a now famous formula: *"To paint is to seek the face of that which has no face."* The process whereby representation comes into being, which imposes the presence of a figure, seems to allow for the subject to be reconstituted at the same time it is lost or damaged, for the very technique of watercolor drowns the image, engulfs, and denies it: *"Faces that will keep appearing to the very end (it is so hard to stifle, to drown anything out definitively)."*[6] The presence of the blurred, hazy, and unstable figure immediately implies its absence, in a process where *"the discovery of life annuls life."*

A few decades later, Michaux was to "stumble" on this same theme again but, in contrast to the first watercolors of the late forties, here he no longer added an underlining pen stroke, which was the only way of stemming the spread of the image over the paper. *"The 'flash' of the colors swimming past on the sheet of water where I place them, that is what I like in watercolor. The small color-giving heap that collapses into tiny particles, these movements and not the final stopping, the painting . . . Papers that drink, a lot, wildly, perseveringly, deeply, that is what speaks to me more than the colors, which indeed I only throw in like bait, as developers, as masses to pull apart . . . Aquarelle water, as vast as a lake, water, omnivorous demon, snatcher of islands, maker*

6. In *Passages (1937–1950)* (Paris: Le Point du Jour/NRF, 1950), p. 94. English translation by David Ball in *Darkness Moves. An Henri Michaux Anthology: 1927–1984* (Berkeley: University of California Press, 1994), p. 311.

Composition, 1967–68
Ink and acrylic on paper
50 × 65 cm

Composition, 1981
Gouache on paper
68 × 50 cm

of mirages, dyke breaker, overflower of worlds . . . I watch with a joy at first secret then more and more overt the line of my drawing drifting in the water and the infiltration gaining ground everywhere."[7]

Here again the liquidity of the medium enables Michaux to abandon all rigidity, all *"particular intentions,"* all will. The hand gives full rein to its febrility, to its inner tension as it unconstrainedly develops the idea in the movement. The threatening water draws attention to the precariousness of the figure and this throbbing instability fascinates and obsesses the painter. No doubt, these sheets gave him the illusion of touching on the limits of our destiny, as a way of grasping all the more effectively the founding act, of perceiving the passage from non-being to being and of coming as close as possible to the original gesture that first emerged from the magma, from formlessness, from nothingness. The search for identity is endless and

7. *Ibid.*, pp. 115–117.

the figure, a true anamnesis, functions as a reservoir of images. It is often blurred, broken down, it grows diffuse even within its own contours, seeming to rise up from the surface of the paper while the clusters of dots and the eddies often evoke scrutinizing eyes staring at the viewer – the other, or oneself. Creating a new, intense vision of the body, Michaux here expresses his attempt to transform our conception of the world and of humanity's place within it.

Composition, 1981
Watercolor on paper
51 × 42 cm

Composition, 1981
Watercolor on paper
49 × 40 cm

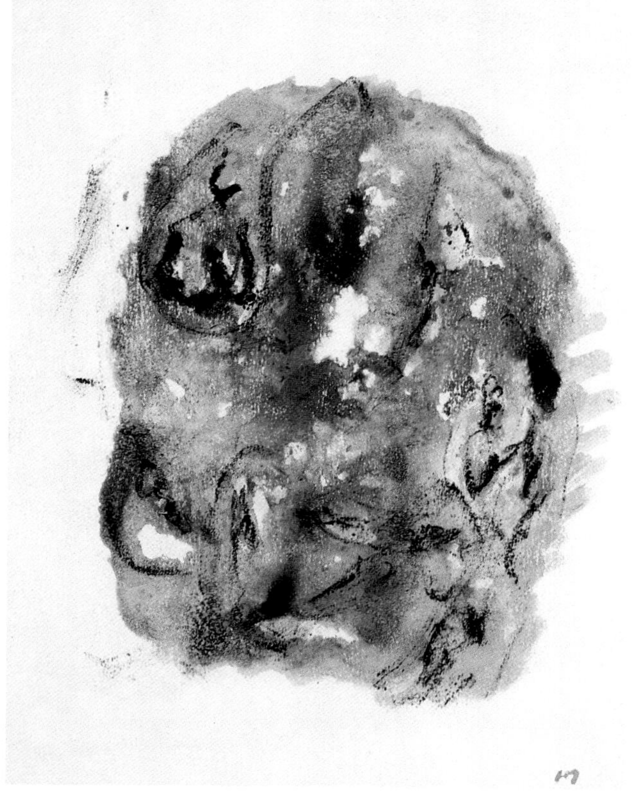

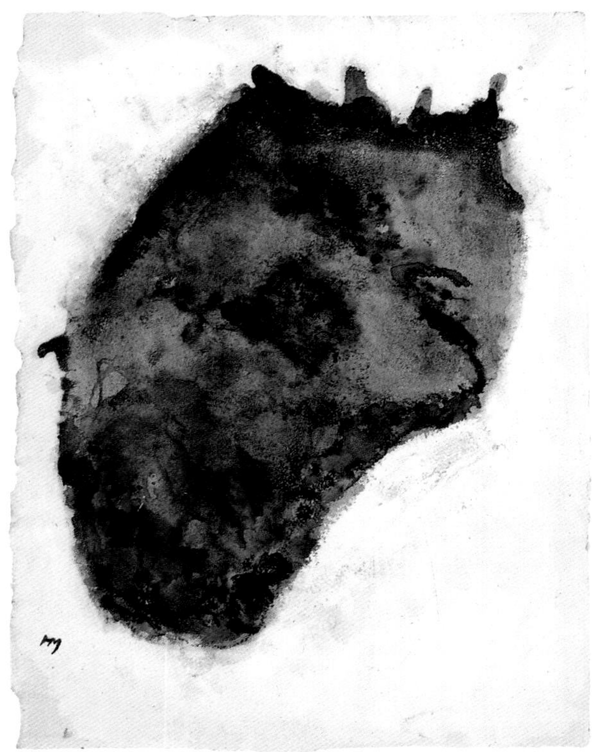

Composition, 1981
Watercolor on paper
50 × 41 cm

Composition, 1981
Watercolor on paper
50 × 40 cm

Ink Again and Forever, Like a Daily Chronicle

A writer, Michaux stuck with ink as his favored medium for painting. This paradoxical continuity is central to his exploratory movement between two practices that are normally very distinct, and to his *"living in this gap."*[8] By this technique he interfered with the process of writing and pushed it towards the *"beyond words"* to which he had been tending ever since he began as a writer. For Michaux, risk was a necessary antidote to the confidence trick that had confirmed and brought him existence and recognition.
The first ink drawings appeared in 1954 and would continue right up to the end, sometimes mixed with gouache or acrylic. Generally speaking, India ink allowed for the immediate transcription of movement, of febrility and, even more, of tumult, chaos, jostling, falls fights, and defeats. Dated 1974, the five ink drawings in the Renault collection exploit the constantly replenished reservoir of forms that Michaux set free in the form of an increasingly varied repertoire of signs. In 1951, at the time of the first *Mouvements*, which were published in book form, the signs were isolated: *". . . I gave life to one or two or three forms, but always one of them faster, one of them a favorite, more diabolically fast than all the others . . . even if this meant that it remained very poor in other respects, I gave it an incredible*

8. Jean Starobinski, "Témoignage, combat et rituel," *La Gazette de Lausanne*, 14 January 1967.

mobility, of which I was the double and the motor . . . I charged it with electricity . . ."[9]

While some of the ink drawings rework the "fabric" of the mescaline drawings, albeit with greater density of style and a more directed architecture, others break away from it, creating links between the signs as if trying to imitate the principles of writing. The line now seems to possess a more generous rhythm, a looser vibration, which makes the mesh slacker. The composition, if we can still speak of composition, suggests a page of writing that has abandoned all syntax and, under the sway of an impulsive chaotic action, lets itself be overcome by the unacceptable, by that which comes from the ignorance that preceded writing – anti-writing, the mark. Michaux plays on this kind of deviated sign, revolts against it: *"Now, to the marks. Well, I loathe them. I love water, but them, no. They disgust me. I just have to keep making them jump, run, climb, clamber. In their current state, they are odious to me and really just marks that mean nothing to me. So I fight with them, I whip them, I want to be rid at once of their flaccid stupidity, to galvanize them, make them distraught, exasperated, to marry them monstrously in spite of themselves to everything that moves, to the unnameable multitude of beings, of non-beings, of rages to be, to all things from here or elsewhere, insatiable desires or nodes of force, that are destined never to be concretized . . . A* Tachiste, *if I am one, who cannot tolerate* taches *[marks].*"[10] In this speech made at the private view at the Galerie Cordier in 1959, Michaux warns the critics of the day against a misguided association, not to put him under the heading of Tachisme or Art Informel, a term coined by Paulhan.[11] His art, he insists, is unique and cannot possibly be confused with the action painting of Pollock, whose liberation of painterly gesture, harking back to the automatisms of the Surrealists, resulted in the drip paintings, that is to say, the creation of a homogenous pictorial space where line modifies structure to rhythms that are ultimately highly repetitive. Signs here are too unruly to fit in a kind of ritual that would structure the page, even if sometimes the movement seems more disciplined. When it is thrown onto the surface, the ink can only be vagabond, its trajectory constantly threatened with splashes. These are never totally abstract but, rather, anthropomorphic, as Francis Bacon points out: *"It is more factual; it suggests more. Because after all, this painting, and most of his paintings, have always been about delayed ways of remaking the human image, through a mark*

9. Henri Michaux in "Postface," *Mouvements* (Paris: Editions Le Point du Jour, NRF, 1951).

10. In (cat.) *Henri Michaux*, Galerie Michel Cordier, Paris, 1959.

11. Jean Paulhan, *L'art informel*, (Paris: Gallimard/NRF, 1962).

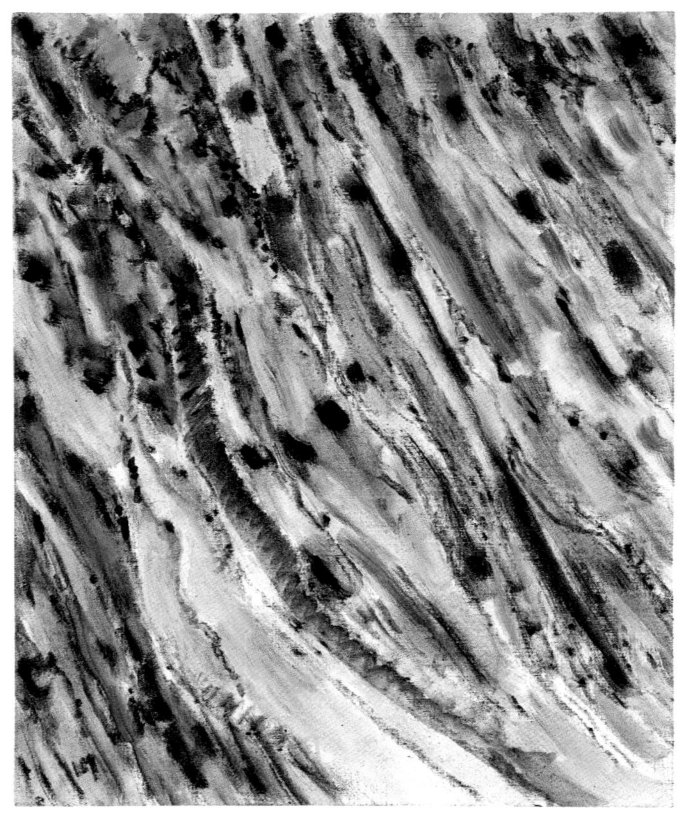

Composition, 1983
Oil on Pavatex
37 × 24 cm

Composition, 1983
Oil on Pavatex
42 × 35 cm

12. David Sylvester, *Interviews with Francis Bacon* (London: Thames and Hudson, 1985), pp. 61–63.

13. In *Paix dans les brisements* (Paris: Editions Karl Flinker, 1959).

that is totally outside an illustrational mark but yet always conveys you back to the human image – a human image generally dragging and trudging through deep ploughed fields or something like that. They are about these images moving and falling and so on." [12] Clustered or scattered over the paper, the signs fill the space with strange stories, traces, or false sketches of battles, of crazed crowds, of sarabands and wild bacchanalias ravaging huge tracts of land: *"The devastation was greater. The speed greater still. In a soundless throbbing, there was accentuation, there was augmentation, there was thrust, there was intensity, there was enormity, there was paroxysm, there was dislocation, there was overstimulation, and as if by the effect of scores of tiny acts of sabotage, there was chaos."* [13] The dialogue between the destruction and construction of the pictorial surface is a precise reflection of the state of mind of the artist

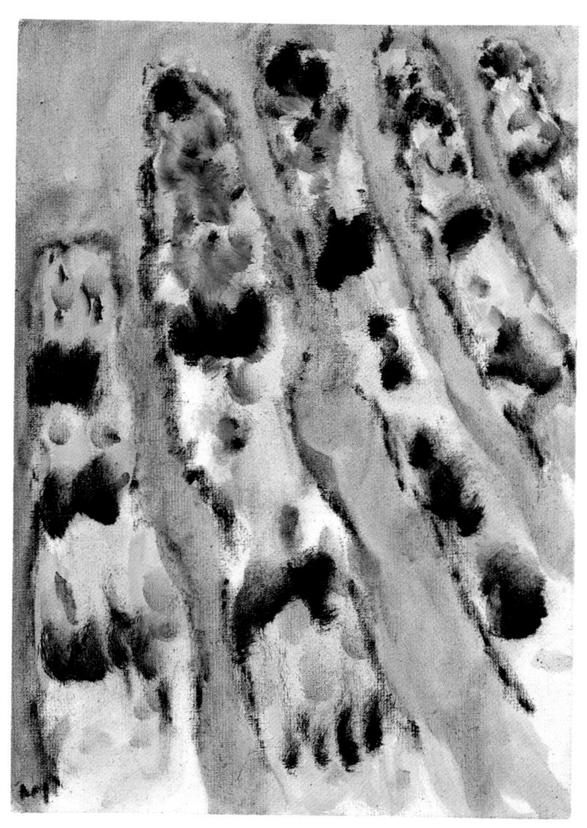

Composition, 1983
Oil on Pavatex
35 × 24 cm

as he unremittingly transposes the strange experience of living beauty irremediably condemned to decrepitude.

With Acrylic, Figures Like New Apparitions

The discovery of a new medium guarantees a new experience, which, a priori, can only mean failure and be a source of tension, and therefore of immediacy of expression. *Arrachements* (Wrestings or Wrenchings) is the title of the first acrylics. These have a real material presence because of their thickness on the paper, however relative, in comparison to the ink drawings. The style is hasty, scratchy, almost graffiti-like. These *"instantaneous and fleeting deposits,"* as Michaux named them,[14] are inscribed on the surface or, rather, emerge in a larval form whose uncertainty is underlined by a more

14. *Ibid.*, reprinted in A. Pacquement and R. Bellour, *Michaux Peinture* (Paris: Gallimard, 1993), p. 182.

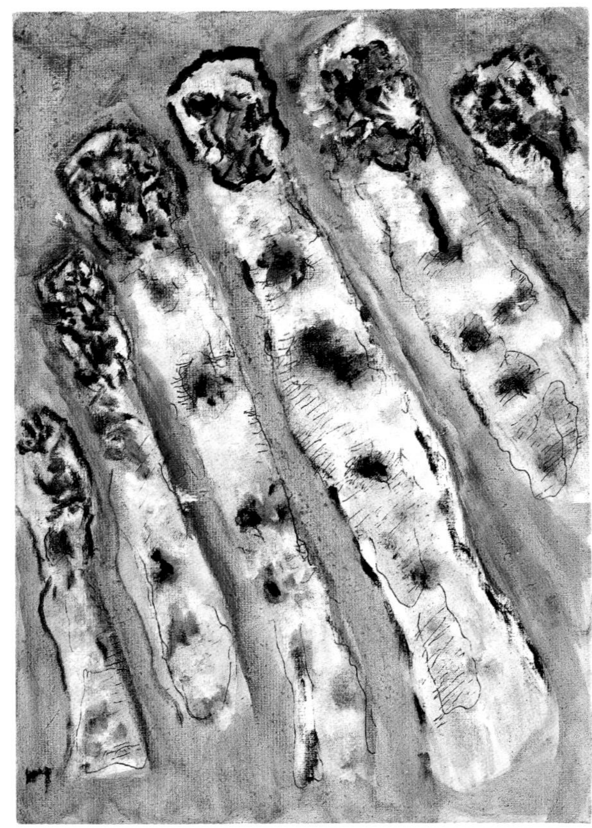

Composition, 1983
Oil on Pavatex
35 × 26 cm

Composition, 1983
Oil on Pavatex
35 × 26 cm

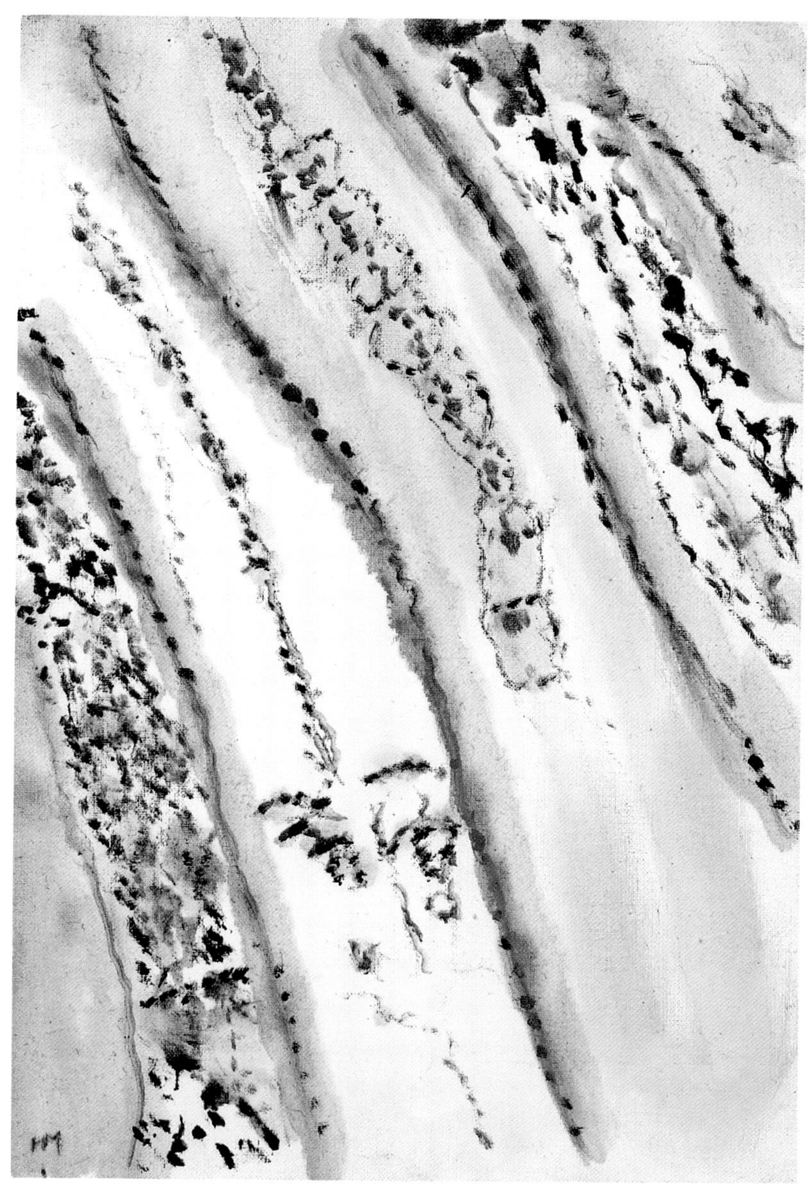

Composition, 1983
Oil on Pavatex
42 × 29 cm

Composition, 1983
Oil on Pavatex
42 × 35 cm

or less emphatic marking of the contours. The almost systematic refusal of color highlights the similarity of finish to the inks but allows him to play on the different values of black. The effect of relief thus obtained intensifies the dynamism of the signs and, above all, causes them to float in *"a universe that no longer wants to take shape,"* as transfigured signs in whose hollow sockets we glimpse an empty gaze. Masks, skeletons, or skulls loom out of the formlessness and skitter into nothingness. Michaux's art oscillates between figuration and disfigurement as the expression of an impossible reality, *"between Appearance and Nothingness, between the deceptive form of being and its absence: a vibration between two unrealities."* [15]

An Art of Disfigurement

Today, almost fifteen years after his death, Michaux is no longer here to insist on his marginality. Perhaps he is losing something of his mystery? It is true that his work is part of a singular expressive movement that made its mark on our century, alongside that of Fautrier, Giacometti, and Artaud, among others. Whether we call it *art autre* (other art) in accordance with Michel Tapié's expression, or borrow the term used by Bernard Ceysson for the exhibition at Saint-Etienne in 1990, *écriture griffée* (scratched or clawed writing), Michaux's art belongs to a moment of history when representation had lost its credibility. The loss of bearings and past references had inaugurated an *"age of suspicion"* for which balanced, rational order, and earlier stylistic forms had become dubious. But this era of suspicion was still without that *"faculty of indifference"* that Cioran advocated, so that man would not be impelled by *"the fascination of the impossible"* and follow the ways of perdition.

While the image had been made impossible by an intolerable reality – the ideology of extermination and crimes against humanity, now revealed for the first time – this did not mean it had been evacuated as it had in the first decades of the century by the nascent abstract art movement. Rather, its representation was vitiated and impaired: *"The first reality experienced by the painter is not metaphysical but physical: it is his material . . . the fluidity of resistance of his vehicle, the vehicle of his thought, of his expressive energy, at the same time as colored pigment. Many things, if not indeed all the things we imagine to be preconceived, are born of these nuptials with matter: the concepts and conceptions of art are consubstantial with practice . . . One cannot overstate*

15. Emil Cioran, *Précis de décomposition* (Paris: Gallimard, 1949).

the importance of the action of the material, of the tool, and also of the media used in the variation of aesthetic doctrines." [16]

At the time, painting, as well as sculpture, was developing within a logic of the disintegration of the figure, or of disfigurement, and was showing the first signs of a prehistory of formlessness. *"My intention was that this drawing should not give the figure any definite form, that, on the contrary it should not prevent this figure from taking on this or that particular form, that it should maintain it in a position as a general concept, as immateriality."* [17] The image is condemned in favor of its materiality. The works mark the final ascendancy of matter over form, the sign of the victory of creation over the culture against which the artist fought and opposed his preference for *"unworthy"* materials. The choice of this *"primitive"* approach, in the image of the Lascaux man *"who created the world of art where the communication of spirits begins,"* is the only possible way to reappropriate means of expression.

Here, what Georges Duthuit called *"a damaged art"* (*art abîmé*) meets *"the art of the abyss"* (*de l'abîme*), as Samuel Beckett described it when speaking of Bram van Velde. *"For what is left of the representable if the essence of the object is to refuse representation? . . . An endless unveiling, veil after veil, plane on plane, of imperfect transparencies, an unveiling before what cannot be unveiled, nothingness, the thing once again. And burial in the unique, in a place of impenetrable proximities, a cell painted on the stone of the cell, an art of incarceration."* [18] In a painting of excess, in Bataille's terms, or a painting of paucity, in Cioran's, matter and its resistance govern form, thus expressing the return to zero level. It is an immersion in the psyche to explain a spiritual malaise, human behavior on the brink of chaos. For many, these marginal forms of expression, born of the experience of penury in the dark years of war, represented an attempt to restore an authentic rapport with art, regardless of style.

16. Jean Dubuffet, *Prospectus et tous écrits suivants* (Paris: Gallimard/NRF, 1967).

17. *Ibid.*

18. Samuel Beckett, "La peinture des van Velde ou le monde et le pantalon," *Les Cahiers d'art*, Paris, 1945–46, and "Peintres de l'empêchement," in *Derrière le miroir*, no. 11/12, Paris, June 1948.

Catalogue of the collection

PIERRE ALECHINSKY

Escalator, 1983
Acrylic on paper mounted on canvas
150 × 120 cm *(p. 47)*

Roue d'herbe, 1983
Acrylic on paper mounted on canvas
155 × 170 cm *(p. 46)*

ARMAN

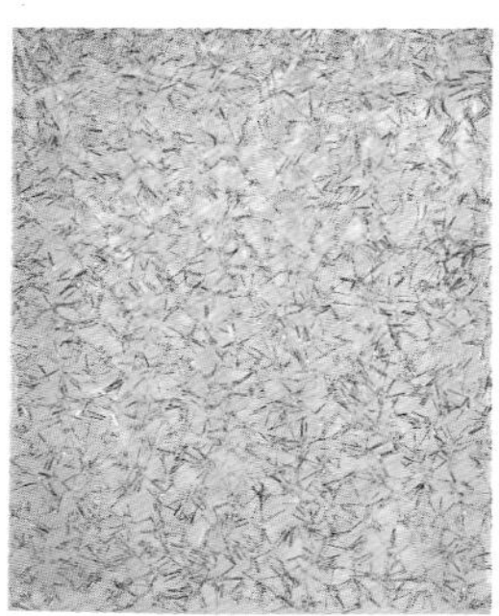

Accumulation of mechanical elements, 1974
Wedges in plexiglass
200 × 160 × 6 cm

Composition, 1974
Oil with imprints from objects on canvas
149 × 200 cm

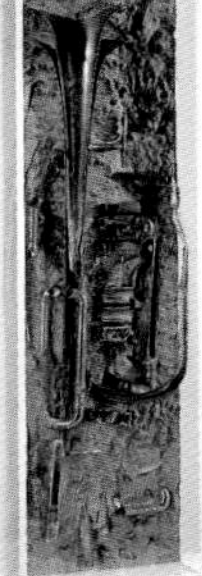

Pieces of trombone in concrete, 1973–1974
85 × 29 × 11 cm

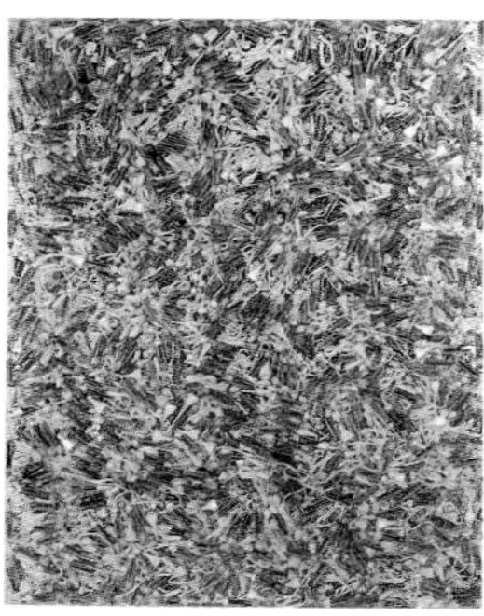

Accumulation of mechanical elements, 1974
Engines and white wires in plexiglass
200 × 160 × 12 cm

Accumulation, 1974
Scrapers in plexiglass
200 × 160 × 12 cm

Accumulation of mechanical elements, 1969
Joints in plexiglass
230 × 160 cm

Accumulation Renault n° 162, 1968
Cutaway engine in plexiglass
34 × 40 × 57 cm

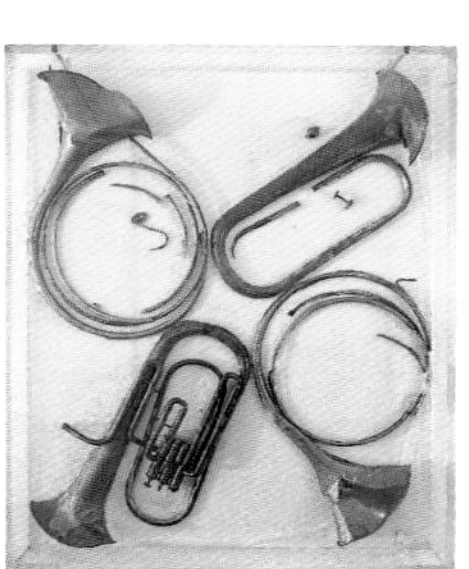

Accumulation of mechanical elements, 1973
Sawn copper elements in plexiglass
100 × 120 cm

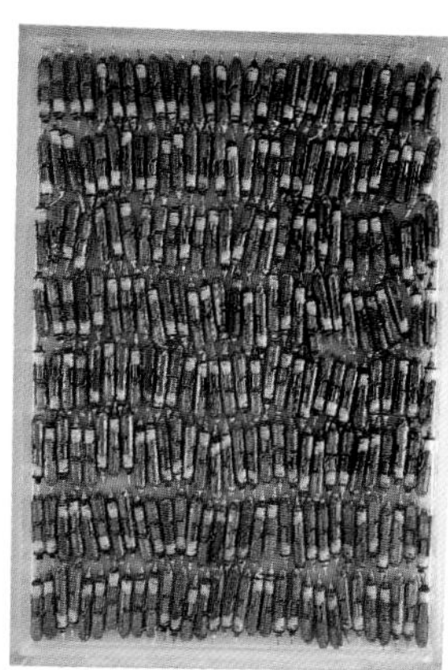
Accumulation of mechanical elements, 1973
Spark plugs in plexiglass
79 × 120 cm

Accumulation Renault, 1974
Renault engine parts (cylinder heads) screwed on painted wooden panel
247 × 628 cm
Renault corporate headquarters, Quai du Point-du-Jour, 8th floor *(p. 58)*

Accumulation Renault, 1974
Renault engine parts (water pumps) screwed on painted wooden panel
247 × 618 cm *(p. 66)*

Composition, 1974
Oil with imprints from objects on canvas
70 × 80 cm

Composition, 1974
Oil with imprints from objects on canvas
70 × 80 cm *(p. 62)*

Composition, 1974
Oil with imprints from objects on canvas
70 × 82 cm

Composition, 1974
Oil with imprints from objects on canvas
74 × 80 cm

Composition, 1974
Oil with imprints from objects on canvas
74 × 80 cm

Composition, 1974
Oil with imprints from objects on canvas
70 × 62 cm

Composition, 1974
Oil with imprints from objects on canvas
149 × 200 cm *(p. 63)*

Accumulation of mechanical elements, 1974
Springs in plexiglass
200 × 200 × 16 cm *(p. 60)*

Accumulation of mechanical elements, 1974
Headlights in plexiglass
200 × 200 × 16 cm *(p. 56)*

Accumulation of mechanical elements, 1974
Fan blades in plexiglass
200 × 200 × 7 cm *(p. 61)*

Accumulation of mechanical elements, 1974
Joints in plexiglass
200 × 200 × 16 cm *(p. 57)*

Accumulation of mechanical elements, 1974
Break parts in plexiglass
200 × 200 × 12 cm *(p. 55)*

Bows, 1970
Oil and silk-screen on canvas
208 × 154 cm

Violin Neeks, 1970
Oil and silk-screen on canvas
160 × 210 cm

POL BURY

Untitled, 1971
Stainless steel, magnets and motor, no. 2/8
40 × 20 × 20 cm

ALEXANDRE CALDER

Untitled, 1970
Gouache on paper
77 × 112 cm

JEAN DEGOTTEX

Les Obliques, 1980
Brick wall
200 × 966 cm
Rueil-Malmaison technical center,
functions room *(p. 26)*

JEAN DEWASNE

Composition murale, 1974
Oil-based paint on metal
8 panels: 248 × 960 cm
Ground floor *(p. 25)*

Composition murale, 1974
Oil-based paint on metal
8 panels: 248 × 960 cm
First floor *(p. 25)*

Composition murale, 1974
Oil-based paint on metal
8 panels: 248 × 960 cm
Second floor *(p. 25)*

Composition murale, 1974
Oil-based paint on metal
8 panels: 248 × 960 cm
Third floor *(p. 25)*

Composition murale, 1974
Oil-based paint on metal
12 panels: 300 × 88 cm

JEAN DUBUFFET

Le moment critique, 1974
Vinyl on canvas
276 × 185 cm

Scène tragique (site avec deux personnages), 1974
Vinyl on canvas
273 × 186 cm

Motif à croix bleue, 1971
Vinyl paint on cut-out plywood
150 × 195 cm

Le buisson, 1972
Vinyl paint on cut-out plywood
197 × 197 cm

Le roman burlesque, 1974
18 works in 22 elements

1. ***Grande parade***
   Vinyl paint on cut-out plywood
   221 × 385 cm *(p. 98)*
2. ***Nuages***
   Vinyl paint on cut-out plywood
   152 × 364 cm *(p. 99)*
3. ***Motif à l'homme couché***
   Vinyl paint on cut-out plywood
   135 × 190 cm *(p. 97)*
4. ***Motif horizontal***
   Vinyl paint on cut-out plywood
   99 × 188 cm *(p. 97)*
5. ***Logologie***
   Vinyl paint on cut-out plywood
   216 × 303 cm *(p. 96)*
6. ***Cortège funèbre***
   Vinyl paint on cut-out plywood
   230 × 368 cm *(p. 94)*
7. ***Nuage***
   Vinyl paint on cut-out plywood
   101 × 230 cm *(p. 94)*
8. ***Décor funèbre***
   Vinyl paint on cut-out plywood
   245 × 446 cm *(p. 95)*
9. ***Trois personnages***
   Vinyl paint on cut-out plywood
   232 × 362 cm
   From left to right: 225 × 102 – 228 × 94 – 232 × 136 cm *(p. 93)*
10. ***Développement horizontal***
   Vinyl paint on cut-out plywood
   99 × 242 cm *(p. 93)*
11. ***Tumulte à deux personnages***
   Vinyl paint on cut-out plywood
   225 × 329 cm *(p. 92)*
12. ***Développement horizontal***
   Vinyl paint on cut-out plywood
   112 × 270 cm *(p. 89)*
13. ***Tour***
   Vinyl paint on cut-out plywood
   233 × 94 cm *(p. 87)*
14. ***Site avec deux personnages dont l'un est couché***
   Vinyl paint on cut-out plywood
   217 × 329 cm *(p. 88)*
15. ***Tour***
   Vinyl paint on cut-out plywood
   239 × 109 cm *(p. 89)*
16. ***Cheval-jupon***
   Vinyl paint on cut-out plywood
   171 × 219 cm *(p. 87)*
17. ***Automobile***
   Vinyl paint on cut-out plywood
   160 × 259 cm *(p. 86)*
18. ***Paysage avec trois personnages dont l'un est assis***
   Vinyl paint on cut-out plywood
   215 × 388 cm *(p. 86)*

Chateau de vent souffle, 1971
Epoxy painted with polyurethane
94 × 110 × 50 cm *(p. 81)*

Site à l'homme assis, 1969
Polyester painted with polyurethane
60 × 64 × 38 cm *(p. 103)*

Le mur bleu, 1967
Polyester painted with polyurethane
350 × 710 × 110 cm *(p. 82)*

Salon d'été, maquette no. 1/10, 1974
Epoxy painted with polyurethane
(black and blue)
565 × 474 cm *(p. 29)*

Territoire aux deux explorants,
1974
Vinyl on canvas
204 × 130 cm *(p. 104)*

Le citadin, 1974
Vinyl on canvas
208 × 130 cm *(p. 70)*

Paysage épisodique, 1974
Vinyl on canvas
203 × 130 cm *(p. 85)*

Paysage avec villa et personnage,
1974
Vinyl on canvas
195 × 130 cm *(p. 105)*

Compagnonnage en site urbain,
1974
Vinyl on canvas
195 × 130 cm *(p. 84)*

Fiston la Filoche, 1966–1967
Transfer on polyester
154 × 61 × 37 cm *(p. 80)*

Scène à l'invalide, 1974
Vinylic paint on polystyrene
50 × 85 × 14 cm *(p. 102)*

Le vaisseau, 1971–1972
Acrylic on klégecell
292 × 385 cm *(p. 74)*

Le convoi, 1971–1972
Acrylic on klégecell
295 × 384 cm *(p. 75)*

Lice tapisse, 1971–1972
Acrylic on klégecell
293 × 390 cm *(p. 76)*

Château de vent souffle, 1971–1972
Acrylic on klégecell
298 × 332 cm *(p. 77)*

Parade nuptiale, 1971–1972
Acrylic on canvas mounted
on klégecell
164 × 487 cm *(p. 101)*

ERRÓ

Untitled, 1985
Serie of 60 collages

Untitled, 1985
Collage on paper
34 × 27 cm

Untitled, 1985
Collage on paper
42 × 30 cm

Untitled, 1985
Collage on paper
34 × 26 cm

Untitled, 1985
Collage on paper
50 × 43 cm

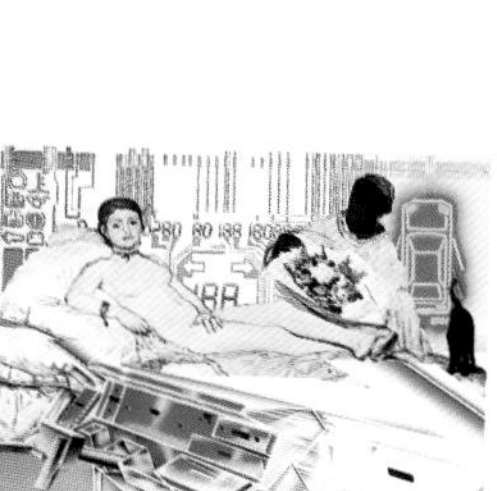

Untitled, 1985
Collage on paper
50 × 43 cm

Untitled, 1985
Collage on paper
38 × 50 cm

Untitled, 1985
Collage on paper
34 × 20 cm

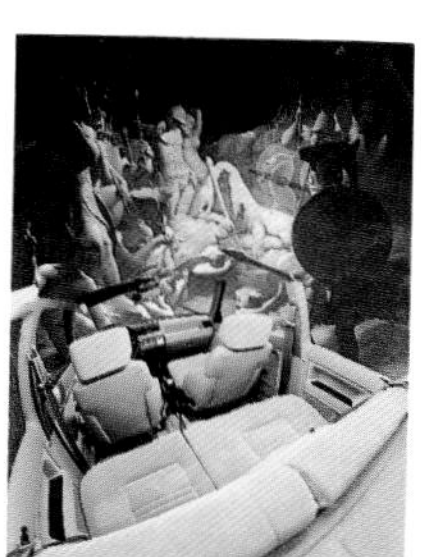

Untitled, 1985
Collage on paper
34 × 30 cm

Renault Scape, 1984
Oil on canvas
200 × 300 cm *(p. 40)*

Motor Scape (Renault 5), 1984
Oil on canvas
200 × 300 cm *(p. 41)*

JEAN FAUTRIER

Tête, 1940
Bronze, no. 7/9
17 × 16 × 17 cm

Tête, 1940
Bronze, no. 9/9
16 × 12 × 10 cm

F.P. 120 "Brisures," 1960
Oil on canvas
88 × 130 cm

SAM FRANCIS

Untitled, 1978
Acrylic on canvas
135 × 365 cm *(p. 51)*

DOMINIQUE GAUTHIER

Opéra-épopée: enlèvement des Sabines, 1982
Oil and acrylic on canvas
91 × 212 cm

Opéra-épopée: enlèvement des Sabines, 1982
Oil and acrylic on canvas
215 × 255 cm

Opéra-épopée: Laacon, 1982
Oil and acrylic on canvas
199 × 129 cm

Untitled, 1982
Oil and acrylic on canvas
200 × 200 cm

Médée n° 1, 1982
Oil and acrylic on canvas, felt pen and pencil on paper glued on canvas, metal rods and plastic parts fixed to a stretcher
227 × 160 cm

Médée n° 13, 1982
Oil and acrylic on canvas, felt pen and pencil on paper glued on canvas, metal rods and plastic parts fixed to a stretcher
230 × 275 cm *(p. 52)*

Médée n° 3, 1982
Oil and acrylic on canvas
300 × 285 cm

Médée n° 13, 1982
Oil and acrylic on canvas
300 × 285 cm

Médée n° 1 Triangle noir, 1982
Oil and acrylic on canvas
300 × 285 cm

Peinture en forme de nô n° III, 1981
Oil and acrylic on canvas
350 × 390 cm

Pour la couleur rose V, 1981
Oil and acrylic on canvas
320 × 500 cm

Pour la couleur rose II, 1981
Oil and acrylic on canvas
380 × 420 cm

Pour la couleur rose III, 1981
Oil and acrylic on canvas
300 × 365 cm

Opéra-épopée: Laacon (sic), 1982
Oil and acrylic on canvas
400 × 320 cm

Opéra-épopée 2 : enlèvement des Sabines, 1982
Oil and acrylic on canvas
300 × 300 cm

ALBERT GLEIZES

Personnage féminin, 1919
Oil on canvas
89 × 68 cm

Tableau familier, 1923
Oil on canvas
61 × 92 cm

SIMON HANTAÏ

Silk-screen on Formica, 1977
Rueil-Malmaison technical center
Staff restaurant *(p. 166)*

Silk-screen on Formica, 1977
Rueil-Malmaison technical center
Staff restaurant
West wall *(p. 169)*

Silk-screen on Formica, 1977
Rueil-Malmaison technical center
Cafeteria *(p. 170)*

Silk-screen on Formica, 1977
Rueil-Malmaison technical center
Cafeteria *(p. 171)*

Silk-screen on Formica, 1977
Rueil-Malmaison technical center
Staff restaurant
East wall *(p. 172)*

Silk-screen on Formica, 1977
Rueil-Malmaison technical center
Staff restaurant
East wall *(p. 173)*

HANS HARTUNG

Composition, 1950
Oil on canvas
38 × 100 cm

ANDRÉ LANSKOY

Composition,
Oil on canvas
195 × 96,5 cm

JULIO LE PARC

Ondes 144, 1974
Oil on canvas
130 × 196 cm

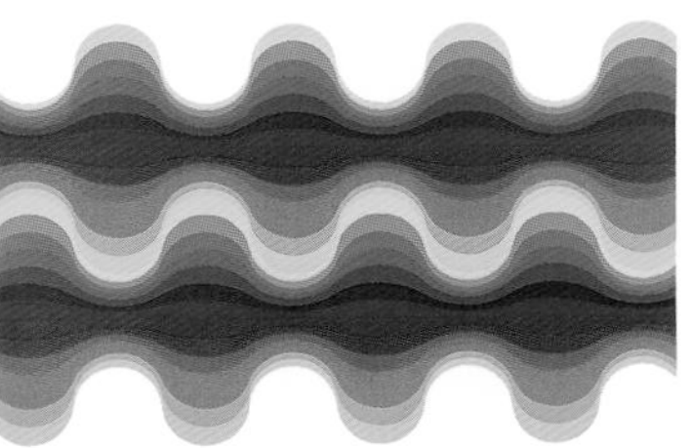

Ondes 136, 1972
Oil on canvas
130 × 193 cm

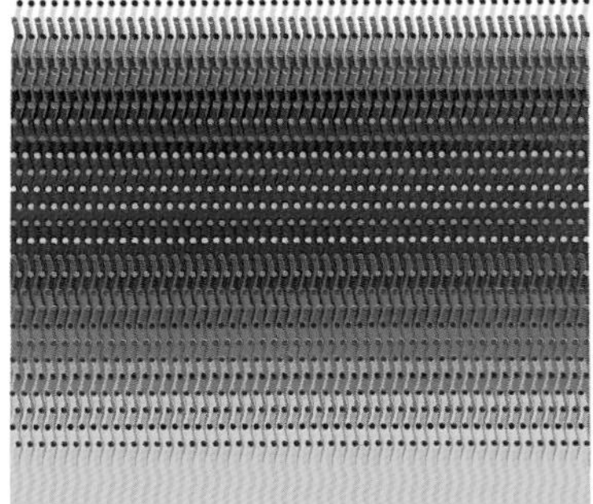

Volume virtuel, 1974
Oil on canvas
200 × 200 cm

ROBERTO MATTA

60-Quand?, 1970
Oil on canvas
154 × 139 cm *(p. 44)*

Wieser tennis, tennis anyone, 1974
Graphite and wax crayons on paper
50 × 71 cm *(p. 45)*

Pen totototo, 1967
Graphite and wax crayons on paper
50 × 65 cm *(p. 45)*

Faire resonne un obstacle, 1978
Graphite and wax crayons on paper
50 × 66 cm *(p. 45)*

Les feux du psycho-obstacle, 1972
Graphite and wax crayons on paper
50 × 65 cm *(p. 45)*

HENRI MICHAUX

Composition, 1980
Ink on paper
70 × 89 cm

Composition, 1968
Acrylic and ink on paper
70 × 88 cm

Composition, 1968
Acrylic and ink on paper
57 × 77 cm

Composition, 1980
Ink on paper
73 × 90 cm

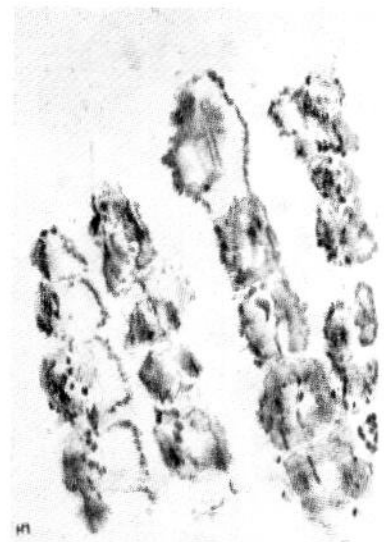

Composition, **1983**
Oil on Pavatex
42 × 29 cm

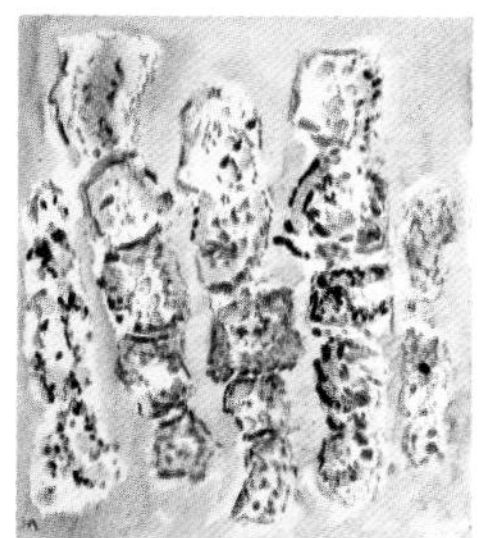

Composition, **1983**
Oil on Pavatex
43 × 35 cm

Composition, 1967
Acrylic on paper
72 × 91 cm

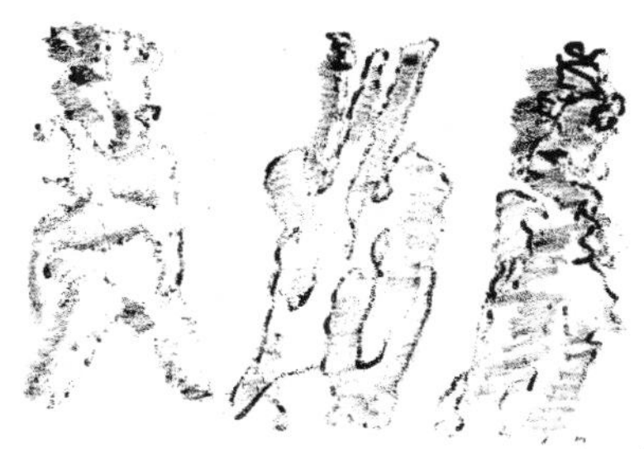

Composition, 1967
Acrylic on paper
71 × 90 cm

Composition, 1967
Acrylic on paper
73 × 92 cm

Composition, 1981
Watercolor on paper
51 × 42 cm *(p. 183)*

Composition, 1981
Watercolor on paper
49 × 40 cm *(p. 183)*

Composition, 1981
Watercolor, ink and gouache on paper
63 × 45 cm *(p. 176)*

Composition, 1981
Gouache on paper
68 × 50 cm *(p. 182)*

Composition, 1967–1968
Acrylic and ink on paper
50 × 65 cm *(p. 180)*

Composition, 1967–1968
Acrylic and ink on paper
50 × 65 cm *(p. 181)*

Composition, 1981
Watercolor on paper
50 × 40 cm *(p. 184)*

Composition, 1981
Watercolor on paper
50 × 41 cm *(p. 184)*

Composition, 1967–1968
Acrylic on paper
72 × 91 cm *(p. 176)*

Composition, 1967–1968
Acrylic on paper
72 × 92 cm *(p. 177)*

Composition, 1968
Acrylic on paper
71 × 90 cm *(p. 178)*

Composition, 1967
Acrylic and ink on paper
50 × 65 cm *(p. 180)*

Composition, 1974
Acrylic on paper
76 × 107 cm *(p. 178)*

Composition, 1983
Oil on Pavatex
35 × 26 cm *(p. 174)*

Composition, 1983
Oil on Pavatex
35 × 26 cm *(p. 188)*

Composition, 1983
Oil on Pavatex
37 × 26 cm *(p. 188)*

Composition, 1983
Oil on Pavatex
35 × 24 cm *(p. 187)*

Composition, 1983
Oil on Pavatex
37 × 24 cm *(p. 186)*

Composition, 1983
Oil on Pavatex
42 × 29 cm *(p. 189)*

Composition, 1983
Oil on Pavatex
42 × 35 cm *(p. 186)*

Composition, 1983
Oil on Pavatex
42 × 35 cm *(p. 190)*

JUAN MIRÓ

Untitled, undated
Ink and crayon on paper
123 × 94 cm

Untitled, undated
Bronze, no. 2/8
31 × 38 × 25 cm

LISA PANG

Untitled, 1982
Oil on canvas
153 × 203 cm

Untitled, 1982
Oil on canvas
153 × 203 cm

Untitled, 1982
Oil on canvas
153 × 203 cm

Untitled, 1982
Oil on canvas
153 × 203 cm

Untitled, 1982
Oil on canvas
153 × 203 cm

ROBERT RAUSCHENBERG

Untitled, 1984
Silk-screen and acrylic on canvas
258 × 206 cm *(p. 43)*

NIKI DE SAINT-PHALLE

The White Goddess, 1963
Objects, wool, and paint on panel
178 × 110 *(p. 38)*

JESÚS RAFAEL SOTO

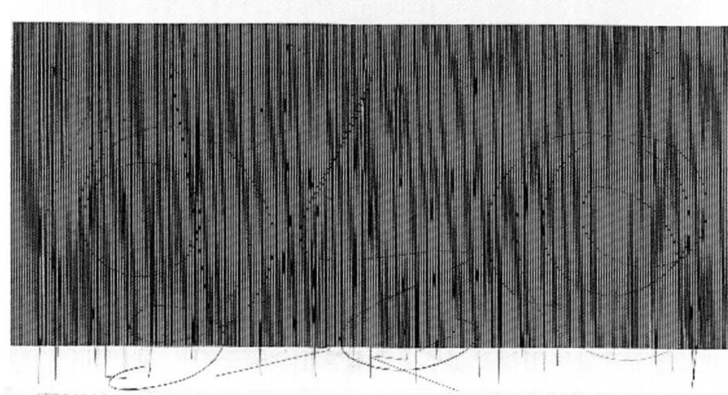

Ecritura Espiral, 1974
Wood and metal
102 × 170 cm

Aquarella, 1972
Wood and metal
121 × 204 cm

Vibration, 1974
Wood and metal
Renault corporate headquarters,
Quai du Point-du-Jour, staff restaurant
(p. 133)

Grande Écriture, 1974
Renault corporate headquarters,
Quai du Point-du-Jour, lobby *(p. 128)*

Carrés vibrants, 1974
Renault corporate headquarters,
Quai du Point-du-Jour, lobby,
central aisle *(p. 130)*

Progression, 1974
Wood and metal
Renault corporate headquarters,
Quai du Point-du-Jour, staff restaurant
(p. 137)

Vibration, 1974
Wood and metal
Renault corporate headquarters,
Quai du Point-du-Jour, staff restaurant
(p. 136)

Progression, 1974
Wood and metal
Renault corporate headquarters,
Quai du Point-du-Jour, staff restaurant
(p. 126)

Gran Amarillo, 1974
Wood and metal
202 × 142 × 42 cm *(p. 138)*

Gran Blanco, 1974
Wood and metal
202 × 142 × 42 cm *(p. 139)*

TAKIS

Untitled, 1974
Screws, coils, graphite, and magnets
fixed on painted wooden panel
171 × 318 × 2 cm
Renault corporate headquarters,
Quai du Point-du-Jour, corridor
between the cafeteria and elevators
(p. 163)

Untitled, 1974
Screws, coils, graphite, and magnets
fixed on painted wooden panel
171 × 318 × 2 cm
Renault corporate headquarters,
Quai du Point-du-Jour, corridor
between the cafeteria and elevators
(p. 158)

ANTONI TÀPIES

Untitled, 1950
Ink with gouache highlights and black
tape on paper
68 × 197 cm *(p. 48)*

DOMINIQUE THIOLAT

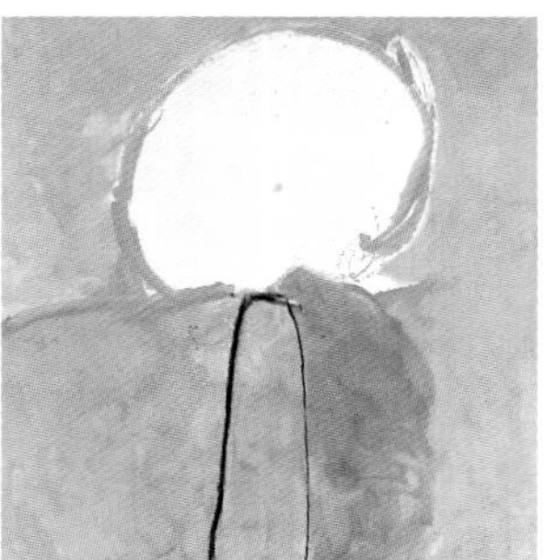

Untitled, 1978–1979
Acrylic on canvas
206 × 193 cm

Untitled, 1978–1979
Acrylic on canvas
206 × 193 cm

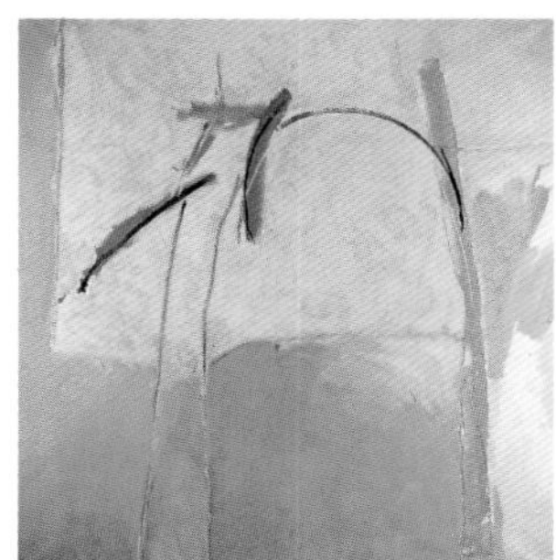

Untitled, 1978–1979
Acrylic on canvas
206 × 174 cm

Untitled, 1978–1979
Acrylic on canvas
206 × 193 cm

Untitled, 1978–1979
Acrylic on canvas
195 × 165 cm

JEAN TINGUELY

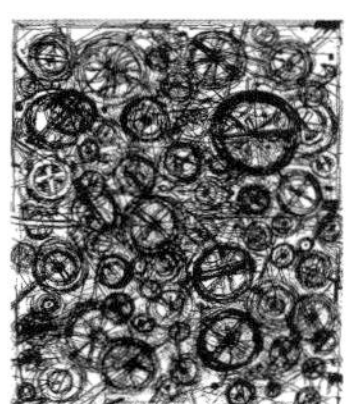

Untitled, undated
Pencil and pastel on paper
78 × 52 cm *(p. 151)*

Meta Pandemonium, 1981
Ink with gouache highlights and
papers glued on cardboard
50 × 90 cm

Cenodoxus, 1981
Gouache on cardboard
50 × 75 cm

Untitled, undated
Ink on paper
70 × 84 cm *(p. 151)*

Untitled, undated
Ink on paper
68 × 53 cm

Requiem for a Dead Leaf, 1967
Painted steel and various elements
305 × 1105 × 80 cm *(p. 146)*

Bascule V, 1967
Painted steel and various elements
90 × 200 × 50 cm *(p. 150)*

Eos VIII, 1966
Painted steel and various elements
180 × 220 × 120 cm *(p. 150)*

Eos XII, 1967
Painted steel and various elements
178 × 188 × 76 cm *(p. 149)*

LUIS TOMASELLO

Study for mural decoration,
conference room, 1974
Felt pen on tracing paper
47 × 75 cm

Pierre-Dreyfus Auditorium, 1974
Renault corporate headquarters,
Quai du Point-du-Jour *(p. 20)*

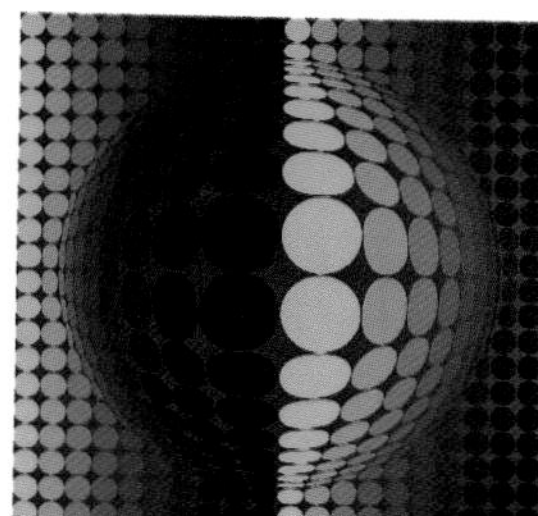

Re-Na, 1968–1974
Oil on canvas
180 × 180 cm

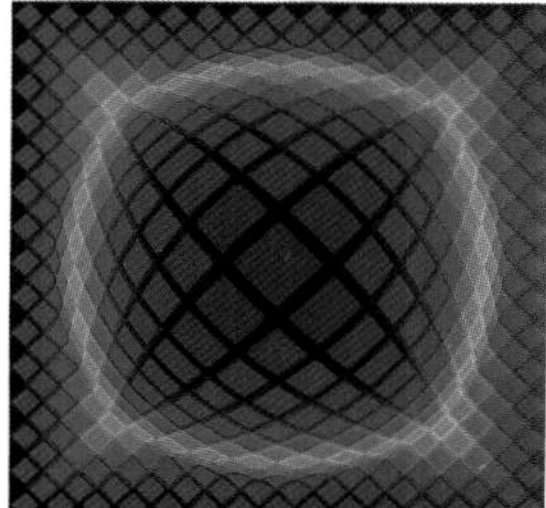

Vega Blue, 1970
Oil on canvas
160 × 160 cm

Betelgeuse négatif, 1974
Silk-screen on aluminum
200 × 200 cm *(p. 122)*

Riu-Kiu positif-négatif, 1974
Silk-screen on aluminum
150 × 200 cm

Riu-Kiu négatif, 1974
Silk-screen on aluminum
150 × 200 cm

Tlinko négatif, 1974
Silk-screen on aluminum
200 × 200 cm

Tau-ceti négatif, 1974
Silk-screen on aluminum
200 × 200 cm *(p. 122)*

Kei Ho positif-négatif, 1974
Silk-screen on aluminum
150 × 200 cm

Andromède négatif, 1974
Silk-screen on aluminum
200 × 200 cm

Kei Ho positif-négatif, 1974
Silk-screen on aluminum
150 × 200 cm

Eridan positif, 1974
Silk-screen on aluminum
200 × 200 cm

Tau-Ceti positif, 1974
Silk-screen on aluminum
200 × 200 cm

Betelgeuse négatif, 1974
Silk-screen on aluminum
150 × 200 cm

Kass positif, 1974
Silk-screen on aluminum
150 × 200 cm

Betelgeuse, 1974
Silk-screen on aluminum
150 × 200 cm

Cassiopée ***négatif***, 1974
Silk-screen on aluminum
200 × 200 cm

Eridan positif, 1974
Silk-screen on aluminum
150 × 200 cm

Eridan négatif, 1974
Silk-screen on aluminum
200 × 200 cm

Kass, 1974
Silk-screen on aluminum
150 × 200 cm

Kei Ho positif, 1974
Silk-screen on aluminum
150 × 200 cm

Gamma négatif, 1974
Silk-screen on aluminum
200 × 200 cm

Andromède positif, 1974
Silk-screen on aluminum
200 × 200 cm *(p. 123)*

Novae régressif-progressif, 1974
Silk-screen on aluminum
200 × 200 cm *(p. 122)*

Betelgeuse, 1974
Silk-screen on aluminum
150 × 200 cm

Tlinko positif, 1974
Silk-screen on aluminum
200 × 200 cm

Novae régressif-progressif, 1974
Silk-screen on aluminum
200 × 200 cm

Novae régressif-progressif, 1974
Silk-screen on aluminum
200 × 200 cm

Gamma positif, 1974
Silk-screen on aluminum
150 × 200 cm

Kei Ho positif, 1974
Silk-screen on aluminum
200 × 200 cm

Eridan, 1974
Silk-screen on aluminum
150 × 200 cm

Betelgeuse, 1974
Silk-screen on aluminum
200 × 200 cm

Preliminary studies on paper
for the series of silk-screens
on aluminum, 1973 *(p. 124)*

C. 2 Kola, 1949
Oil on paper
40 × 38 cm

C. 3 Chisola, 1949–1953
Oil on paper
36 × 34 cm

B. 4 Kerman 2, 1952
Oil on paper
32 × 42 cm *(p. 120)*

C. 14 Basilian 4, 1953
Oil on paper
38 × 35 cm *(p. 120)*

166 Sirs-Kek, 1953
Oil on canvas
75 × 116 cm *(p. 117)*

Tonk, 1954
Oil on canvas
168 × 100 cm *(p. 111)*

Gordium PS positif, 1951
Oil on canvas
195 × 160 cm *(p. 109)*

Tlinko 22, 1955
Oil on canvas
190 × 190 cm *(p. 110)*

Yanina II, 1956
Oil on canvas
148 × 120 cm *(p. 114)*

Algenib II, 1956
Oil on canvas
152 × 81 cm *(p. 118)*

Unova, 1960
Oil on canvas
155 × 141 cm *(p. 119)*

FR. Kodd, 1965
Oil on canvas
180 × 180 cm

CTA 102, 1965
Oil on canvas
170 × 170 cm *(p. 106)*

Freg 1.2, 1965
Oil on canvas
180 × 180 cm *(p. 66)*

Pokol, 1973
Oil on canvas
160 × 161 cm

Basq, 1973
Oil on canvas
158 × 117 cm *(p. 121)*

Tridim S., 1968
Oil on canvas
200 × 100 cm

Perokta, 1973
Oil on canvas
75 × 75 cm

Andromède négatif, 1974
Silk-screen on aluminum
200 × 200 cm

Tau, 1973
Oil on canvas
144 × 135 cm

Meh 2, 1967
Oil on canvas
100 × 150 cm

Sonora AE, 1973
Oil on canvas
120 × 80 cm

Tridem VER, 1968–1973
Oil on canvas
104 × 108 cm

Select Bibliography

Pierre Alechinsky. Exhibition catalogue, Galerie Nationale du Jeu de Paume. Paris: Editions du Jeu de Paume, 1998.

Michel Butor and Michel Sicard. *Pierre Alechinsky*. Exhibition catalogue, Abbaye de Sénanque. Paris: Editions Renault, Art et Industrie/Editions Galilée, 1984.

Arman, rétrospective. Exhibition catalogue, Galerie Nationale du Jeu de Paume. Paris: Editions du Jeu de Paume, 1998.

Arman, accumulations Renault, 1967–1970. Exhibition catalogue, Galerie Georges-Philippe Vallois, Paris, 1995.

Arman. *Mémoires accumulés*. Conversations with Otto Hahn. Paris: Editions Belfond, 1992.

Pol Bury. *Les colonnes animées de Pol Bury*. Paris: Maeght Editeur, 1973.

Jean Frémon. *Jean Degottex*. Paris: Editions du Regard, 1986.

Jean Dewasne, antisculptures, cerveaux mâles. Exhibition catalogue, ARC/Musée d'Art Moderne de la Ville de Paris. Paris: Editions Renault, Recherches, Art et Industrie, 1975.

Michel Thévoz. *Dubuffet*. Geneva: Editions Albert Skira, 1986.

Jean Dubuffet. *Catalogue des travaux de Jean Dubuffet*. Catalogue raisonné in 40 vols. Paris: Editions de Minuit, 1976.

Errò. Catalogue raisonné, vol.1, 1974–1986. Paris: Editions Incitation à la Création/Fernand Hazan; vol. 2, 1984–1998. Paris: Editions Fernand Hazan.

Sam Francis, les années parisiennes, 1950–1961. Exhibition catalogue, Galerie Nationale du Jeu de Paume. Paris: Editions du Jeu de Paume, 1996.

Pontus Hulten. *Sam Francis*. Kunst- und Austellungshalle der Bundesrepublik Deutschland, Cantz, 1993.

Dominique Gauthier. Arlequinades I et Arlequinades II. Exhibition catalogue, Les Filles du Calvaire, Art Contemporain, Paris, 1998.

Georges Didi-Huberman. *Simon Hantaï, L'étoilement*. Paris: Editions de Minuit, 1998.

Simon Hantaï. Exhibition catalogue, Musée National d'Art Moderne. Paris: Editions du Centre Georges Pompidou, 1985.

Gottfried Honneger. Exhibition catalogue, Musée d'Art Moderne de la Ville de Paris, Centre International de la Création Artistique de Sénanque-Gordes, Galerie Nouvelles Images, The Hague, 1978.

Jean Clay. *Julio Le Parc*. Madrid, 1976.

Frank Popper. "Julio Le Parc." *Naissance de l'art cinétique*. Paris: 1967.

Roberto Matta, Dessins 1936–1989. Paris: Editions Galerie de France, 1990.

Roberto Matta. Exhibition catalogue, Musée National d'Art Moderne. Paris: Editions du Centre Georges Pompidou, 1985.

Alfred Pacquement and René Bellour. *Michaux peinture*. Paris: Gallimard, 1993.

Henri Michaux, rétrospective. Exhibition catalogue, Musée National d'Art Moderne, Centre Georges Pompidou, Paris; Solomon R. Guggenheim Museum, New York; Musée d'Art Contemporain, Montreal, 1978.

Liga Pang. Exhibition catalogue, Abbaye de Sénanque. Centre International de Création Artistique, 1984.

Robert Rauschenberg, A Retrospective. Exhibition catalogue, The Solomon R. Guggenheim Museum, New York, 1998.

Mary Lynn Kotz. *Rauschenberg, Art and Life*. New York: Harry N. Abrams, 1990.

Jean-Pierre Raynaud. Exhibition catalogue, Galerie Nationale du Jeu de Paume. Paris: Editions du Jeu de Paume, 1998.

Denyse Durand Ruel. *Jean-Pierre Raynaud*. Catalogue raisonné, 1962–1973. Paris: Editions du Regard, 1998.

Niki de Saint-Phalle. Exhibition catalogue, Musée National d'Art Moderne. Paris: Editions du Centre Georges Pompidou, 1980.

Niki de Saint-Phalle, les nanas au pouvoir. Stedelijk Museum, Amsterdam, 1967.

Jesús Rafael Soto, rétrospective. Exhibition catalogue, Galerie Nationale du Jeu de Paume. Paris: Editions du Jeu de Paume, 1997.

Gérard-Georges Lemaire. *Soto*. Collection "Mains et merveilles." Paris: Editions la Différence, 1997.

Takis, rétrospective. Exhibition catalogue, Galerie Nationale du Jeu de Paume. Paris: Editions du Jeu de Paume, 1993.

Dominique Vieville. *Takis*. Paris: Editions du Regard, 1993.

Antoni Tàpies. Exhibition catalogue, Galerie Nationale du Jeu de Paume. Paris: Editions du Jeu de Paume, 1994.

Tàpies, peintures, encres, et vernis, 1982–1983. Exhibition catalogue, Abbaye de Sénanque. Paris: Editions Renault, Recherches, Art et Industrie, 1983.

Dominique Thiolat, in *Daniel Templon*, 1978–1983.

Jean Tinguely. Exhibition catalogue, Jean Tinguely Museum, Basel, 2 vols. Basel: Editions Museum Jean Tinguely, and Berne: Benteli Verlags, 1996.

Pontus Hulten. *Jean Tinguely, une magie plus forte que la mort*. Paris: Le Chemin Vert, 1987.

Luis Tomasello. Centre Noroît, Arras, 1991.

B. Dahhan. *Victor Vasarely ou la connaissance d'un art moléculaire*. Paris: Denoël/Gonthier, 1979.

Werner Spies. *Victor Vasarely*. Cologne: Dumont-Schauberg and New York: Harry N. Abrams, 1971.

ISBN : 2 85025 678 1

Design: Studio Aparicio
Typesetting: Cursives
Correction: Jian Too
Sub-editor: Régine Cuzin
Renault MCAV

Photoengraving: Seleoffset, Turin
Printing: Ages, Turin
Printed in the EU